CW00649285

REMAINS

Historical and Literary

CONNECTED WITH THE PALATINE COUNTIES OF

Lancaster and Chester

VOLUME XXXII — THIRD SERIES

MANCHESTER:

Printed for the Chetham Society

1986

TO MY PARENTS

INDUSTRY BEFORE THE INDUSTRIAL REVOLUTION

NORTH-EAST LANCASHIRE
*c.*1500–1640

John T. Swain

MANCHESTER

Printed for the Chetham Society
1986

Copyright © The Chetham Society 1986

Published for the Society by
Manchester University Press
Oxford Road, Manchester M13 9PL, UK

British Library cataloguing in publication data
Swain, John T.
Industry before the industrial revolution North-east Lancashire, c.1500–1640.—(Remains historical and literary connected with the palatine counties of Lancaster and Chester. 3rd series)
1. Pendle (Lancashire)—Industries—History
I. Title   II. Series
338.09427′645   HC257.P4/

ISBN 0–7190–1340–2 *cased*

Photoset by Wilmaset, Birkenhead, Wirral

Printed in Great Britain at the University Printing House, Oxford
by David Stanford, Printer to the University

CONTENTS

FIGURES AND TABLES

ABBREVIATIONS

The bibliography contains details of all primary and secondary sources cited, and therefore abbreviations have been used throughout in the footnotes.

PREFACE

This book is a revised version of a Cambridge doctoral thesis which was submitted in 1983. I am indebted to the Economic and Social Research Council (formerly the Social Science Research Council) for funding three years as a research student. In addition, I also wish to express my thanks to the Cambridge Historical Society and to the Managers of the Ellen McArthur Fund for providing some financial assistance towards the cost of completing my thesis.

I should like to express my gratitude to the staff of the various record offices at which I have worked, particularly the Lancashire Record Office and the Public Record Office. I have benefited greatly from the advice and criticism of many teachers, colleagues and friends, whom I hope will forgive me if I do not mention them all by name; but I should particularly like to thank Dr Joan Thirsk, Professor D. C. Coleman and Professor W. H. Chaloner. Above all, my greatest debt is to my supervisor, Dr John Hatcher, who has proved a constant source of encouragement, helpful advice and constructive criticism, for which I am extremely grateful. Those shortcomings and errors which remain, however, are my sole responsibility.

Author's note All dates before 1752 in this book are in Old Style, except that the year is taken to begin on January 1st. Spelling and punctuation have been modernised in all quotations.

CHAPTER I

INTRODUCTION

Lancashire's significant contribution to the industrial revolution is well known. What is less well known, however, is the extent to which industrial and craft activities were practised in Lancashire well before the industrial revolution, and, secondly, the important contribution that this early experience was to have in helping to shape later industrial developments. The purpose of this book is to examine the role played by industry in the economy of north-east Lancashire during the sixteenth and early seventeenth centuries.

The subject of industry before the industrial revolution has recently attracted a good deal of attention due to a debate on the origins of the industrial revolution begun in 1972 by Franklin Mendels. Mendels argues that the first stage of the industrialisation process, which he terms 'proto-industrialisation', ought to be seen as the expansion of traditional rural industry (the second stage in Mendels' model is the factory or mechanised stage).[1] Proto-industrialisation as a concept has undergone a series of modifications and re-definitions.[2] Much of the debate, however, is largely peripheral for our purposes, since the literature relates mainly to the eighteenth and nineteenth centuries. Moreover, there is a danger that the debate on proto-industrialisation is becoming over-theoretical, with insufficient attention paid to regional and local diversity.[3]

Despite this renewed attention on industry in the early modern period, there has been relatively little examination of Lancashire's economy during the Tudor and Stuart period. This contrasts strongly with the considerable amount of research done on the county during the industrial revolution. The neglect of early modern Lancashire may be connected to a belief that Lancashire's contribution to national economic development must have been small before the industrial revolution, due to the comparative poverty of the area – Lancashire was the poorest taxed county in England in terms of assessed wealth per acre, according to the subsidies of 1514 and 1515 (though it should be noted that the Welsh and the northernmost English counties were exempt).[4] Little had changed by the 1630s, for the Ship Money assessment of 1636 shows that Lancashire was the second poorest English county.[5] However, this relative lack of wealth makes the transformation wrought by the industrial revolution all the more remarkable and significant, and therefore emphasises the need for further examination of pre-industrial Lancashire, in order to establish what were the economic and social conditions peculiar to the county which helped to facilitate industrialisation.

There are three studies of particular note which concentrate on industry in early modern Lancashire. First, Wadsworth and Mann investigated the rise of the Lancashire cotton industry between 1600 and 1780.[6] This is an outstanding pioneering work, but since its publication in 1931, many additional sources have become available, thanks to the establishment of county record offices. Secondly, Norman Lowe's M.A. thesis on the textile industry in sixteenth-century Lancashire, which was published in 1972, is an important contribution, particularly in its use of probate inventories.[7] Thirdly, John Langton has published a detailed account of the geography of the coal industry in south-west Lancashire between 1590 and 1799.[8] A justifiable criticism of all of these studies, however, is that industry has not been examined as part of the local economy. It is necessary to look in depth at the interaction of demography, agriculture, lordship and landholding before a proper understanding of the working of industry may be achieved.

This more comprehensive approach is obviously only possible if the amount of source materials to be worked through is manageable. In practice, this means that the area and period studied must be limited to sensible proportions. The boundaries of this study have been drawn to cover part of north-east Lancashire, primarily Colne manor and the forests of Trawden and Pendle, during the period from 1500 to 1640.

The pre-industrial economic history of north-east Lancashire has not been extensively researched. The most recent book of note, G. H. Tupling's classic study of Rossendale, was written nearly sixty years ago.[9] This work is particularly strong on lordship and landholding in the medieval and early modern periods, and on the textile industry from the seventeenth century onwards. Again, a number of documents, such as probate records, are now easily accessible, but were not available to Tupling, and so there are many new questions and avenues of research to be investigated. The area covered by the present study does not overlap with that examined by Tupling. Indeed, Colne manor and the forests of Trawden and Pendle have received extremely little attention in academic literature, though more in popular fiction, thanks to the trial of the Pendle witches in 1612, which inspired the writing of two historical novels.[10] The only important academic research on this district for the early modern period is a book by Sarah Pearson on the houses of the area between 1560 and 1760, and an article by Mary Brigg on Pendle forest during the seventeenth century.[11]

The Colne area is a distinctly upland district, lying at a level above the 300 foot contour, and much of the forests of Trawden and Pendle lie 600 feet above sea level. Pendle Hill dominates the landscape, rising to a peak of 1,831 feet. To the west of Pendle, by contrast, is the relatively low-lying Ribble valley. The geological formation of the Colne district belongs to the carboniferous system, that is, millstone grit, coal measures and carboniferous limestone. Most of the Colne area is composed of millstone grit, and, to a lesser extent, of coal measures. Uppermost, there are vast tracts of peat and boulder clay, with some outcrops of coal.[12]

Superimposed upon this rather bleak picture was a complex system of lordship and secular and ecclesiastical government. Colne manor and the forests of Trawden and Pendle were constituent elements of the Honor of Clitheroe, which was part of the Duchy of Lancaster's extensive holdings in the north of England. Thus the lord was an absentee, that is the King, for the Duchy of Lancaster had been part of Crown lands since Henry IV's accession in 1399.[13]

The ecclesiastical structure did not coincide with seigneurial boundaries, thus making life difficult for the historian using documents drawn from both sources. Colne manor and the forests of Trawden and Pendle formed part of the huge parish of Whalley, which contained 10,000 communicants in 1563.[14] This parish was divided into dependent chapelries which were referred to as parishes and which kept their own parish registers. Pendle forest was divided between four chapelries. Most of the forest came within the jurisdiction of Newchurch in Pendle chapelry, but some other sections of the forest were found in the chapelries of Padiham, Burnley and Colne. Higham with West Close Booth, and Heyhouses were in Padiham chapelry; Burnley chapelry included Reedley Hallows, Filly Close and New Laund Booth; Barrowford Booth was in Colne chapelry. Colne manor and Trawden forest were both included in Colne chapelry. The remainder of Colne chapelry consisted of the small areas of Foulridge and Little Marsden.[15] For greater clarification of these boundaries, the reader is referred to Map 1.

For purposes of secular government, Colne manor and the forests of Trawden and Pendle were part of Blackburn Hundred, which was divided into sub-units called townships. The forests of Pendle and Trawden were not divided, but Colne manor was split between the townships of Colne and Marsden (the latter included Little Marsden, which was part of Ightenhill manor).[16]

The term 'township' must not be confused with 'town', for in Lancashire a village or even a hamlet might be described as a township. Colne itself was the only part of our area which was called a town by contemporaries; in 1579, it was stated that 'the towns of Rochdale, Clitheroe, Colne and Burnley are market towns of great resort and trade'.[17] On the other hand, a document of 1610 refers to 'the town or village of Colne'.[18] Many of Colne's inhabitants owned land and pursued an agricultural livelihood,[19] and therefore it would be nonsense to speak of urban society.[20] In 1664, there were only 196 households in Colne township,[21] and since the area of the township must have exceeded that of the town, the size of the town of Colne cannot have been greater than a few hundred people, even by the middle of the seventeenth century after a period of considerable population growth.[22]

INDUSTRY IN THE MIDDLE AGES

There are numerous signs of the presence of industry in the Colne area during the Middle Ages. This took a number of forms, including cloth production, coal and iron mining, slatestone quarrying, tanning and brewing.

Before the beginning of the reign of Edward III (1327), there were at least four fulling mills in existence in Lancashire, situated at Burnley, Colne, Manchester and Wyresdale.[23] The siting of two of these mills in north-east Lancashire is testimony to the early development and importance of the cloth trade in this area. The first reference to the fulling mill at Colne is found in the ministers' accounts for Michaelmas 1295–6, but it is clear that this was not the first year of its operation, since expenses of 12s 8d for repair of the mill were also noted.[24] Similarly, the Burnley mill was first

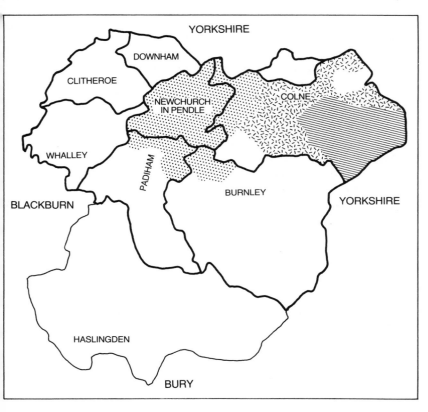

Colne manor   Trawden forest   Pendle forest

—— Boundaries of chapelries
cited in the text

MAP I Whalley Parish
(Based on a map in Farrer and Brownbill *V.C.H.Lancs.*, vol. 6, p. 348)

mentioned in these accounts, where it was recorded that it had been built 'anew', at a cost of £2 12s 6½d.[25] Thus it is apparent that the level of cloth production in this district must have been substantial by the late thirteenth century to justify the presence of two adjacent mills. Indeed, the decision of the lords of the Honor of Clitheroe to construct these mills in the first place must have been motivated by an awareness that a considerable local cloth trade already existed, and therefore that large profits might be made by using seigneurial powers to force tenants to pay to have their cloth fulled at the lord's mill.

The lords of the Honor of Clitheroe did not operate these fulling mills on their own account, but leased them to 'farmers'. High rents were received from these lessees in the 1290s and 1300s, for the rent from Colne fulling mill stood at £1 13s 4½d in 1295–6, and at £1 4s 0d in 1304–5.[26] Rents were never again to reach this level. An inquisition post mortem of February 1311 gives the rent as just 6s 8d,[27] and in 1323–4, 13s 6d was received from the lessee of the mill.[28] This low level of rent obtained in 1323–4 may have been due to a number of factors, such as the political instability of the period, particularly the pillage which followed the revolt of Thomas, Earl of Lancaster in 1322 (who was lord of the Honor of Clitheroe), and also that produced by Bruce's army and by the raids of men from Craven.[29] Rents had recovered slightly by 1341–2, when 18s was received for the fulling mill,[30] but by the early fifteenth century, rents were severely reduced again, standing at only 6s 8d in 1422–3 and 10s in 1439–40.[31] By 1529–30, the rent from the fulling mill had increased slightly to 13s 4d.[32]

It must be remembered that there was no free market economy during the Middle Ages because the influence of lordship, both strong and weak, had an important bearing on the level of rent obtained. Nevertheless, the rents of Colne fulling mill suggest that cloth production was probably at a high level in the 1290s and 1300s, but subsequently fell substantially. Furthermore, Colne does not appear to have shared in the great expansion of the cloth industry, which was so evident in the West Riding of Yorkshire during the fifteenth century.[33]

Coal mining in the Colne area had been established early. The ministers' accounts for 1295–6 refer to 'sea' coal valued at 10s sold in Trawden forest, and in 1304–5, sea coal worth 16s was obtained in Colne manor.[34] However, the receipts for Trawden forest in 1323–4 were just 2s 6d.[35] (but it is probable that the factors discussed above also applied to coal mining). By 1341–2, receipts for Trawden had recovered somewhat, registering 6s 8d.[36] Part of the demand for coal came from outside the area, for the monks of Bolton Priory purchased coal in the Colne area in the reign of Edward III, and they may have bought Colne coal in 1294 for use in their forge.[37]

By the early fifteenth century, the coal mines were leased. The annual rent for the mines in Trawden forest in 1422–3 was 13s 4d.[38] Rents began to rise, reaching 30s in the 1430s and 1440s, but did not rise above 6s 8d during the remainder of the century.[39] The political instability of the period may have been partly responsible for the low levels of rent received.

Coal mining was also recorded in Pendle forest, at least as early as the 1320s.[40] However, it must be doubted whether this mining was actually taking place within the precincts of Pendle forest proper, for in the fifteenth century, rents for coal mines at Padiham and Broadhead (which were both in Ightenhill manor) were recorded under Pendle forest.[41]

Iron ore was also mined in Trawden and Pendle forests in the early fourteenth century. This must have been conducted on an extensive scale, for iron ore mining, together with the right to gather old brushwood, was sufficiently profitable to generate an annual rent of £8 13s 4d in Trawden in 1323.[42] Both Trawden and Pendle forests contained a forge for iron ore in 1341–2; the rent received was 3s per week in both cases, but whilst the mine in Pendle had operated for 17½ weeks, that in Trawden had been worked for just four weeks, possibly suggesting difficulties of extraction.[43] There appears to be no reference to the mining of iron ore in this area during the fifteenth century.[44]

Other industries were also practised in this district during the later Middle Ages. For example, the right to quarry slate was leased throughout the fifteenth century; this quarry was situated at Longfurlong Head in Marsden (but was recorded under Trawden forest).[45] In addition, both brewing and tanning were found, for licences were awarded in Colne manor in 1323 to three women to brew ale, and to two men to tan hides.[46] The presence of tanners is not at all surprising, for, as we shall show, the forests contained large cattle farms during this period.

In order to understand the reasons for the patterns of industrial activities found, it is useful to examine the very different economic organisation of manor and forest in the Honor of Clitheroe during the later Middle Ages. Turning firstly to Colne manor, an analysis of the fluctuations in rent receipts is extremely instructive. In 1242, rent from Colne manor stood at £20 7s 1d.[47] By 1304–5, rent from land was £22 17s 1½d, whilst the grain and fulling mills were worth an additional £12 6s 0d.[48] In 1323–4, land rents had risen substantially to £25 14s 11d and mill rents had increased slightly to £12 13s 6d.[49] Total land rents continued to rise, and had reached £26 12s 3¾d by 1341–2, though mill rents had fallen somewhat to £10 10s 0d.[50]

The rising level of total receipts from land rents in Colne manor during the later thirteenth and early fourteenth centuries suggests that the demand for land was increasing, implying in turn considerable local population growth. Analysis of the structure of landholding confirms that more land was brought into cultivation during this period. For example, 10½ acres were 'approved' in 1304–5.[51] In 1323, an extent of the manor records that there were 310 acres and 2 rods of 'rodland' (land 'ridded' or improved from the waste), though exactly when this land had been brought into cultivation is unclear. In addition to rodland, there were eleven oxgangs of land in 1323 (at least ten of which were leased out to the tenants) and eight freehold tenancies.[52] Thus, there was no direct seigneurial involvement in farming activity in Colne manor at this time.

By 1399–1400, land rents had increased slightly to £27 10s 6½d, but mill rents had fallen dramatically to £2 6s 8d,[53] presumably due to a severe reduction in the demand for the mills' services following the decimation of the population by the Black Death. During the fifteenth century, very small plots of land, often less than an acre, were brought into cultivation in Colne and Marsden. Many of these had been improved by 1425, and almost all new parcels had been brought into cultivation by the middle of the century, for land rents stood at £27 14s 3d in 1424–5, £27 19s 11½d in 1449–50, and just £28 0s 6d in 1499–1500.[54] These new parcels of land were leased at a rent of 4d an acre, and therefore it appears that nearly 55 acres must have been improved between 1342 and 1400, and a further 28¼ acres by 1450.

In the forests, we may discern three distinct stages of economic development during the later Middle Ages. They were originally reserved as an area for hunting deer, but under the de Lacys substantial cattle farms (called vaccaries) were established, and the deer were confined to just two parks within the forests, at Ightenhill near Burnley, and at Musbury in Rossendale.[55] By 1295–6, there were five vaccaries operating in Trawden forest and eleven in Pendle. The number of cattle kept in the forests was considerable, especially in Pendle; for example, there were 407 head in Trawden and 906 in Pendle in 1295–6, and 387 and 848 respectively in 1304–5.[56]

This period of vigorous direct management of the forests did not continue uninterrupted. The accounts for 1323–4 show that all the vaccaries in Trawden and Pendle forests had been leased to farmers.[57] The decision to lease the vaccaries may have been a recent one, encouraged by the political upheaval and consequent devastation, since it would clearly have been sensible policy at such a time to transfer the risks of farming to others. Nevertheless, this was not a temporary expedient, for the ministers' accounts of 1341–2 show that the vaccaries in Trawden were then leased. The vaccaries in Pendle were farmed directly at this date, but operated at a more modest level than at the turn of the century, for the total head of cattle kept was only 551.[58] By 1399, direct management of the vaccaries had been abandoned in both Trawden and Pendle, and the forests were leased to farmers.[59] The abandonment of the vaccary system gave opportunities to farmers to develop the pastoral resources of the forests on their own account, but it was only when the tenants were granted security of tenure at the disafforestation in 1507 that they had a real incentive to exploit the forest lands fully.[60]

The vaccary organisation of the forests is likely to have discouraged the development of a sizeable cloth industry in these areas, since the forests were occupied by only a few paid herdsmen and their families, who looked after between seventy and ninety cattle each;[61] they would therefore have been heavily involved in supervising the cattle, making butter and cheese, and tanning hides, and would have had little time to spare for clothmaking. Nevertheless, though the forest population under the vaccary system must have been small, it provided a limited market for those in the manors who produced cloth. In addition, the forests supported a handful of coal miners and iron smelters.[62]

It seems that the Colne manorial population was rising rapidly during the late thirteenth and early fourteenth centuries, and presumably those who were compelled to take on more marginal land would have participated actively in cloth manufacture to supplement their incomes. Thus it is not surprising that large rents were obtained for the fulling mill at Colne in 1295–6 and 1304–5. The decimation of the population by the Black Death must have eased the pressure on holdings and reduced the need for secondary employment in textile production.

This brief summary is in many respects unsatisfactory, but we lack much crucial information on the structure of the local economy during the Middle Ages. Sources for the early modern period proved to be far more prolific, and demonstrate the crucial importance of industry, particularly clothmaking, in the Colne area.

THE SOURCES FOR THE PERIOD 1500–1640

Whilst a number of important sources have been utilised in this study, there are three which proved to be of primary significance, namely probate records, Honor of Clitheroe court rolls, and Duchy of Lancaster administrative and legal records.

Wills and inventories have been employed extensively throughout this study. All the available wills and inventories of testators from Colne chapelry and Pendle forest for the period up to 1640 have been examined (there are 332 wills and 253 inventories in all).[63] Inventories are invaluable for analysis of agricultural practices, wealth distribution and industrial activities; wills have been used primarily to discover the patterns of inheritance arrangements. It must be stressed that analysis of wills and inventories is not a straightforward task, for there are many pitfalls, and problems of interpretation. However, used with care, probate records are an indispensable asset.

Manor court rolls have been used to a relatively small extent by early modern economic historians, which is surprising since they are useful sources of information on manorial customs and of data on land transfers. The Clitheroe court rolls are a fairly well preserved series which survive fully from 1507. We are extremely fortunate that all the rolls which are extant for the period up to 1567 are in print;[64] these represent nearly half of the rolls which are relevant for our period.[65] The existence of these printed court rolls must have influenced Tupling in his choice of Rossendale as an area for study, but the other rolls, including those for Colne, Trawden and Pendle, have been little used. Though working through the original court rolls is a time-consuming exercise, the effort was rewarded by making possible an analysis of sales, mortgages and leases.[66]

The Duchy of Lancaster records are a well-organised and catalogued collection. Great use was made of documents relating to estate management (principally rentals, ministers' accounts and special commissions) and of litigation brought before the Duchy Chamber at Westminster (which includes pleadings, depositions, and decrees and orders).[67] Litigation has to be handled carefully, since by definition statements by litigants or their supporters are *parti pris*. Nevertheless, amongst dozens of very mundane cases concerned largely with disputed title to land, there are several interesting suits about cloth manufacture and coal mining which provide crucial information on the structure of these industries.

On the other hand, there are a number of potentially important sources which have not survived at all, or which exist for only a part of our period. Examples of the former include accounts of the overseers of the poor and of local collieries. The absence of colliery accounts is particularly regrettable, since in order to obtain information on local coal mining activities, we are forced to depend largely on less reliable sources, such as statements of litigants.

Several of our sources are extant for only a portion of the period under review. The most serious losses occur in the chapelry register records, for the Colne register does not begin until 1599, and for Newchurch in Pendle, we have just fifteen isolated years of usable Bishops' transcripts, beginning in 1602. The registers for Burnley and Padiham commence in 1562 and 1573 respectively, but are not of central importance, since they contain only small sections of Pendle forest.[68] In addition, there are no inventories and only two wills extant for the early sixteenth century; indeed, probate records do not become fairly plentiful until the last quarter of the sixteenth century. Quarter Sessions records are not available until 1590, and the series of recognisance rolls does not begin until 1626 (with the exception of the isolated year 1606).[69] Churchwardens' accounts have only survived for Padiham from 1623, and are generally uninformative.[70] Gentry household accounts exist only from 1582.[71] Thus it is apparent that our sources do not become particularly plentiful or informative until the later sixteenth century.

There are two peculiarities in the source material which must be noted. First, probate records for the Diocese of Chester are divided into *supra* and *infra* categories. *Supra* wills belonged to Esquires and clergy, and to those with personal estates valued at more than £40; these were proved before the Bishop of Chester's Consistory Court. The wills of those whose personal estate was worth less than £40, called *infra* wills, were proved locally by the rural deans, but have survived in very small numbers,[72] and for our area exist for a few isolated years between 1601 and 1621.

The second problem lies not in the organisation of the records but rather in the restrictive ways in which they may be analysed. The range of surnames and forenames used was found to be extremely small, and this naturally greatly increases the problems of nominal record linkage. The surname Hartley was especially common; indeed, in the rental for Trawden forest in 1608, no less than 11 of the 16 copyholders in Trawden itself were called Hartley. Worse still, 7 of these copyholders were named James Hartley.[73] It was common practice to name children, particularly the eldest, after the parents, and therefore we are faced with the likelihood of, for example, more than one James Hartley in many of these households. Hartleys were found in large numbers throughout our area; for example, 117 of the 1,000 burials in Colne chapelry between April 1599 and March 1616 were of people called Hartley. Other surnames were also fairly common; there were 43 persons named Hargreaves buried during the same period, together with 36 called Smith.[74] Thus historians of north-east Lancashire cannot follow the methodology suggested by Macfarlane of linking together all the available documents about each individual,[75] since in many cases it is likely that two references to people with the same name relate to different individuals, not to the same person.

NOTES

[1] Mendels, 'Proto-industrialisation: the first phase of the industrialisation process', p. 241 and *passim*

[2] See especially Kriedte *et al.*, *Industrialisation before industrialisation*, and Mendels, 'Proto-industrialisation; theory and reality'

[3] See, for example, the criticism of the whole theory of proto-industrialisation in Coleman, 'Proto-industrialisation: a concept too many'

[4] Schofield, 'Geographical distribution of wealth in England', pp. 504–6. There was a high degree of continuity in the relative position of Lancashire in 1334 and in 1514–15, for in 1334, Lancashire was the poorest taxed county judging from the lay subsidies, and was 33rd out of 38 counties if clerical wealth is combined with lay wealth

[5] Blackwood, *Lancashire gentry*, p. 3 (quoting from Rogers, *History of agriculture and prices*, vol. 5, pp. 70, 104–5). The poorest county in England in 1636 was Cumberland

[6] Wadsworth and Mann, *Cotton trade and industrial Lancashire*

[7] Lowe, 'Lancashire textile industry' and *Lancashire textile industry*

[8] Langton, *Geographical change and industrial revolution*

[9] Tupling, *Economic history of Rossendale*

[10] Ainsworth, *Lancashire witches*; Neill, *Mist over Pendle*

[11] Pearson, *Rural houses of the Lancashire Pennines*; Brigg, 'Forest of Pendle'

[12] Freeman, *et al.*, *Lancashire, Cheshire and the Isle of Man*, pp. 7–15, 23; Wightman, *Bonnie Colne*, pp. 11–13; Geological survey of Great Britain (drift and solid editions), soil association map of the county of Lancashire

[13] For the organisation of the Duchy of Lancaster, see Somerville, *History of the Duchy of Lancaster*

[14] P.R.O. S.P. 12/31 fol. 86

[15] Ecroyd, *Registers of Whalley*, 1538–1601, pp. vi–vii. Strictly speaking, Heyhouses was not part of Padiham chapelry during this period, but was extraparochial and in the chapelry of St. Mary's Clitheroe. However, the majority of the Heyhouses inhabitants were baptised and buried at Padiham; Laycock, *Registers of Padiham*, vi. Before the dissolution of the monasteries, the forest areas of the Honor of Clitheroe, including Pendle and Trawden, had been in the peculiar jurisdiction of Whalley Abbey; Haigh, *Reformation and resistance*, p. 62. Newchurch in Pendle was consecrated in 1544; Brigg, 'Forest of Pendle', Part 1, p. 67

[16] See Farrer and Brownbill, *V.C.H.Lancs*, vols. 6 and 7

[17] P.R.O. D.L.1/173/M4

[18] P.R.O. D.L.44/828 m.3

[19] The rental for Colne manor in 1650 shows that many in 'Colne' and 'Colne township' owned land; P.R.O. E.317 Lancs. 8 m.18–23

[20] Ramsey argues that the inhabitants of small towns, such as those listed by Leland, should be thought of as countrymen, not as town dwellers; Ramsey, *Tudor economic problems*, p. 11. Cf. Laslett, *World we have lost*, p. 58

[21] See Chapter 5, p. 106.

[22] For the scale of demographic expansion in the sixteenth and early seventeenth centuries, see Chapter 2

[23] Carus-Wilson, 'Industrial revolution of the thirteenth century', p. 48

[24] Lyons, *Two 'compoti'*, pp. 119, 125

[25] *Ibid.*, pp. 122, 126

[26] *Ibid.*, pp. 119, 176

[27] Farrer, *Lancashire inquests, part 2*, p. 6 (reprinted in Farrer, *Court rolls*, vol. 1, p. 487). We should not place too great reliance on data derived from inquisitions post mortem, however, since it was usual to understate valuations; see Farrer, *Court rolls*, vol. 2, xvii, and Latham, 'Inquisitions post mortem', pp. 78–9

[28] Farrer, *Lancashire inquests, part 2*, p. 187. An extent of Colne manor in October 1323 gives a similar rent of 14*s* per annum for the fulling mill; Farrer, *Court rolls*, vol. 1, p. 483

[29] Shaw, *Royal forest of Lancaster*, pp. 366, 368

[30] P.R.O. S.C.6/1091/6

[31] Farrer, *Court rolls*, vol. 1, pp. 493, 495

[32] P.R.O. D.L.29/81/1562

[33] Heaton, *Yorkshire woollen and worsted industries*, Chapter 2

[34] Lyons, *Two 'compoti'*, pp. 119, 176. Mineral coal was called sea coal, to distinguish it from charcoal

[35] Farrer, *Lancashire inquests, part 2*, p. 200

[36] P.R.O. S.C.6/1091/6

[37] Farrer and Brownbill, *V.C.H.Lancs.*, vol. 2, pp. 356–7

[38] Farrer, *Court rolls*, vol. 1, p. 490

[39] P.R.O. D.L.29/76/1499 – D.L.29/79/1535 (Blackburnshire forest), *passim*

[40] Farrer, *Lancashire inquests, part 2*, p. 200, note 1

[41] P.R.O. D.L.29/76/1499 – D.L.29/79/1535 (Blackburnshire forest), *passim*

[42] Farrer, *Court rolls*, vol. 1, p. 483; Farrer, *Lancashire inquests, part 2*, p. 200

[43] P.R.O. S.C.6/1091/6

[44] P.R.O. D.L.29, *passim*; cf. Tupling, 'The early metal trades', p. 4

[45] P.R.O. D.L.29/76/1498 – D.L.29/79/1535 (Blackburnshire forests)

[46] Farrer, *Court rolls of 1323–4*, p. 1

[47] Farrer, *Lancashire inquests, part 1*, p. 157; this figure includes Colne, Alkincoats and Great Marsden. It is unclear whether there were any mills operating at this date, and therefore whether this figure also includes mill rents

[48] Lyons, *Two 'compoti'*, p. 176

[49] Farrer, *Lancashire inquests, part 2*, p. 187

[50] P.R.O. S.C.6/1091/6

[51] Lyons, *Two 'compoti'*, p. 176

[52] Farrer, *Court rolls*, vol. 1, pp. 482–3; vol. 2, xii

[53] Farrer, *Court rolls*, vol. 1, p. 489

[54] P.R.O. D.L.29/89/1633; D.L.29/89/1640; D.L.29/91/1668

[55] Tupling, *Economic history of Rossendale*, p. 15; Smith, *Blackburnshire*, p. 8

[56] Tupling, *Economic history of Rossendale*, pp. 19, 22. The first reference to the vaccaries was apparently in 1242, when the vaccaries and stud farms of John de Lacy were valued at 100 marks (but where they were situated is unclear); Farrer, *Lancashire inquests, part 1*, p. 157. By 1258, there were five vaccaries operating in Pendle, according to an extent of the lands of Edmund de Lacy (*ibid.*, p. 216)

[57] Farrer, *Lancashire inquests, part 2*, p. 200; Shaw, *Royal forest of Lancaster*, pp. 366–7

[58] Shaw, *Royal forest of Lancaster*, pp. 370, 373

[59] Farrer, *Court rolls*, vol. 1, p. 489; Shaw, *Royal forest of Lancaster*, p. 375; Tupling, *Economic history of Rossendale*, p. 32

[60] See Chapter 4

[61] The mean herd size in Pendle and Trawden forest vaccaries in 1295–6 and 1304–5 was 82; Lyons, *Two 'compoti'*, pp. 129–34, 156–61. Cf. Tupling, *Economic history of Rossendale*, p. 22

[62] See above, pp. 6–7

[63] B.I. P.C.Y; L.R.O. WCW *Supra* and *Infra*, DRCh. In addition, there are a few wills and inventories in other collections at the L.R.O. in DDX/19/19; DDBd/60/1, 60/2, 60/6; DDWh/3/5, 3/14, and a few wills are enrolled in the halmote records (DDHCl3). Throughout this book, unless otherwise stated, these additional wills and inventories have been included in the *supra* sample, since they relate to testators with considerable personal estate, invariably more than £40 (the qualification for *supra* status); however, the handful of wills and inventories of children, and of inventories where the goods were not separately listed, have been excluded from the samples

[64] Farrer, *Court rolls*

[65] The original court rolls are at the L.R.O. (DDHCl3)

[66] See Chapter 5. It should be noted that the halmote for Trawden forest was held at Colne and is enrolled under Colne manor; that for Pendle forest was usually held at Higham, and is enrolled under Ightenhill manor

[67] P.R.O. D.L.1, D.L.3, D.L.4, D.L.5, D.L.6, D.L.29, D.L.43, D.L.44

[68] See Chapter 2, pp. 19–20

[69] The early records are printed in Tait, *Lancashire Quarter Sessions records*. The recognisance rolls are catalogued at the L.R.O. under QSB 1

[70] L.R.O. P.R. 2863/2/1

[71] Harland, *Accounts of the Shuttleworths*

[72] Camp, *Wills and their whereabouts*, xxv; Jones, 'Lancashire probate records', pp. 65–6

[73] Farrer, *Court rolls*, vol. 2, p. 402

[74] Ecroyd, *Registers of Colne*, pp. 158–81

[75] Macfarlane, *Reconstructing historical communities, passim*

CHAPTER II

DEMOGRAPHY

Demographic change is of fundamental importance to an understanding of the structure of the local economy during this period. Four main areas have been selected for discussion. First, an attempt has been made to estimate total population size. Secondly, we investigate more precisely the timing of demographic change. Thirdly, an analysis is made of the causes of crisis mortality. Lastly, there follows a discussion of the incidence of illegitimacy over time and space.

THE SIZE OF THE LOCAL POPULATION

In order to estimate total population size, various sources have been investigated. Unfortunately, the 1377 poll tax, which has been used by Russell[1] and others for this purpose, has not survived for the Blackburn Hundred. The 1379 poll tax returns for Pendle and Trawden forests have survived,[2] but it is unclear just how many evaded this tax, and whether it can be used for demographic purposes.[3]

The 1524–5 subsidy has also been used frequently as the basis for estimating population size.[4] This was a tax on all persons having land worth £1 a year, movable goods worth £2 a year, or wages worth £1 a year or more; each person was assessed on whichever category of wealth would yield the most revenue.[5] It included all but paupers, and is thus useful for demographic exercises.[6] In 1524, there were 48 taxpayers in Colne chapelry (excluding Barrowford Booth in Pendle forest), and 16 in Pendle forest.[7] Comparison with the communicants' returns of 1563 and the rental of 1527 suggests very strongly that this assessment was not at all comprehensive.[8] This is disappointing but not surprising, for the Yorkshire subsidy returns of 1524–5 are not comprehensive either.[9]

Communicants' returns are another valuable source of demo-

graphic data. It is regrettable that there are no relevant surviving
chantry certificates of 1547 for this area,[10] and that there are no
communicants' returns for the diocese of Chester in 1603.[11] We are
left with returns for the number of communicants' households in 1563
and 1650.[12] A comparison of these returns shows that population
increased in the chapelries of Colne, Newchurch in Pendle, Burnley
and Padiham, though the relative and absolute extent of this growth
varied considerably. In Colne chapelry, the number of communicants' households rose from 315 in 1563 to 'above 400' in 1650, whilst
in Newchurch in Pendle chapelry, the number of these households
grew from 64 to 150 during this period. Thus, whereas the population
in each chapelry increased by similar amounts between 1563 and
1650, this growth was more spectacular in Newchurch, where the
number of communicants' households more than doubled. Population growth was also noticeable in Burnley and Padiham chapelries
(each of which contained small sections of Pendle forest);[13] in Burnley, the number of communicants' households rose slightly from 278
in 1563 to '300 and upwards' in 1650, whilst in Padiham, there was a
substantial increase in the number of these households, from 106 to
232 between 1563 and 1650.

Various problems attach to the use of communicants' returns.
Those for 1650, with the exception of Padiham, are suspiciously
rounded, and, in the case of Colne and Burnley, imprecise. Furthermore, communicants' returns do not, or at least should not, include
the number of non-communicating, largely Catholic households.
Religious changes, including the receptiveness of the population to
Catholicism and the fervour of state or Catholic priests may have
caused fluctuations in the numbers of non-communicants.[14] More
significantly, the willingness of Catholics to take communion may
have changed over time. A report of c.1590 claimed that many of those
who came to church refused to take communion, and also that most of
those who took communion at Easter refused to do so at any other
time of the year.[15] Another report of c.1591 stated that some Lancashire and Cheshire J.P.s and their wives, children and servants had
not taken communion since the beginning of Elizabeth's reign, and
that many gentlemen and others of 'good countenance' who sometimes attended church, had not taken communion for many years.[16]

It is likely, since the Reformation proceeded slowly in
Lancashire,[17] that the 1563 returns are far closer to a total household
count than are those for 1650. The size of the Catholic population
locally is difficult to estimate, but may have been considerable. For

example, it was reported in the metropolitan visitation of 1595 that there were 42 recusants and 14 non-communicants in Colne chapelry.[18]

Since it seems that considerable caution must be exercised in the use and interpretation of the communicants' returns for 1650, other mid-seventeenth-century sources must be utilised in order to estimate population levels at this time correctly. The hearth tax records for 1664[19] are most suitable for this purpose, for they include the numbers of households chargeable under the tax and also those not chargeable, thus giving a total household count. However, in order to make the hearth tax returns comparable with those for communicants, we need to estimate the numbers of households in each chapelry (the hearth tax returns list households by township, not by chapelry).[20] When this is done, it appears that there were 624 households in Colne chapelry and 134 in Newchurch (and a further 32 and 37 households in the Pendle forest sections of Burnley and Padiham chapelries respectively).

The hearth tax data cast doubt on the reliability of the 1650 communicants' returns, particularly with regard to Colne chapelry, for the contrast between the hearth tax estimate of 624 households in 1664 and the communicants' evidence of 'above 400' households is striking. It therefore seems sensible to discard the communicants' returns of 1650, and to use instead the data obtained from the hearth tax of 1664.

In order to convert the data for household numbers into figures for actual population size, it is necessary to have a multiplier for mean household size. Fortunately, the communicants' returns for Padiham in 1650, which are by far the most reliable, give not only the number of communicants' households (232), but also the number of inhabitants in these households (1,106),[21] which produces a mean household size of 4.77. If this is used as a multiplier for the hearth tax data, it would appear that the size of the population in Colne chapelry in 1664 was about 2,975, whilst that in Newchurch in Pendle was about 640 (with the sections of Pendle forest which lay in Burnley and Padiham chapelries amounting to about 150 and 175 inhabitants respectively).

There are no data available on mean household size in the mid-sixteenth century, but if the same multiplier of 4.77 is applied to the figures derived from the communicants' returns of 1563, it suggests that the population of Colne chapelry at this time was about 1500, and that of Newchurch in Pendle just 300.[22] It is possible, since the population grew considerably between the mid-sixteenth and mid-seventeenth centuries, that mean household size in 1563 was considerably less than 4.77, and therefore that we have overestimated the size of the population in 1563. Nevertheless, it seems safe to infer that between the mid-sixteenth and mid-seventeenth centuries, the population of the chapelries of Colne and Newchurch in Pendle at least doubled in size.[23]

THE CHRONOLOGY OF DEMOGRAPHIC CHANGE

Contemporaries were certainly aware of population growth in this area. For example, Richard Towneley, Esquire, alleged in the mid-1540s that his late father had built a new mill at Padiham for the use of the tenants of Pendle forest 'lately multiplied and increased'.[24] Furthermore, it was alleged in 1596, during another dispute over suit to Carr mill, that where there had been one household in Pendle forest when Lawrence Towneley had been granted his lease for Carr mill (1542), there were now at least twenty. This last estimate was clearly an exaggeration – it was in the interests of the defendants to show that the Pendle population was of such size that Carr mill was overburdened, and that another was needed.[25]

Demographic change prior to 1563 is not easy to establish. Population growth seems to have been particularly rapid in the forest areas after the disafforestation and grant of lands by copy of court roll in 1507.[26] A comparison of the lists of tenants for 1443, 1507 and 1527 illustrates this rapid increase.[27] The number of copyholds in Colne manor, by contrast, hardly increased. However, one should not necessarily assume that the rate of increase of landholdings was proportionate to the rise in population, or indeed reflected it at all, for such an assumption takes no account of changes in the proportion of the landless or of subtenants in the total population, nor of changes in the structure of landholding and inheritance. Nevertheless, the opening up of large tracts of forest land, together with the evidence of the rentals and contemporary comments, suggest beyond reasonable doubt that the forest populations were increasing rapidly in the very early sixteenth century.

For the later sixteenth and early seventeenth centuries, the parish registers offer more reliable evidence on the actual timing of population growth. Unfortunately, the earliest surviving registers (those for Burnley and Padiham chapelries, which begin in 1562 and 1573 respectively)[28] are largely peripheral for our purposes, for each contained only small sections of Pendle forest. The most important register of all, that for Colne chapelry, does not begin until 1599,[29] and that for Newchurch in Pendle appears not to have survived at all. However, we do possess Bishops' transcripts of the Newchurch registers for fifteen years between 1602 and 1637,[30] and, in addition, a nineteenth-century genealogist's copy of the Bishops' transcripts for Newchurch from 1574 is available, but it suffers from under-registration of vital events and should not be relied upon for any individual year.[31]

The Colne register appears, on the whole, to be an accurate compilation, and does not seem to suffer from serious gaps and omissions.[32] Also there is the question of what proportion of vital events, particularly those of Catholics, escaped registration. It was alleged in c.1591 that marriages and christenings in Lancashire and Cheshire were very commonly celebrated in secret by Catholic priests. On the other hand, it was claimed that children baptised according to the laws were subsequently rebaptised by 'massing priests' in some parts of Lancashire,[33] which implies that Catholics' baptisms were recorded in the parish registers. In Colne chapelry it seems that Catholics' vital events, not only burials, but also baptisms and marriages too, were recorded in the register.[34] Nevertheless, some under-registration must have occurred. For example, Roger Blakey, a curate of Colne, was often in trouble for conducting secret illegal marriages for money, and his successor continued the practice.[35]

It is clear from the Colne register that there was a considerable surplus of baptisms over burials in the early seventeenth century. During the period from 1600 to 1639, baptisms exceeded burials by 1,310. This surplus of baptisms over burials was particularly noticeable during the 1600s, when baptisms exceeded burials by 453; subsequently, this surplus declined to 378 in the 1610s, 317 in the 1620s and 162 in the 1630s.[36] The gap between baptisms and burials can be seen clearly in Graph 2.1, where the relative importance of baptisms and burials may also be observed.

The data for the surplus of baptisms over burials suggest that the population was rising rapidly in Colne chapelry, particularly in the 1600s. One important caveat, however, must be stressed. Calculations which are based on the surplus of baptisms over burials do not take migration into account, and will only reflect actual population growth if net migration is zero.[37] Regrettably, data are lacking on both in- and out-migration, but it does seem likely that net out-

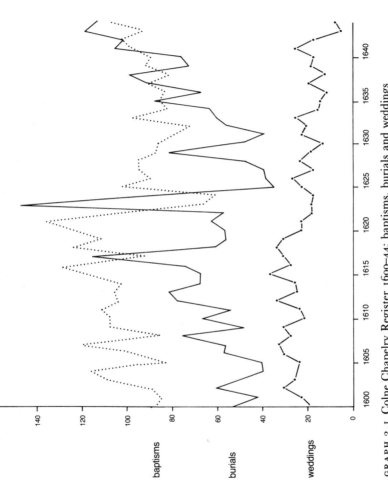

GRAPH 2.1 Colne Chapelry Register 1600-44; baptisms, burials and weddings

migration was occurring on a significant scale in the 1620s and 1630s, since a steep decline in the number of marriages celebrated may be observed, which is out of all proportion to conceivable changes in the age structure of the population or in patterns of marriage behaviour.[38] The explanation for such out-migration in the 1620s may well have been the difficulties caused by the pronounced depression in the local kersey industry,[39] together with the onerous composition payments required by the Duchy from the tenants of Colne manor,[40] and, above all, the crisis mortality of 1623, to which we turn in the next section.

The Newchurch transcripts, though not sufficiently reliable for annual analysis, do indicate the broad trends of demographic change.[41] There was a surplus of baptisms over burials of 268 for the period from 1580 to 1639, or of 307 if the data are corrected for under-registration. It seems that the period of most rapid growth occurred in the 1600s and 1610s.[42]

The Burnley register, which includes a small part of Pendle forest, is especially useful in that it commences in 1562. Indeed, Burnley's demographic history appears to have been quite different from that of Colne, for comparatively little growth took place in the seventeenth century. A fairly rapid increase in population, however, seems to have taken place in the 1560s and 1570s, which was heavily cut back by crisis mortality in 1587–8 and in 1597.[43] Padiham combined elements of both Colne and Burnley, for a surplus of baptisms over burials occurred in the 1570s (and continued in the 1580s, in contrast to Burnley), but was especially noticeable in the 1600s, and, to a lesser extent, in the 1610s.[44]

CRISIS MORTALITY

It has been argued recently by Appleby that north-west England was peculiarly prone to famine, and in this respect differed from much of the rest of the country. He examined the demographic crises of 1587–8, 1597–8 and 1623 in Cumberland and Westmorland, and concluded that famine was a major cause of high mortality in 1597–8 and 1623, and a contributory cause in 1587–8.[45] A recent study of the Lancashire population crisis of 1623 has confirmed Appleby's finding that starvation was a primary cause of the high mortality.[46] The conclusion that starvation was a major determinant of these periods of high mortality is a major revision of previous work.[47]

In 1623 the numbers of burials in the chapelries of Colne, Burnley and Padiham increased by 144%, 165% and 159% respectively (compared with the period from 1618 to 1622).[48] Burial figures began to rise in Colne in the last quarter of 1622, fell somewhat in the next quarter, but subsequently rose to very high levels for the next four quarters. They did not return to normal levels until the spring of 1624.[49] A similar pattern was apparent in both Burnley and Padiham, though burials continued to rise in the first quarter of 1623 in the former, whilst high mortality was not evident until the second quarter of the year in Padiham.[50] Thus, very high mortality occurred in all three chapelries from at least the second quarter of 1623, and persisted into the first quarter of 1624. Mortality also appears to have been high in Newchurch during this time, but did not reach the same level as in the other three chapelries.[51]

By comparing conceptions[52] and burials, it is apparent that conceptions started to fall noticeably in Colne in the last quarter of 1622, and did not recover markedly until the spring of 1624; conceptions therefore followed an inverse pattern to that of burials.[53] Appleby argued that a reduction in the number of conceptions at a time of high mortality was more usually a sign of famine than epidemic disease, since malnutrition was very likely to produce amenorrhoea. He also pointed out, however, that this is a necessary but not sufficient test for the presence of famine, since disease might also reduce the number of conceptions by killing pregnant women and marriage partners, by inducing spontaneous abortions or by encouraging voluntary abstinence, postponement of marriage or flight from the area.[54] Wrigley and Schofield have shown that a 'scissors' movement in conceptions and burials is not in itself conclusive proof of famine, without independent evidence of high food prices.[55] This 'scissors' movement is also present in the data derived from the registers of Burnley and Padiham chapelries,[56] and is also evident in the Newchurch transcripts.[57]

There are other signs of the presence of famine in 1623. First, the absence of a strong seasonal pattern to mortality in 1623–4 suggests that we can rule out the hypothesis that a single epidemic disease was responsible. For example, bubonic plague usually struck in the summer and autumn, dysentery in the late summer, and typhus in the winter, whilst influenza had a quick epidemic course through a community (approximately seven weeks).[58] This of course does not eliminate the possibility that more than one epidemic disease was at work. Nevertheless, we can certainly discount dysentery as a contributory cause of the crisis mortality, since it does not cause a fall in conceptions and kills primarily the young.[59] Only 12% of those who died in Colne chapelry between October 1622 and March 1624 were described in the burial register as infants or children; this compares with 17% in this category between January 1618 and September 1622.[60] This last piece of evidence perhaps conflicts with the hypothesis that starvation was the major killer, for as Appleby pointed out, one of the characteristics of famine was that it killed a high proportion of infants and children, and also the economically marginal.[61] However, whilst the numbers of infants and children dying fell relative to the adult population, in absolute numbers they rose. In addition, whilst the clerk of Colne did not record the deaths of poor migrants, that of Burnley noted the deaths of 9 poor men, women and children in 1623,[62] and 3 poor wanderers or beggars were buried in Padiham between May 1623 and March 1624.[63] There were none described in this way in Burnley or Padiham burial registers in 1621 or 1622.

Secondly, the wide geographical spread of crisis mortality in 1623 suggests that epidemic disease was not the primary factor responsible, for it is unlikely that the same disease or diseases would have struck simultaneously over a wide region, including sparsely populated rural areas.[64] The crisis of 1623 affected most of the parishes in Lancashire, for burials at least doubled in 41 out of 54 parishes, and in only three parishes were mortality levels found to be normal. The worst affected areas lay on the 40 inch per annum rainfall contour and between 600 and 1,000 feet above sea level.[65]

Thirdly, we have local evidence that bad harvests in 1621 and 1622 pushed up grain prices to high levels. The price of wheat stood at 3s 9d or 4s a mett (a local measurement – equivalent to two pecks) in October 1620, but had risen to 9s by November 1621; it was also at this price in August 1623, and even in December 1624, the price of wheat stood at 6s a mett. This was considerably higher than it had been before 1621. The price of oats, the staple diet of most of the population (but especially the poor), rose from 9s 6d a quarter at Michaelmas 1621 to between 20s and 24s a quarter at Michaelmas 1622.[66] Unfortunately, we do not appear to have data on the price of oats in 1623.

Fourthly, we have strong evidence of a pronounced and prolonged depression in the cloth industry at this time.[67] Drake suggests that this was a fundamental cause of the crisis mortality in the West Riding in 1623, since it reduced the earnings of many at a time when additional income was needed to pay for higher prices of food.[68] Appleby also noted the deleterious effects of the depression in the cloth industry, and its contribution to the famine in Westmorland, Lancashire and the West Riding.[69] Lastly, the scale of the composition payments to the Crown by tenants of the manors of the Honor of Clitheroe in 1618 (including Colne), must have exacerbated this loss of income.[70]

Whilst the evidence is by no means conclusive, the hypothesis that famine played a major role in the mortality crisis of 1623 is substantially corroborated.[71] This view is strengthened by an examination of the productivity of arable farming, the structure of landholding and the distribution of wealth in this area. It appears that a large proportion of the population was economically marginal, and that this group increased in number over time, whilst its economic fortunes deteriorated.[72]

ILLEGITIMACY

A report to the Privy Council in c.1591 referred to the 'multitude of bastards' in Lancashire and Cheshire.[73] Laslett has found that Lancashire was an area of high illegitimacy ratios, and claimed that bastardy ratios might reach 9% or 10% over whole decades in certain parishes in Elizabethan Lancashire and Cheshire.[74]

It is thus not surprising to find that there were also high illegitimacy ratios in north-east Lancashire, and that these persisted over long periods of time. For example, the illegitimacy ratio for Colne chapelry between 1600 and 1639 was 11.97%; indeed, in the 1600s, it was as high as 14.74%.[75] This was far higher than the illegitimacy ratios calculated for the chapelries of Newchurch in Pendle, Burnley and Padiham during this period, which were 4.72%, 8.96% and 7.03% respectively.[76] All of these ratios, however, were well in excess of the 'national' average, which was between 2% and 3% from 1600 to 1640.[77]

Another feature which is particularly noteworthy is that illegitimacy ratios rose to a very high level in the late Elizabethan period, and then fell in the 1610s (in the case of Colne and Burnley) and 1620s (Padiham).[78] This pattern roughly follows that found by Laslett in his national sample;[79] it may reflect genuine fluctuations in the incidence of illegitimacy, or alternatively, might indicate a change in the willingness of parish clerks to distinguish between legitimate and illegitimate births.

In order to investigate these questions further, the wills proved at
Chester of *supra* male testators from Colne chapelry and Pendle
forest have been examined for reference to illegitimate children.
Higher levels of bastardy in the early seventeenth century compared
with the later sixteenth century were confirmed. In the period from
1546 to 1599, just 8% of testators who mentioned children in their
wills referred to bastard offspring, compared with 17% between
1600 and 1640.[80] Furthermore, it was noticeable that whilst there
was a higher incidence of illegitimacy in Colne chapelry (excluding
Barrowford) than in Pendle forest, bastardy in north-east Pendle
mirrored that in Colne during the early seventeenth century.[81] It is
therefore not surprising to find that cases of bastardy predominate
amongst the business contained in the Quarter Sessions recognisance rolls relating to this area, 1626–42; no less than 35 of the 61
cases (57%) in which the nature of the business was stated relate to
bastardy.[82]

High levels of illegitimacy persisted, though at fluctuating levels,
over long periods of time. They do not appear to have been tied to
short-term economic change in the way, for example, that the
illegitimacy 'boom' in Terling in the 1590s and 1600s seems to have
been linked to the disruption of courtship and marriage strategies by
the disastrous harvests of the 1590s, set against a background of
economic polarisation in society.[83] Nor can one view the incidence of
illegitimacy simply as a function of poverty, for this is disproved by
the high levels of bastardy found amongst the children of testators
who had at least £40 in personal estate. Nevertheless, the secular rise
in illegitimacy ratios in Burnley and Padiham in the late sixteenth
century may be related to a change in courtship patterns following
the impoverishment of many of the population and the growth in the
numbers of the landless and virtually landless.[84] However, this
argument cannot be developed too far, for increasing illegitimacy
was also apparent amongst the relatively prosperous *supra* testators.
The predominance of lower socio-economic groups amongst the
putative fathers of bastards brought before Quarter Sessions[85] is not
surprising, for these were men who had not indicated their
willingness to help financially with the upbringing of their bastards
(presumably in some cases out of poverty, since upkeep could be
onerous, usually £1 or £1 6s 8d a year in the 1620s and 1630s).[86]

There is some evidence that social stigma was attached to
bastard-bearing. For example, the Pendle witch Elizabeth Device
allegedly bewitched to death John Robinson alias Swyer for

accusing her of bearing a bastard.[87] This may be untypical, for it seems strange that we should find a high level of illegitimacy across the social scale compatible with such a stigma.

CONCLUSION

The demographic data available for the Colne area suggest that the local population approximately doubled in size between the mid sixteenth and the mid seventeenth centuries, despite periods of crisis mortality. It is regrettable that there are no data on age-specific movements of vital events, particularly on mean age at first marriage for women, but the extreme problems of identification of individuals discussed in the last chapter and the absence of parish registers for many years makes family reconstitution impossible. Nevertheless, the demographic picture is reasonably clear, and it will become apparent in subsequent chapters that population growth had implications of fundamental importance for the health of the local economy and the structure of industry.

NOTES

[1] Russell, *British medieval population*, Chapter 6
[2] P.R.O. E.179/130/28
[3] Stephens, *Sources for English local history*, p. 27
[4] Cornwall, 'English population' and 'English country towns', *passim*; Spufford, *Contrasting communities*, pp. 10ff. One should note that the muster rolls of 1522, which Cornwall used in conjunction with the subsidy, appear not to have survived for this area
[5] Smith, *Land and politics*, p. 264
[6] Thirsk, 'Sources of information on population', pp. 130–1
[7] P.R.O. E.179/130/87, indenture 20 Dec. 1524 for Blackburn Hundred. This lists a single taxpayer in Foulridge, 18 in Colne, 18 in Marsden, 11 in Trawden and 16 in Pendle
[8] The communicants' returns of 1563 (B.L.Harleian 594, fol. 102) record 315 households in Colne chapelry and 64 in Newchurch in Pendle chapelry in September 1563. The former figure includes Barrowford Booth in Pendle forest and the latter does not include the sections of Pendle forest in the chapelries of Burnley and Padiham. In both cases, the difference between the subsidy and the communicants' returns is large. The rental of 1527 (P.R.O. D.L.43/15/15, printed in Farrer, *Court rolls*, vol. 2, pp. 377–83) lists a total of 92 copyhold tenancies in Colne manor, Trawden forest and Little Marsden. This compares with 47 taxpayers in Colne, Marsden and Trawden in 1524. Similarly, whilst 16 paid tax in Pendle forest in 1524, there were 100 copyhold tenancies in the forest (excluding Ightenhill Park and Sabden Hey) in 1527

[9] Thirsk, 'Sources of information on population', p. 131

[10] The use of chantry certificates for estimating population size has been suggested by, amongst others, Thirsk, 'Sources of information on population', pp. 131–2, and by Drake, *Historical demography: problems and projects*, p. 82

[11] This was also noted by Appleby, *Famine in Tudor and Stuart England*, p. 26. For the surviving returns, see Hollingsworth, *Historical demography*, p. 83

[12] B.L.Harleian 594, fol. 102; Fishwick, *Lancashire and Cheshire church surveys*, pp. 164–8

[13] See Chapter 1, p. 3.

[14] On religious changes in Lancashire, see especially Haigh, *Reformation and resistance*, and Richardson, *Puritanism in north-west England*

[15] Raines, 'State of the county of Lancaster', p. 3

[16] P.R.O. S.P.12/240, fol. 222v

[17] See Haigh, *Reformation and resistance*, Chapter 14, and 'Continuity of Catholicism', especially pp. 45, 50, 67–8

[18] L.R.O. MF4a

[19] P.R.O. E.179/250/11, Parts 3 and 7

[20] To obtain an estimate for the population of Colne chapelry from the hearth tax, it is necessary to calculate the number of households in Barrowford Booth, which was included under Pendle forest in the hearth tax, but which formed part of Colne chapelry. The evidence of the Protestation Oath of March 1642 (L.R.O. MF25; the original is in the House of Lords Record Office) was used for this purpose, in which it was found that Barrowford constituted 33% of the inhabitants of Pendle forest. If it is assumed that this proportion was the same in 1664, the number of households in Barrowford may be estimated at 101 (out of a total of 304 households in the whole of Pendle forest). Using the same methodology, the number of households in Newchurch was 134, and there were 32 and 37 households in the Pendle forest sections of Burnley and Padiham chapelries. There were 523 households recorded in the hearth tax returns for Colne, Marsden, Trawden and Foulridge, and if we add our estimate of the number of Barrowford households (101), we produce an estimate of 624 for the number of households in Colne chapelry

[21] Fishwick, *Lancashire and Cheshire church surveys*, p. 164

[22] It is impossible to calculate the size of the small sections of Pendle forest which lay in Burnley and Padiham chapelries, for there is no way of calculating what proportion of their respective chapelries they represented

[23] For further details, see Swain, 'Industry and economy', pp. 25–33

[24] P.R.O. D.L.1/15/T7

[25] P.R.O. D.L.1/208/A39

[26] See Chapter 4, for a discussion of the significance of the disafforestation

[27] See Table 5.1

[28] Farrer, *Registers of Burnley*, and Laycock, *Registers of Padiham*

[29] Ecroyd, *Registers of Colne*

[30] L.R.O. DRB 2/262

[31] L.R.O. P.R.2862/2/1. This is based on the Bishops' transcripts at Chester, and is dated 1 October 1897. Though it begins in 1574, there are,

on the transcriber's admission, many illegible entries for the early years. In addition, these transcripts are arranged alphabetically, and thus an illegible entry or a partly destroyed section in the Bishops' transcripts would be lost. The transcriber was concerned with genealogical, not demographic, questions. Whilst not reliable for any individual year, these transcripts may be used to detect broad changes over long periods of time

32 The main deficiency in the Colne register is that occasionally small sections of the baptism register are illegible; though the total number of entries may be ascertained, there may be a very slight tendency to understate the number of baptisms due to the possibility of the baptism of twins, who would be recorded on the same line. The same applies to illegitimacy ratios, which may be affected very slightly by this, and by the very occasional omission of an illegitimate baptism. See Ecroyd, *Registers of Colne, passim*

33 P.R.O. S.P.12/240, fol. 222v; these points are also noted in Raines, 'State of the county of Lancaster', p. 1

34 The prominent local Catholic families, such as the Towneleys, Blakeys, Houghtons, Waltons, Bannisters and Shireburns appear in baptism and wedding registers, as well as in the burial register; see Ecroyd, *Registers of Colne, passim*. For the names of prominent local recusants, see L.R.O. MF 4a, Metropolitan Visitation for 1595; see also the subsidy returns E.179/131/317, E.179/131/322, E.179/131/330 (1625–9) in which recusants and non-communicants' fines are recorded

35 Haigh, *Reformation and resistance*, pp. 238–9

36 Ecroyd, *Registers of Colne, passim*

37 Wrigley and Schofield, *Population history of England*, p. 185

38 See Graph 2.1. The average number of weddings per annum in Colne chapelry was 27 in the 1600s and 29 in the 1610s; it then fell sharply to 21 in the 1620s and to 18 in the 1630s

39 See Chapter 6, pp. 127–38, 142–4

40 See Chapter 4, pp. 61–5

41 If we compare the 15 (old style) years of surviving and usable Bishops' transcripts (L.R.O. DRB 2/262) for 1602, 1607–8, 1610, 1617, 1620–1, 1625, 1628–30, 1633–5 and 1637 with the totals calculated from the genealogist's transcripts (L.R.O. P.R.2862/2/1), it is apparent that there was under-registration. For the period 1602–17, baptisms were under-registered by an average of 4.8 per annum and burials by 3.8; under-registration was less noticeable for the period 1620–37, for baptisms were under-registered by an annual average of just 1.3 and burials by 1.4

42 It seems necessary to inflate the totals of baptisms and burials to combat the problem of under-registration, and it has been assumed that the data for 1580 to 1599 should be inflated by the same proportions as those figures for the 1600s and 1610s. The total for 1605, which is missing, has been estimated by using an average of the data for 1600–4 and 1606–19. No attempt has been made to use the data for the period 1574–9, since it is clear from the genealogist's transcripts that these years were largely illegible or damaged. The surplus of baptisms over burials for the sub-periods 1580–99, 1600–19 and 1620–39 were 78, 131 and 59, or 98, 151 and 58 if the data are corrected for under-registration

[43] Farrer, *Registers of Burnley*, *passim*. The figures for the surplus of baptisms over burials were as follows: 93 (1563–9), 119 (1570s), −102 (1580s), 33 (1590s), 65 (1600s), 143 (1610s), 58 (1620s), 101 (1630s). For a graph illustrating the annual totals of baptisms, burials and weddings, see Swain, 'Industry and economy', Graph 2.2, p. 42

[44] Laycock, *Registers of Padiham*, *passim*. The Padiham register is defective in certain years and the exact figures should not be relied upon too heavily during these periods; in addition, there are a small number of entries which may have been either baptisms or burials; see Swain, 'Industry and economy', p. 36, fn. 44. The surplus of baptisms over burials was as follows (a ? indicates that the register for part of the period was defective): 57 to 61 (1574–9), 59 to 61 (1582–9), 14? (1590s), 156 (1600s), 75 (1610s), − 6 to −10? (1620s), 46 to 52 (1630s)

[45] Appleby, 'Disease or famine?' and *Famine in Tudor and Stuart England* (especially Chapters 7–9)

[46] Rogers, *Lancashire population crisis*, pp. 26–7. I am grateful to Dr Richard Smith for drawing my attention to this study

[47] For example, Howson argued that plague was responsible for high mortality in north-west England in 1586–8, 1596–8 and 1622–3, though he noted that these years were also periods of scarcity and famine; Howson, 'Plague, poverty and population', p. 33. Sharpe France claimed that the high mortality of 1622–4 was caused by typhus and cannot be connected with any scarcity in England, for there were neither contemporary accounts of famine nor high grain prices. As will be seen later, he was certainly wrong in his assertion that prices of food did not rise. He was also completely wrong in stating that Padiham and Colne chapelries escaped this mortality. France, 'Plague in Lancashire', pp. 51–2. More recently, Shrewsbury argued that Lancashire was hit by epidemic disease in 1623, which may have been a combination of plague, smallpox and typhus. He argued that smallpox may have been present in Blackburn in 1623, and in Rochdale the seasonal pattern of the high mortality between 1 July 1623 and the end of February 1624 suggests the presence of plague followed by typhus. Shrewsbury, *History of bubonic plague*, pp. 311–13. The greatest drawback in these works is that mortality is not studied systematically, month by month, in conjunction with baptisms and grain prices. The dubious assumption underlying all of this work is that peaks of mortality must have been caused by disease alone

[48] Based on the burial registers; see Ecroyd, *Registers of Colne*, Farrer, *Registers of Burnley*, and Laycock, *Registers of Padiham*, *passim*

[49] The quarterly figures for burials in Colne chapelry, 1622–4, were as follows: 13, 10, 8, 28 (1622); 18, 35, 44, 50 (1623); 33, 16, 14, 14 (1624). See Swain, 'Industry and economy', Graph 2.3, p. 46

[50] In Burnley chapelry, 1622–4, quarterly burials were as follows: 17, 15, 10, 24 (1622); 29, 30, 42, 48 (1623); 27, 15, 7, 6 (1624). Quarterly burials in Padiham, 1622–4, were as follows: 7, 7, 3, 4 (1622); 9, 20, 17, 13 (1623); 20, 8, 3, 10 (1624). It should be noted that there is a gap in the burial register from 12 March until 27 April 1624, which, according to the curate, was because the register had been taken away; Laycock, *Registers of Padiham*, pp. 86–7. See Swain, 'Industry and economy', Graph 2.4, p. 47

[51] In the old style year 1623, there are 38 burials recorded, compared with 20 (1618), 11 (1619), 12 (1620), 31 (1621), 29 (1622), 13 (1624) and 15 (1625); L.R.O. P.R.2862/2/1. However, these figures should not be taken as reliable, for the Bishops' transcripts which survive for 1620 record 13 burials (not 12); in 1621, there were 37 burials (not 31), and in 1625, there were 16 burials (not 15); see L.R.O. DRB 2/262

[52] Conception is defined as baptism less nine months; this assumes that baptism occurred immediately after birth, but we have no evidence that this was not the case. See Appleby, *Famine in Tudor and Stuart England*, pp. 116, 239, and Drake, *Historical demography: problems and projects*, p. 105. See also Berry and Schofield, 'Age at baptism', where it is argued that it was not until towards the end of the eighteenth century that long intervals between birth and baptism became common

[53] Conceptions per quarter in Colne chapelry, 1622–4, were as follows: 25, 24, 21, 14 (1622); 8, 18, 10, 15 (1623); 18, 33, 20, 25 (1624). See Swain, 'Industry and economy', Graph 2.3, p. 46

[54] Appleby, *Famine in Tudor and Stuart England*, p. 118

[55] Wrigley and Schofield, *Population history of England*, p. 329

[56] Quarterly conceptions in Burnley, 1622–24, were as follows: 11, 18, 10, 8 (1622); 13, 12, 10, 9 (1623); 7, 25, 28, 12 (1624). In Padiham during this period, quarterly conceptions were: 7, 4, 7, 3 (1622); 3, 2, 1, 2 (1623); 4, 11, 1, 8 (1624). It should be noted that the Padiham data for the second and third quarters of 1623 are defective, for there were no baptisms recorded between 29 February and 17 June 1624; Laycock, *Registers of Padiham*, pp. 86–7. See Swain, 'Industry and economy', Graph 2.4, p. 47

[57] In the old style year 1623, there were 14 baptisms recorded in the genealogist's transcripts; this compares with 30 (1618), 18 (1619), 24 (1620), 41 (1621), 21 (1622), 17 (1624), 24 (1625) and 27 (1626); L.R.O. P.R.2862/2/1. When compared with the surviving Bishops' transcripts, these figures are seen to be slightly unreliable; there are 26 baptisms recorded in the Bishops' transcripts for 1620 (not 24), 41 in 1621 (also in the genealogist's transcripts) and 23 in 1625 (not 24); L.R.O. DRB 2/262

[58] There is a good summary of the salient characteristics of major epidemic diseases in Rogers, *Lancashire population crisis*, Appendix II, pp. 31–3. See also Appleby, *Famine in Tudor and Stuart England*, pp. 97–106, 119–20

[59] Appleby, *Famine in Tudor and Stuart England*, p. 120

[60] Ecroyd, *Registers of Colne*, pp. 185–93. Of 208 burials recorded between October 1622 and March 1624, 19 were described as infants, and 6 as children ('liberi'), or son or daughter ('fil' or 'junior'). This compares with a total of 273 burials recorded between January 1618 and September 1622, of which 31 were described as infants and 16 as children ('fil'). This methodology for determining the proportion of infant and child deaths is very crude, for Eversley pointed out that for every child not described as 'fil' in the burial registers, another was incorrectly described as 'fil', even though he was in his twenties. However, he argued that it is safe to assume that these cases cancel each other out. Eversley, 'Exploitation of Anglican parish registers', p. 71. Nevertheless, the accuracy of registration of infant and child mortality in Colne is doubtful, for Rogers found in his Lancashire

sample of parishes that 44% of deaths between 1611 and 1630 (excluding 1623) were of children and 35% in 1623; Rogers, *Lancashire population crisis*, p. 15. This compares with 23% and 10% in Colne during the same periods

[61] Appleby, *Famine in Tudor and Stuart England*, p. 118

[62] Farrer, *Registers of Burnley*, pp. 236–9

[63] Laycock, *Registers of Padiham*, pp. 85–6

[64] Appleby, *Famine in Tudor and Stuart England*, p. 117

[65] Rogers, *Lancashire population crisis*, pp. 11, 29–30; Appleby, *Famine in Tudor and Stuart England*, p. 147; Smith, 'Population and its geography', p. 214

[66] L.R.O. DDPt 1. These accounts are not separately catalogued or foliated. I am extremely grateful to Dr. William King for pointing out to me the existence of these accounts. It is essential to use local prices where possible; Appleby's use of southern price data is a major deficiency in his argument. Appleby, *Famine in Tudor and Stuart England*, pp. 106, 125, 190

[67] See Chapter 6, pp. 127–38, 142–4

[68] Drake, 'Elementary exercise', pp. 432, 435–6. See also Drake, *Historical demography: problems and projects*, p. 109

[69] Appleby, *Famine in Tudor and Stuart England*, pp. 146, 148–9, 183

[70] See Chapter 4, pp. 61–5

[71] This area appears to have been particularly prone to famine, for the Burnley and Padiham chapelry registers record severe mortality crises in 1587–8 and 1597–8, which seem to have been caused, in part at least, by famine; see Swain 'Industry and economy', pp. 52–5

[72] See Chapters 3 and 5

[73] P.R.O. S.P. 12/240 fol. 222, article 1; fol. 222v, article 18

[74] Laslett and Oosterveen, 'Long-term trends in bastardy', p. 255. They quote the example of the parish of Eccles in Lancashire, which had an illegitimacy ratio of 7.2% during the period, 1581–1640; *ibid.*, p. 278. See also Laslett, *Family life and illicit love*, chapter 3, which is a revised version of this article. Keith Wrightson has argued that south Lancashire was an area of high bastardy ratios and that ecclesiastical discipline before 1640 may have been peculiarly weak. See Wrightson, 'Nadir of English illegitimacy', p. 180, and also Wrightson's thesis, 'Puritan reformation of manners', p. 54, in which the illegitimacy ratios for Rochdale, Eccles, Standish, Chorley and Sefton are presented by decade. The highest ratio recorded (10%) was for Sefton, 1631–40

[75] Ecroyd, *Registers of Colne, passim*. During the period from 1600 to 1639, a total of 3,910 baptisms were recorded, of which 468 were described as bastards; in the 1600s, 145 out of 984 baptisms were of illegitimate children. See Swain, 'Industry and economy', Table 2.8, p. 57

[76] The Newchurch ratio has been calculated from the fifteen surviving years of Bishops' transcripts, 1602–37, in which 17 out of 360 recorded baptisms were of illegitimate children; L.R.O. DRB 2/262. In Burnley chapelry, there were 256 illegitimate baptisms out of a total of 2,857 between 1600 and 1639; in Padiham chapelry, 87 out of 1,238 baptisms recorded between 1600 and 1639 fell into this category; Farrer, *Registers of Burnley*, and Laycock, *Registers of Padiham, passim*. See Swain, 'Industry and economy', Table 2.8, p. 57

[77] Laslett, 'Comparing illegitimacy over time and between cultures', pp. 14, 24

[78] See Swain, 'Industry and economy', Table 2.8, p. 57. In Colne, the illegitimacy ratio stood at nearly 15% in the 1600s, but subsequently fell to around 11% in the 1610s, 1620s and 1630s. In Burnley, the illegitimacy ratio fluctuated in the later sixteenth century, but was as high as 11% in the 1600s and then fell to between 8% and 9%, 1610–1639. In Padiham, the ratio stood at 3% in the 1580s, but rose to 8% in the 1590s, 9% in the 1600s and $9\frac{1}{2}$% in the 1610s; it then fell to 3% in the 1620s, increasing to 6% in the 1630s

[79] Laslett, 'Comparing illegitimacy over time and between cultures', pp. 14, 18

[80] L.R.O. WCW *Supra, passim*. In the period 1546–1599, 51 out of 63 male testators from Colne chapelry and Pendle forest referred to children, and only 4 of these mentioned having illegitimate children; in the period from 1600 to 1640, 99 out of 129 male testators mentioned having children and 17 of these referred to bastard offspring. See Swain, 'Industry and economy' Table 2.9, p. 59

[81] *Ibid.* Of those male testators from Colne chapelry (minus Barrowford) in the period to 1599 who mentioned children, 15% referred to illegitimate children (27 out of 36 testators mentioned children, and 4 of these referred to their bastard children), but no illegitimate offspring were noted in the 27 wills of male testators from Pendle forest. In the period from 1600 to 1640, 20% of male Colne testators who mentioned children referred to bastard offspring (55 out of 71 testators mentioned children, and 11 of these referred to illegitimate children), and similarly 20% of male testators in Barrowford and Roughlee mentioned bastard children (15 out of 21 testators referred to children, and 3 of these mentioned illegitimate offspring), compared with only 10% of male testators in the rest of Pendle forest (29 out of 37 male testators referred to their children and 3 of these mentioned bastards)

[82] L.R.O. QSB 1/9 – QSB 1/269a

[83] Levine and Wrightson, 'Social context of illegitimacy', pp. 165, 170–2

[84] See Chapter 5

[85] Of the 29 cases in Colne, Pendle and Trawden, 1626–1642, where the occupations of the bastards' fathers are given, 6 were described as yeomen, 14 as husbandmen, 2 as clothiers, 3 as woollen weavers, 1 as a feltmaker, 2 as colliers and 1 as a miller; L.R.O. QSB 1, *passim*

[86] Annual maintenance by the father to the mother was assessed at £1 in 2 cases (QSB 1/17/39, QSB 1/29/33) and at £1 6s 8d for 12 years in another 2 cases (QSB 1/53/17, QSB 1/197/29). In another case, the father was ordered to pay £2 a year for 4 years, and then take the child into his own house and bring him up until the age of 12 (QSB 1/53/18). The size of these payments can best be judged by comparison with daily wage rates; in the 1620s and 1630s, for example, a slater was usually paid 4d, excluding the food which he was given, whilst a mower received 6d; see Swain, 'Industry and economy', pp. 341–3

[87] Crossley, *Potts' discovery of witches*, F3

CHAPTER III

AGRICULTURE

In this chapter, we investigate the nature of agricultural practice in Colne chapelry and Pendle forest in the sixteenth and early seventeenth centuries. It will be shown that, due to the harshness of the climate and the unproductiveness of the land, the predominant form of agriculture was pastoral. This took the form of stock-raising and dairying, especially the former. Thus there was a degree of continuity between medieval and early modern agriculture in this area.

In a survey of Lancashire agriculture drawn up in 1795, John Holt concluded that 'the north-east part of the county, Blackburn, Clitheroe, Haslingden etc. is rugged, interspersed with many rivulets with a thin stratum of upper soil'.[1] His opinion was shared by the forest tenants of the Honor of Clitheroe, who in 1609 noted the 'extreme barrenness of that soil and coldness of that country'.[2] Yet natural conditions were not entirely unfavourable, for the high level of rainfall, though unpromising for arable cultivation, helped to ensure that a good supply of grass was available.[3] Under these circumstances, it was not unnatural that agriculture should have been predominantly pastoral.

This region has been classified by Joan Thirsk under the general heading 'open pasture'; specifically as one of, 'cattle and sheep rearing, sometimes with dairying'.[4] However, attempts to establish more precisely the relative importance of arable and pastoral farming in the Colne district are not as easy as might at first be supposed.

One way of assessing the relative importance of arable and pasture is to calculate the proportion of land described as arable, meadow and pasture in sources such as surveys and final concords. Many rentals have survived for this area, but we do not have a survey which gives the precise acreage devoted to arable, meadow and pasture. Nevertheless, such evidence is available for the adjacent manor of Ightenhill, where it was found in 1617 that 42% of the acreage for which rent was paid was designated as arable, 12% as meadow and 46% as pasture. In addition, there were 2,254 Lancashire acres of commons and wastes which might be used as pasture.[5] It is unlikely that land use in Colne manor and in the forests of Trawden and Pendle differed greatly from that prevailing in Ightenhill manor.

Further evidence is provided by Rodgers' study of final concords for the period from 1450 to 1558. Rodgers calculated the proportion of land described as arable, meadow and pasture, but he excluded wasteland, since he found that it varied enormously and erratically from one area to another. Whilst, as Rodgers admitted, the exclusion of waste represents a weakness in the analysis (since the distinction between pasture and waste must have been rather arbitrary in many cases), we do have a rough guide to land use. Rodgers found that in the Rossendale uplands in east Lancashire, arable constituted a consistently low proportion of the recorded productive acreage, rarely more than 40%, and pasture amounted to at least as much as arable. In Colne, Rodgers calculated that 49% of the land was described as arable, 26% as meadow and 25% as pasture, compared with 38%, 16% and 46% respectively for the Rossendale region as a whole. By contrast, between 55% and 62% of productive land was under the plough in the more arable regions in Lancashire.[6] Thus both sources suggest that agriculture in the Colne area was largely pastoral, but with a significant amount of arable cultivation.

There is one particular difficulty, however, in the above approach. It seems that it was extremely difficult to distinguish between arable, meadow and pasture in north-east Lancashire during this period, since land use may have varied from year to year. This was specifically noted in a survey of Rochdale in 1610,[7] and so acreages of arable, meadow and pasture given in surveys or final concords may have been largely notional, or representative only of a single (possibly atypical) year's practice. Thus it seems sensible to look for further and possibly more reliable evidence.

It has been noted by Overton that a rough guide to the relative importance of arable and pasture is provided by a calculation of the ratio of the valuation of crops to livestock in probate inventories, which, he argues, measures 'the ratio by value of working capital tied up in these two branches of farming'.[8] Following Overton's method, 35 *supra* inventories of male testators, drawn up during the period 1558–1640, and relating to property in Colne chapelry and Pendle forest, were surveyed.[9] Only August, September and October inventories were used, these being the months of harvest.[10] It was found that livestock represented 69.6% of the total figure for livestock and crops, corroborating the previous findings that the pastoral sector was predominant in the Colne district.

Turning to the agricultural organisation and regulation of land, it is unclear whether common arable fields existed in Colne manor in the early sixteenth century. In 1510, the Colne jury presented 'the tenants of Trawden and Winewall for trespassing in Colne fields in passing over arable land there with their horses'.[11] Tupling has interpreted this as evidence of open arable fields in Colne.[12] However, the meaning of 'Colne fields' is open to question; indeed, it has been noted that even reference to 'townfield' or 'common field' does not always provide firm evidence of open and common fields.[13] On the contrary, the multiplicity of field names recorded in the Colne halmote rolls is suggestive of a large number of small, enclosed fields. For example, the following areas are mentioned in the period up to 1540: Broadfield, Colne fields, Eastfield, Greenfield, Hanefields, Judfields, Marsden fields, Newfield, Priestfield, Southfield, Westfield and Winter field. Furthermore, other areas were explicitly described as enclosures; for example, Blackstub Heys, Coldwell field, Lower Walkerfield, Nether Hey and Smith Close.[14] Some enclosures were in larger areas designated as 'fields'; thus Laithe Flatt and Little Kirk Hey were both situated in Southfield.[15] This suggests that Southfield at least had once been held in common.

In the forests, the booths were leased to a number of tenants at the disafforestation in 1507.[16] Some portions of these were held in common initially, but were subsequently subdivided by pleas of partition. For example, in 1529 the Trawden jury made an award that the vaccary of Beardshaw Booth should be divided according to the rent of each tenant.[17] Similar developments occurred in Pendle; in 1546 the jury there ordered that the 'mean ground' in Over and Nether Roughlee should be divided in proportion to the rents of the various holdings.[18] The exact agricultural use of this 'mean ground' is unclear.

In order that all might receive a fair share in the commons and wastes, it was obviously necessary to establish some regulations governing their use, even in areas such as Colne manor where the commons and wastes were extremely plentiful.[19] Many tenants were fined in the halmotes of Colne manor, Trawden and Pendle forests for overstocking the commons with more livestock than they were permitted.[20] The usual method of allocating a share in the commons and wastes seems to have been to limit the number of livestock which might be pastured according to the size of a tenant's holding. Thus in 1518, the Trawden jury ordered that no tenant from Wycoller or Winewall was to have more beasts in Netherdene than he ought to have 'for his stint or by virtue of his holding'.[21] In some land transactions, the accompanying rights of pasture were explicitly mentioned. In 1631, John Robinson of Goldshaw in Pendle surrendered a messuage and 20 acres at Deerstones, together with 'liberty to pasture 20 sheep, viz. 20 sheep gates'.[22]

The commons and wastes were not only of value as a source of pasture, for tenants of Colne manor were also entitled to collect turf, slate, limestone and other stones, sand, gravel, marl, clay, sods, heath, furling and gorse, providing that it was used only on their own holdings.[23] These tenants were thus unwilling to see their commons enclosed, and they declared in 1594 that the commons and wastes represented

their greatest stay of living, and that the same inhabitants are therefore very unwilling that the said moors, wastes and commons or any part thereof should be improved or enclosed, for that the same should as well tend to the great prejudice of their said common and profits, in so much as no enclosure can be had leaving sufficient, as also to the great impoverishing of the said inhabitants, but especially of the poorer sort now much relieved by the said commons.[24]

It was therefore of great importance that the Duchy compelled the tenants of Colne manor to accept individual portions of waste in 1618.[25] Some implications of this development are discussed in subsequent chapters. Many who could not afford to enclose their allotted portions were compelled to sell part or all of their shares, thereby alienating many valuable rights and reducing their capacity to keep as many livestock as previously.[26] Conversely, for those who could afford to undertake the necessary expenses of enclosure, they might then pasture as many beasts as they wished on their portion of waste.

The low profitability of agriculture in this area is well illustrated by the following extract from a petition of the forest tenants of Rossendale, Pendle, Trawden and Accrington in 1608. They claimed that since the disafforestation in 1507,

not only in the enclosure of the same copyholds and the continual manuring and tilling thereof, being before that time in respect both of the nature of the country and the soil thereabouts extremely barren and unprofitable and as yet capable of no other corn but oats and that but only in dry years and not without the continual charge of every third year's new manuring, but also in the building of their houses and habitations thereon having no timber there nor within many miles thereof, and having from time to time ever since enjoyed the same and therefore paid a rent and fine at the first as much or more and now very near the value thereof, have nearly disposed, employed and placed all the fruit and increase of their ancestors and their own labours and industries and the estates and maintenance of themselves, their families and posterities upon the same copyholds . . .[27]

We should not accept the tenants' claims uncritically, for the petition was designed to persuade the Duchy that the tenants were too poor to afford to purchase the freehold of their estates. The picture was certainly not as bleak as the tenants painted it; for example, inventories of the forest tenants demonstrate that crops other than oats were grown, such as barley and wheat.[28] Nevertheless, as we noted in the last chapter, the strong evidence of starvation in 1623 following the bad harvests of 1621–2.[29] gives some indication that oats could only be grown successfully in dry years.

Tenants were clearly anxious to maintain or improve the fertility of their holdings. The above quotation suggests that it was common practice to manure holdings every three years. However, only 22% of *supra* testators' inventories listed manure explicitly. This proportion must be regarded as a minimum, for in all cases manure was valued cheaply (in no cases at more than £1) and therefore in some inventories appraisers may not have bothered to record it.[30]

Other fertilisers employed in this area included both marl and lime. Norden claimed in 1607 that Lancashire and other counties had benefited from the use of marl,[31] and this was reiterated by John Holt in his survey of Lancashire agriculture in 1795: 'marl is the great article of fertilisation and the foundation of the improvements in the agriculture of this county'.[32] Marl was certainly available in this locality, for marl pits were noted in Lower Laund in 1537 and in Higham in 1561 (both of which were in Pendle forest).[33] Some field names clearly display the use of marl. For example, the lands of the Barcrofts, a gentry family of Lodge in Pendle, included closes called 'Tom Marled', 'John Marled', 'Old Marled' and 'Little Marled' in 1578;[34] other instances included a small close of meadow land at Haughead in Pendle called 'The Marled', and two other closes there called 'Giles Marled' and 'Marled Earth',[35] and also 'Marled Scar' in Trawden forest.[36]

Kerridge has argued that increased costs and diminishing returns applied with marl; the land became glutted, and lime or manure was then needed to rectify the situation. Furthermore, he argued that this saturation point had been widely reached in the Lancashire plain towards the end of the sixteenth century, and subsequently lime was increasingly used instead.[37] It is possible that this development occurred in the Colne district too, and that this helps to explain the noticeable increase in the proportion of inventories listing lime or limestone in the early seventeenth century compared with the period up to 1600.[38] However, it would be dangerous to develop this argument too far, since lime was also used in the making of mortar, the demand for which presumably increased due to population growth during this period.

Lime was certainly in use as a fertiliser in this area. For example, lands called 'Old Limed' and 'New Limed' in Higham Booth in Pendle were noted in 1600.[39] Sometimes the use of lime was stipulated as part of a leasing arrangement. In 1588, Robert Robinson was to occupy a house and two closes at Laund in Roughlee for a period of twelve years, but was not to plough or sow any part of the land before first liming it.[40]

Another way of preserving soil fertility was to ensure that the land was not cropped too frequently. For example, when John Moore leased a messuage and closes in Higham Booth in Pendle in 1621 for a term of seven years, he stipulated that his tenant was only to plough and sow a third of the premises at any one time, and then for not more than two years.[41] It is impossible to determine how typical this arrangement was, for this is the only example found of such a clause, but it may be the case that a higher proportion of land was usually cropped by subtenants, and was often under the plough for a longer period, and therefore Moore felt it necessary to limit this.

It is difficult to gauge the effect of these various measures on arable productivity, since we lack the necessary data to calculate seed-yield ratios, which is the type of measure most usually employed. The most straightforward way of calculating such a ratio is to use data from farm account books, but the gentry household accounts which have survived for this area do not supply the appropriate information.[42] Whilst the fertility of gentry land may have been untypical of arable productivity in general (due possibly to possession of better quality land or more efficient estate management), it would at least have provided a guide to the upper limits of arable productivity which might be attained. Appleby found that, despite vigorous management and a period of good harvests (with the exception of 1600), the average seed-yield ratio for oats on the Westmorland demesne lands of the Lowthers was just 2·5:1 during the period from 1598–9 to 1604–5.[43] Agricultural conditions in north-east Lancashire appear to have been fairly similar to those prevailing in Westmorland, and it is unlikely that arable productivity in the Colne district differed significantly from that found in Westmorland.

A less direct method of measuring arable productivity has been employed by Overton, who used probate inventories to calculate yields per acre. He divided the mean acreage before the harvest by the mean volume of grain after the harvest, and sidestepped the problems of omissions, or the sale or purchase of grain after the harvest by working with unit valuations of grain.[44] However, the probate inventories of testators from the Colne area record neither the acreage under crops before the harvest, nor the volume or weight of grain harvested, but only the valuation of corn.[45] Thus we cannot use local probate inventories to estimate arable productivity.

Other similar problems present themselves in attempting to establish which crops were grown in this area. First, as we have stated, inventories do not record acreages under crops or the volume or weight of different harvested crops, so the relative importance of each type of grain cannot be established precisely. Secondly, inventory appraisers often used the term 'corn' rather than specifying the type of grain. However, as Brigg and King have noted, it seems that corn and oats were synonymous, since 'corn' was often used in the phrase 'corn and barley'.[46] Furthermore, in no inventory were 'corn' and 'oats' found separately. This view is reinforced by the fact that in some inventories, oats and corn were run together as 'oatcorn'.[47]

Many inventories contain evidence of arable cultivation; no less than 155 of 195 *supra* male testators (79%) owned either seeds or growing or harvested corn. Wheat was explicitly referred to in only 25 inventories (13%). It is likely that wheat had been purchased and not grown by some testators, and therefore this proportion is probably an over-estimate of the extent of wheat cultivation. Where wheat was valued separately, it was usually in small amounts. Barley was listed more frequently in inventories; 55 (28%) recorded it. Though some barley may have been purchased, clearly some was turned into malt; 89 inventories (46%) recorded either barley or malt. Where listed separately, barley was often valued at £1 or less.[48]

Thus the infrequency with which each type of grain was listed and valued separately, and the uncertainty as to the meaning of 'corn' makes precise quantification impossible, but it seems that oats were the predominant crop, which is a finding supported by the petition of the forest tenants quoted above.[49] References to crops other than oats, barley and wheat in the sample were extremely rare; rye was mentioned just once, peas once and beans twice.[50]

Crops seem to have been largely spring sown, for, with two exceptions, there is an absence in inventories of references to grain sown before April.[51] This is not surprising, for Holt noted in 1795 that common oats were sown in Lancashire in April, early oats in May and June, and barley in April and May.[52] The two exceptions found relate to wheat, for sown wheat was recorded in inventories drawn up in January and February.[53] Holt pointed out that the time for seeding wheat was from mid-September until the end of October.[54] However, not all Lancashire wheat was sown at this time, for 'March wheat' was recorded in a Pendle inventory of 1569.[55]

It is impossible to estimate either the proportion of households which were self-sufficient in grain, or the amount of corn imported from outside the area. Clearly, this would have varied from year to year with the state of the harvest. Though at least 79% of *supra* male testators grew some grain, this group was by no means typical of the population as a whole.[56] The existence of 'badgers' from the Colne district, who were licensed to trade in corn, implies that there must have been a fairly active market for corn.[57] Some farms were able to produce a surplus of corn for the market even in bad years, for on 31 August 1600, at a time of a poor harvest, George Spencer sold all the oats from 10 acres at Filly Close in Pendle to a badger from Burnley.[58] However, Filly Close was in a relatively low-lying area and was therefore untypical of the Colne district as a whole. Indeed, the data on the size of holdings and the distribution of wealth suggest that many must have been compelled to purchase a large proportion of their food requirements at the market, even in years of good harvests. When harvests were extremely bad, as in 1621–2, starvation might result.[59]

Turning to the nature and extent of pastoral agriculture, we have shown that animal husbandry rather than arable cultivation was the dominant branch of farming activity. The Colne district was primarily cattle country; 78.8% of the total valuation of *supra* male testators' livestock consisted of cattle. Cattle were found in varying numbers in virtually all *supra* inventories of male testators; no less than 181 of 195 inventories (93%) recorded them.[60] An analysis of the geographical distribution of cattle over time is presented in Table 3.1.[61]

One of the problems with using a mean valuation is that it is open to distortion by an extreme value, which is particularly serious if the size of the sample is small. For example, if the inventory of Richard Towneley Esquire of Carr Hall (who owned 74 cattle) is removed from the sample for north-east Pendle, 1621–40, the mean which results is just 7·67, not 14·3. It seems sensible, therefore, to place more trust in the median figures.

The sample for Trawden forest is much too small to rely on the data for sub-periods, but the overall median of 18·0 cattle per inventory suggests that this was an area of large herds. This conclusion is in accordance with the data available on the distribution of wealth, which indicate that this was the most prosperous part of our area.[62] Pendle forest was also involved in cattle farming to a considerable extent; the median herd size in both the north-east and in the rest of the forest was 12·0. Herds in Colne manor were far smaller, for here the median herd size was just 6·0 cattle.

However, notable changes in herd sizes were clearly apparent over time. Judging by both mean and median figures, average herd sizes dropped very sharply in Colne manor and also fell in north-east Pendle forest in the 1600s and 1610s, whilst those in Trawden forest and the rest of Pendle forest rose. Part of the explanation for the former development may be that price inflation resulted in more poorer people being transferred from the *infra* to the *supra* categories. It is certainly true that *infra* testators owned relatively few cattle; the median number for *infra* male testators from Colne chapelry and Pendle forest during the period from 1601 to 1621 was 1·0, and the mean 1·5.[63] Nevertheless, this hypothesis is contradicted by the fact that average herd sizes rose in the rest of Pendle forest (and also in the very small sample for Trawden forest). An alternative hypothesis is that the changes in average herd sizes are connected with the distribution of land. It will be shown that whilst copyholds became subdivided in Colne manor and north-east Pendle forest during this period, those in Trawden forest and the rest of Pendle forest did not become fragmented significantly.[64] Subdivision of land restricted a tenant's ability to keep as many cattle on his holding over the winter, whilst it reduced the number of cattle which

Table 3.1 Geographical fluctuations in herd sizes in supra inventories of
male testators from Colne chapelry and Pendle forest, 1558–1640

Period	Colne manor			Trawden forest			North-east Pendle forest			Rest of Pendle forest			Colne chapelry and Pendle forest		
	No.	Mean	Median	No.	Mean	Median	No.	Mean	Median	No.	Mean	Median	No.	Mean	Median
to 1600	17	13·9	13·0	5	14·6	17·0	8	17·8	17·0	11	11·0	7·0	44	13·9	13·5
1601–20	27	8·5	5·0	2	17·5	17·5	14	16·5	14·5	20	14·1	13·0	70	12·3	10·0
1621–40	12	9·0	5·0	8	16·6	19·5	10	14·3	7·0	12	16·2	13·5	47	13·0	9·0
Total	56	10·3	6·0	15	16·1	18·0	32	16·1	12·0	43	13·9	12·0	161	12·9	10·0

he might pasture on the commons and wastes during the summer. In areas where land did not become fragmented, an expansion of animal husbandry was more feasible.

In the 1620s and 1630s, there were little significant changes in median herd sizes, with the exception of north-east Pendle forest, where there was a pronounced fall from 14·5 to 7·0. Elsewhere, the median herd size in Colne manor remained static, whilst those in Trawden forest and the rest of Pendle forest increased slightly. At first sight, these movements might appear to be explicable in terms of a continuation of trends in landholding previously discussed. Yet fragmentation of copyholds also became apparent in the rest of Pendle forest between 1608 and 1650, and to a slight extent in Trawden forest too,[65] but this did not produce a reduction in median herd sizes. We can only conclude that holdings in these areas must have been sufficiently large initially to permit some subdivision without giving rise to a serious shortage of pasture.

Seasonal variations in herd sizes were also apparent, but these were not very extreme. The median herd size in the first quarter of the year stood at 9·5, but rose to 11·0 between April and June; in the third quarter of the year, the median herd size fell to 10·0, where it remained for the last quarter of the year.[66] Thus it is clear that there was no winter slaughtering of cattle on a significant scale, which corroborates the findings of Brigg and King.[67] The increase in herd sizes in the second quarter can be attributed to the birth of calves, whilst the subsequent fall was presumably due to sales of cattle at the Michaelmas 'beast fair',[68] and to some culling of weak or old stock before the onset of winter.

It is important to note that herd sizes varied not only by location, over time and by season, but also, as we would expect, by occupation. The largest herds were naturally owned by Esquires and gentlemen, whose median herd sizes amounted to 53·5 and 19·0 respectively. Next came yeomen, with an average of 15·5 head. Interestingly, the median size of clothiers' herds (12·0) was higher than that of the husbandmen (6·5), and many of those with non-agrarian occupations were found to keep cattle.[69] The implication of this last finding will be discussed in subsequent chapters.[70]

Within the pastoral sector, it is important to establish as precisely as possible the relative importance of stock-raising and dairying. One guide to this is to ascertain the relative proportion of beef and dairy cattle in the herds of this area. In Table 3.2, we have treated all types of cattle, irrespective of age, sex or type, as one unit; the

Table 3.2 Proportion of dairy cattle to all cattle in supra inventories of male testators from Colne chapelry and Pendle forest, 1558–1640

Period	Colne manor		Trawden forest		North-east Pendle forest		Rest of Pendle forest		Colne chapelry and Pendle forest	
	%	No.	%	No.	%	No.	%	No.	%	No.
to 1600	36	(237)	33	(73)	35	(142)	59	(122)	41	(612)
1601–20	46	(230)	34	(35)	34	(231)	37	(265½)	39	(842½)
1621–40	46	(108)	34	(133)	38	(143)	35	(194)	37	(612)
Total	42	(575)	34	(241)	35	(516)	41	(581½)	39	(2066½)

ratio of 'kine' and cows to the total number of cattle has been calculated in order to discover the varying proportion of dairy animals over time and space.[71]

It must be stated at the outset that these data only represent a rough guide to the relative importance of beef and dairy animals. First, all oxen are included, whether for fattening or for draught purposes.[72] However, this is not a serious difficulty since plough oxen would eventually be fattened for meat when they became too old to be used as draught animals. Secondly, it is probable that some heifers were being used for dairy purposes, but again this is not a great problem, since only 5% of cattle were described as heifers or 'whies'.[73] Conversely, presumably some of the cows were barren and therefore were being fattened for beef.[74]

Nevertheless despite these qualifications the data clearly demonstrate the predominance of beef cattle in all areas, but especially in Trawden and north-east Pendle forests. However, important changes seem to have been apparent over time, for whilst the beef–dairy balance of herds in Colne manor swung relatively towards dairy animals in the early seventeenth century, the reverse occurred on a much larger scale in the rest of Pendle forest.

The explanation for these developments can be found by correlating herd sizes with the proportion of dairy animals kept (Table 3.3).[75]

It is clear that the proportion of a herd devoted to dairying varied inversely with the size of the herd; small livestock farmers

Table 3.3   Herd sizes correlated with cattle type in supra inventories of male testators from Colne chapelry and Pendle Forest, 1558–1640

Herd size	Dairy cattle, as a % of all cattle	
	%	No.
1–5	75	(124)
6–10	56	(288)
11–15	38	(268)
16–20	36	(386)
21–30	33	(697½)
31–40	29	(132)
41 and above	24	(171)
Total	39	(2,066½)

concentrated mostly on dairying, whilst larger farmers were proportionately more involved in stock-raising. There are two probable reasons for this. First, the returns on capital invested were more rapid in dairying than they were in stock-raising, and moreover the dairy farmer enjoyed a regular income for part of the year, in contrast to the stock farmer whose expenditure was continuous but whose income from sales of cattle was sporadic. Dairying was therefore ideally suited to the requirements of the small farmer.[76] Secondly, it is probable that there was insufficient local demand for dairy products, since there were no very large concentrations of people nearby in urban centres. The dairy produce of the small farmer might supply the needs of his household and leave some over for sale, but there was little incentive for the larger farmer to specialise in dairying.

The reason for the noticeable increase in the proportion of dairy animals in Colne manor, and the reverse development in the rest of Pendle forest now becomes clear, for we have noted the sharp fall in average herd sizes in Colne manor during the early seventeenth century and the increase in the rest of Pendle forest.[77] As herds became smaller in Colne, an increasing proportion of dairy animals were kept; as herds grew in the rest of Pendle forest, farmers concentrated proportionately more on stock-raising.

Colne was clearly well known as a market for cattle; by 1610, three fairs were held there for the sale of cattle. The first, for 'cattle and other merchandise' took place on February 24th, but was stated in 1610 to be of fairly recent origin. The other two fairs, on May 1st and September 29th, were held purely for the sale of cattle, and by implication had been longer established than that in February.[78] These fairs must have attracted a considerable number of people. For example, the Shuttleworths, a gentry family of Smithills (near Bolton) and Gawthorpe made frequent trips to Colne fair to buy cattle. Their family accounts, and those of the Walmsleys of Dunkenhalgh contain many references to the purchase of all types of cattle, especially oxen, between 1586 and 1631. In May 1586, the Shuttleworths bought two oxen from William Hudson in Colne, and a year later purchased two more from a Mr. Blakey.[79] Similarly, the Walmsleys purchased an ox from Henry Hartley at Colne fair in 1625.[80] Other cattle bought in Colne by these families included a bull, a heifer, twinters and cows.[81]

The Shuttleworths also purchased some butter in the Pendle area, though this occurred only after they had moved from Smithills to Gawthorpe near Burnley. In 1600, they bought 5 stones of butter from

'Goodwife Grymshe of Mowerhylles', and another stone from 'John wife Moore of Higham' in 1613.[82] Usually, the amounts of butter and cheese recorded in inventories were small, suggesting that dairy production was largely designed for household consumption.[83]

Data from inventories suggest that there was some increase in dairying activity during the early seventeenth century. In the period up to 1600, 17% of *supra* testators' inventories listed churns, cheese-making equipment, milkhouses, dairies or butteries, compared with 31% between 1601 and 1640. Furthermore, the proportions possessing butter and cheese up to 1600 were 27% and 33% respectively, compared with 37% and 38% between 1601 and 1640.[84] The proportion of testators with dairy equipment should be regarded as the minimum possible, for presumably some was concealed under the general description 'wooden vessels', and few inventories systematically recorded rooms. Conversely, some households had probably purchased their butter and cheese, rather than making it themselves. Thirsk has argued that some farmers in this area were turning to dairying rather than stock-raising by the beginning of the seventeenth century.[85] This evidence supports her contention, as does that for herd composition (but with the important exception of the rest of Pendle forest).[86]

Cattle, whether for draught, rearing or dairying, were not the only livestock kept in this district. Indeed, 87 of the 195 *supra* male testators from this area (45%) owned sheep. In general, flocks were small; the mean flock size, where stated, was just 26·0 and the median 19·5;[87] the largest stated flock size was only 114.[88] Furthermore, relatively little capital was invested in sheep, for they represented just 7·8% of the total valuation of livestock, which was exactly a tenth of that invested in cattle.[89] Trawden forest testators were the most heavily involved in sheep farming, as indicated by the proportion with sheep (79%) and the average flock size (78·0). In the other areas, between a third and a half of male testators owned sheep, but often only ten to twenty animals.[90] Poorer testators were even less likely to keep sheep; only a single *infra* male testator's inventory for the period from 1601 to 1621 (1 out of 15), listed them.[91]

It was far more usual to find horses than sheep in inventories; 155 of the *supra* male testators (79%) owned horses; half of these owned only one horse, and a third kept two.[92] The maximum number of horses recorded in any one inventory was 13, belonging to Richard Towneley Esquire of Carr Hall.[93] Poorer testators were far less likely to own horses, for only 3 of 15 *infra* male testators possessed a horse, and each of these had only one.[94] Nevertheless, despite the small number of horses usually kept, they represented a significant proportion of *supra* testators' investment in livestock (11·7%).[95] Horse furniture recorded in inventories suggests that horses were used for riding, for transportation of goods in pack saddles and for draught (carts and wains). It is unclear whether horses were sometimes used for ploughing instead of oxen.[96]

Swine were present in 75 of the *supra* male testators' inventories (38%), but invariably in small numbers. Usually only a single pig was kept; the maximum was eight.[97] Pigs seem to have been kept purely as a source of food for the household. Relatively little capital was invested in them — just 1·4% of the total valuation of all livestock — but despite their cheapness none of the fifteen *infra* male testators owned swine.

Poultry was kept by 111 of the *supra* male testators (57%) but was usually valued at just a few shillings. Poultry represented 0·3% of the total valuation of these testators' livestock. *Infra* male testators seem to have been little involved in poultry farming; only a single inventory in 15 recorded them.

In an age before the advent of cheap sugar, honey was often employed as a sweetening agent. Hives were recorded in 12 *supra* males' inventories (6%), though none of the *infra* male testators owned them.[98] Some owned just a share in a hive; thus John Baldwin, a yeoman of Wheathead in Pendle owned half of two hives valued at 10s in 1620.[99] Others were involved in bee-keeping in a much bigger way. For example, a labourer named John Whitehead of Little Marsden left 14 hives and 3 quarts of honey valued at £7 4s 0d at his death in 1618. His hives were situated at houses throughout the area (but largely in Pendle) and were in many cases shared with others.[100] Clearly bee-keeping was a specialist activity, and not without its dangers to the uninitiated. It was alleged in 1638 that a husbandman named John Bulcock had stolen a hive at Blackmoss in Pendle from a wool webster called Stephen Dugdale, but he had been so badly stung that he was forced to keep his swollen hands in his pockets at a funeral the following day, in order to hide his guilt. Not surprisingly, this disrespectful behaviour aroused Dugdale's suspicions, and the case was brought before Quarter Sessions.[101]

Inventories leave no trace of any fishing activity, yet it is apparent from the court rolls that several individuals were involved in this. The absence of fish in inventories is partly due to the fact that fish in common waters belonged to the lord, whose permission was required before fishing could commence,[102] and partly because live fish were not regarded as chattels and therefore could not be put into an inventory.[103] Several amercements are to be found where men fished without licence in this area, most of which concerned Pendle forest.[104] Some individuals were deterred from fishing neither by the lack of a licence, nor by the fines of the halmote juries. For example, John Kingstones was a persistent offender who was fined a shilling for fishing with nets in Pendle Water in 1529, 1537, 1538 and 1542.[105] It is impossible to estimate what proportion of this illicit fishing was brought to the attention of the juries, but it is clear that fishing must have represented a source of food and income for some inhabitants of the Colne district.

The agricultural set-up of this area helps to explain one of the peculiarities in the occupational structure, namely the relatively infrequent reference to labourers in all sources. Only one example of a labourer's will has been found,[106] but this would not necessarily be surprising even in areas where labourers were quite common, since the poor did not often make wills.[107] However, in a sample of 203 occupations of males from Colne chapelry and Pendle forest, derived from Quarter Sessions recognisance rolls from 1626 to 1642 (which is likely to be more representative of the whole population), only one labourer was discovered.[108] Similarly, there is not a single reference to a labourer in 733 occupations listed in the Burnley baptism and burial registers from 1653 to 1660.[109]

Arable farming is obviously far more labour-intensive than past-oral, and within the pastoral sector, dairying is more labour-intensive than stock-raising.[110] Since we have shown that this area concentrated primarily on stock-raising, one reason for the paucity of references to labourers is clear. Furthermore, as Kussmaul has suggested, animal husbandry was associated with the hiring of relatively more permanent workers (who would be designated as 'servants'), in contrast to arable farming, where comparatively more temporary workers (day labourers) were employed.[111] It is difficult to verify this hypothesis for the Colne area, since the absence of a listing makes it impossible to compare the numbers of servants relative to labourers with any precision. Servants were predominantly young and unmarried, and therefore would tend not to be represented proportionate to their actual numbers in wills or parish registers.[112] In our Quarter Sessions sample for the Colne district, four servants were recorded and only one labourer,[113] but it is unclear whether these servants were actually employed in husbandry.

In conclusion, we have failed to unearth any evidence from the Colne district of what Kerridge has called 'The Agricultural Revolution'.[114] Changes there certainly were, but none may be termed revolutionary or far-reaching. Arable productivity was still very low in the early seventeenth century, and appears to have been insufficient in bad years (such as 1623) to feed the rapidly rising population. However, problems were not only caused by the absolute level of agricultural productivity, but also by the structure of lordship and landholding, to which we now turn.

NOTES

[1] Holt, *Agriculture of the county of Lancaster*, p. 8

[2] P.R.O. D.L.5/19 fol. 395

[3] Holt, *Agriculture of the county of Lancaster*, p. 3; Fussell, *English dairy farmer*, p. 73

[4] Thirsk, 'Farming regions of England', p. 4

[5] Farrer, *Court rolls*, vol. 2, pp. 404–8, 411

[6] Rodgers, 'Land use in Tudor Lancashire', pp. 81–2, 85–6, 94–5

[7] Fishwick, *Survey of Rochdale*, p. x; quoted by Thirsk, 'Farming regions of England', p. 85 and by Kerridge, *Agricultural revolution*, p. 166

[8] Overton, 'Agricultural change in Norfolk and Suffolk', p. 97

[9] Ten inventories are unusable, since appropriate items are not valued separately. Livestock includes cattle, sheep, horses, swine, poultry and bees. Crops include oats, meal, wheat, barley, malt, hay and corn. It proved impossible to exclude items such as hay since hay was usually valued with corn. Thus the calculations exaggerate the importance of arable crops somewhat. The inventories are from L.R.O. WCW *supra, passim*

[10] Inventories drawn from these months have been used for this purpose by Frost, 'Yeomen and metalsmiths', p. 32, and by Yelling, 'Probate inventories and the geography of livestock farming', p. 115

[11] Farrer, *Court rolls*, vol. 1, p. 250

[12] Tupling, *Economic history of Rossendale*, p. 100

[13] Baker and Butlin, *Field systems in the British Isles*, p. 33

[14] Farrer, *Court rolls*, vol. 1, pp. 244, 250, 261, 272, 287, 291, 306, 325, 328, 335, 342, 343

[15] *Ibid.*, p. 342

[16] For further information on the disafforestation, see chapter 4, pp. 56–7

[17] Farrer, *Court rolls*, vol. 1, pp. 294–8

[18] *Ibid.*, vol. 2, p. 192

[19] There were 2,200 Lancashire acres of commons and wastes in Colne manor in 1617. See Chapter 5, p. 70

[20] Farrer, *Court rolls*, vols. 1 and 2, *passim*; L.R.O. DDHCl3, *passim*

[21] Farrer, *Court rolls*, vol. 1, p. 268

[22] L.R.O. DDHCl3/114, Pendle forest, 1st halmote, 27 October 1631

²³ P.R.O. D.L.5/27 fols. 1314, 1322

²⁴ P.R.O. D.L. 5/19 fol. 126

²⁵ See Chapter 4, pp. 61–5

²⁶ See Chapter 5, pp. 81–3

²⁷ L.R.O. DDTa 216 fol. 3–3v (copies of this petition may be found in M.C.L. L1/38/3/1 and W.R.O. D/DZ.A4, Towneley MSS, fols. 58–58v). This has been quoted in part by Brigg, King and Thirsk; Brigg, 'Forest of Pendle', Part 1, p. 71; King, 'Economic and demographic development of Rossendale', p. 105; Thirsk, 'Farming regions of England', p. 85 (Thirsk misquotes part of the text as 'not without the continual change of every third year's new manuring')

²⁸ L.R.O. WCW inventories, *passim*

²⁹ See Chapter 2, pp. 22–5

³⁰ L.R.O. WCW *Supra* inventories, *passim*. In a total of 215 usable inventories, 48 listed dung, manure, 'manner' or 'worthing'. 'Manner' and 'worthing' are local names for manure

³¹ Thirsk and Cooper, *Seventeenth century economic documents*, p. 111. 'Marl' was a fertiliser made of lime and clay

³² Holt, *Agriculture of the county of Lancaster*, p. 111

³³ Farrer, *Court rolls*, vol. 2, pp. 120, 306

³⁴ L.R.O. DDHCl3/60, Pendle forest, 2nd halmote, 10 June 1578

³⁵ L.R.O. DDHCl3/82, Pendle forest, 1st halmote, 17 Dec. 1601

³⁶ L.R.O. DDHCl3/104, Trawden forest, 1st halmote, 23 Oct. 1621

³⁷ Kerridge, *Agricultural revolution*, pp. 247–8, 342

³⁸ See Chapter 8, pp. 182–3

³⁹ L.R.O. DDHCl3/82, Pendle forest, 2nd halmote, 22 May 1600

⁴⁰ L.R.O. DDHCl3/70, Pendle forest, 2nd halmote, 16 May 1588

⁴¹ L.R.O. DDHCl3/103, Pendle forest, 2nd halmote, 9 May 1621

⁴² The gentry household accounts which are available are those of the Shuttleworths of Smithills and Gawthorpe, and the Walmsleys of Dunkenhalgh. Harland, *Accounts of the Shuttleworths, passim*; L.R.O. DDPt 1, *passim*

⁴³ Appleby, *Famine in Tudor and Stuart England*, pp. 65–6

⁴⁴ Overton, 'Agricultural change in Norfolk and Suffolk', pp. 69–72

⁴⁵ L.R.O. WCW inventories, *passim*

⁴⁶ Brigg, 'Forest of Pendle', Part 1, p. 80; King, 'Economic and demographic development of Rossendale', pp. 104–5

⁴⁷ L.R.O. WCW inventories, *passim*. John Mangnolls, a yeoman of Great Marsden, owned 'oat corn' valued at £22 in 1624. L.R.O. WCW *Supra* will 1612, inventory 1624

⁴⁸ L.R.O. WCW *Supra* inventories, *passim*

⁴⁹ See above, pp. 37–8

⁵⁰ Rye and groats valued at 5s were listed in the inventory of Bernard Shuttleworth of Winewall in Trawden, dated 1582; L.R.O. DDWh 3/5. Peas and beans were recorded in the inventory of Richard Hargreaves of Higham in 1601; L.R.O. WCW *Supra*, will and inventory, 1601. Beans were listed in the inventory of James Emott of Laneshaw Bridge in 1640; L.R.O. WCW *Supra* inventory 1640

⁵¹ L.R.O. WCW *Supra* inventories, *passim*

⁵² Holt, *Agriculture of the county of Lancaster*, p. 65

[53] John Crankshaw of Hunterholme, yeoman, owned 'wheat sown upon the ground' valued at 50s on 15 January 1618; L.R.O. WCW *Supra* inventory 1618. In an inventory dated 25 February 1620, the possessions of Christopher Hartley of Barrowford included wheat sown; L.R.O. WCW *Supra* inventory 1620

[54] Holt, *Agriculture of the county of Lancaster*, p. 65

[55] John Hancock, a gentleman of Lower Higham in Pendle owned 'March wheat' valued at 4s 8d on 4 March 1569; L.R.O. WCW *Supra* will and inventory, 1569. Joan Thirsk has also noted that a March or summer wheat, sown in the spring, was known in the northern counties. Thirsk, 'Farming techniques', p. 169

[56] For a discussion of the representativeness of inventories, see Chapter 6, pp. 132–5

[57] See Chapter 8, p. 187

[58] Tait, *Lancashire Quarter Sessions records*, p. 74. This has also been noted by Brigg, 'Forest of Pendle', Part 1, p. 82. 1600 was a bad harvest nationally; see Bowden, 'Statistical appendix', pp. 820, 854; it was deficient locally too – see Swain, 'Industry and economy', p. 335

[59] See Chapters 2 and 5

[60] A total of 152 inventories were usable for this calculation; 43 others either recorded no livestock or did not value each category of livestock separately. L.R.O. WCW *Supra* inventories, *passim*

[61] L.R.O. WCW *Supra* inventories, *passim*. It proved impossible to use 20 inventories, since the number of head was not given

[62] See Chapter 5, pp. 93–5

[63] L.R.O. WCW *Infra* inventories, *passim*

[64] See Chapter 5, pp. 71–2

[65] *Ibid.*

[66] L.R.O. WCW *Supra* inventories of male testators from Colne chapelry and Pendle forest, 1558–1640, *passim*. The size of each sample was 42, 45, 32 and 41 inventories respectively

[67] Brigg, 'Forest of Pendle' Part 1, p. 84; King, 'Economic and demographic development of Rossendale', pp. 93–4

[68] See below, p. 47

[69] L.R.O. WCW *Supra* inventories, *passim*. The size of each sample was as follows: Esquires 2, gentlemen 3, yeomen 86, clothiers 5, husbandmen 28. Obviously, some of these median figures should not be relied upon too heavily, due to the small samples involved. For further details, see Swain, 'Industry and economy', Table 3.3, p. 81

[70] See Chapters 6 and 8

[71] L.R.O. WCW *Supra* inventories, *passim*. This methodology has been employed by King, 'Economic and demographic development of Rossendale', p. 90

[72] Oxen are not systematically distinguished according to their function

[73] A 'whie' was a young heifer

[74] For example, John Robinson of Roughlee in Pendle owned 2 'drape' (barren) kine in 1616; L.R.O. WCW *Supra*, will and inventory, 1616. No attempt has been made to transfer cows stated to have been barren to the beef category, since the extreme rarity of references to barren cows

suggests that many appraisers did not trouble to differentiate between types of cows

[75] L.R.O. WCW *Supra* inventories, *passim*

[76] Bowden, 'Agricultural prices, farm profits and rents', p. 672

[77] See above, pp. 42–4

[78] P.R.O. D.L.44/828. There were also Pedlars' fairs on 3rd May and 1st October

[79] Harland, *Accounts of the Shuttleworths*, Part 1, pp. 27, 38

[80] L.R.O. DDPt 1

[81] Harland, *Accounts of the Shuttleworths*, Part 1, pp. 103, 142, 161; L.R.O. DDPt 1, *passim*

[82] Harland, *Accounts of the Shuttleworths*, Part 1, pp. 130, 207

[83] L.R.O. WCW *Supra* inventories, *passim*

[84] L.R.O. WCW *Supra* inventories, *passim*. The size of the sample was 59 or 60 inventories for the period up to 1600, and 158 or 160 inventories for the period 1601–40 (some inventories were damaged and hence were unusable for certain calculations). For further details, see Swain, 'Industry and economy' Table 3.6, p. 87

[85] Thirsk, 'Farming regions of England', pp. 85–6

[86] See above, Table 3.2

[87] L.R.O. WCW *Supra* inventories, *passim*. A total of 50 of the 87 sheep-owning *supra* male testators' inventories stated the size of the flock

[88] This was found in the inventory of William Hanson of Emmott Lane in Colne; L.R.O. WCW *Supra*, will and inventory, 1595

[89] L.R.O. WCW *Supra* inventories, *passim*. The size of the sample is 152 inventories

[90] *Ibid.* For further details, see Swain, 'Industry and economy', Table 3.7 and pp. 88–9

[91] L.R.O. WCW *Infra* inventories, *passim*

[92] L.R.O. WCW *Supra* inventories, *passim*. The number of horses was stated in 152 of these inventories; 75 testators kept one horse, and 50 owned two

[93] L.R.O. WCW *Supra*, will and inventory, 1630

[94] L.R.O. WCW *Infra* inventories, *passim*

[95] L.R.O. WCW *Supra* inventories, *passim*

[96] King was also unable to resolve this. King, 'Economic and demographic development of Rossendale', pp. 98–9. It is certainly true that oxen were used for ploughing, since there are a number of references in inventories and accounts to yokes of oxen

[97] L.R.O. WCW *Supra* inventories, *passim*. Of the 75 inventories which mentioned swine, 72 stated numbers. Again, Richard Towneley possessed the most swine. L.R.O. WCW *Supra*, will and inventory, 1630

[98] L.R.O. WCW *Infra* and *Supra* inventories, *passim*

[99] L.R.O. WCW *Supra* will and inventory, 1620

[100] L.R.O. WCW *Supra* will and inventory, 1618

[101] L.R.O. QSB 1/197/10–13, 47

[102] A number of individuals were fined for fishing 'without licence of the steward'; for example, Farrer, *Court Rolls*, vol. 2, pp. 152–3

[103] Overton, 'Agricultural change in Norfolk and Suffolk', p. 30

[104] Of 16 amercements for this offence, 13 were in Pendle forest, 2 in Trawden forest and 1 in Colne manor. Farrer, *Court Rolls*, vol. 1, pp. 378, 454; vol. 2, pp. 47, 97, 122, 127, 152–3, 166, 168, 193, 243, 313. L.R.O. DDHCl3/67, Pendle forest, 2nd halmote, 21 April 1585; DDHCl3/68, Trawden forest, 2nd halmote, 12 April 1586; DDHCl3/99, Pendle forest, 2nd halmote, 19 June 1617

[105] Farrer, *Court rolls*, vol. 2, pp. 97, 122, 127, 152–3

[106] That of John Whitehead of Little Marsden. WCW *Supra*, will and inventory, 1618

[107] See Chapter 6, pp. 133–4

[108] L.R.O. QSB 1, *passim*. See Swain, 'Industry and economy', table 6.14, p. 253

[109] L.R.O. P.R. 3027/1/2. See Swain, 'Industry and economy', Table 6.15, p. 256

[110] Skipp, *Crisis and development*, p. 54; Thirsk, 'Farming regions of England', pp. 13–14; Everitt, 'Farm labourers', pp. 433–5; Bowden, 'Agricultural prices, farm profits and rents', p. 672; Kriedte, *et al.*; *Industrialisation before industrialisation*, pp. 14, 27

[111] Kussmaul, *Servants in husbandry*, p. 104

[112] *Ibid.*, p. 5

[113] L.R.O. QSB 1, *passim*. See Swain, 'Industry and economy', Table 6.14, p. 253

[114] Kerridge, *Agricultural revolution, passim*

CHAPTER IV

LORDSHIP

It will be shown in this chapter that, with the exception of the copyhold dispute in the early seventeenth century, Duchy of Lancaster lordship in this area was extremely benevolent. This was of great financial benefit to those who held land as Duchy tenants, and compensated somewhat for the agricultural difficulties which they faced.

The most significant development in lordship in the Honor of Clitheroe during the sixteenth century was the disafforestation of 1507. By the end of the fourteenth century, the forest vaccaries had ceased to hold the lord's stock, and instead were mostly leased to farmers, who in turn sublet to husbandmen.[1] However, on 1 April 1503, Henry VII leased 'certain meadows, pastures, feeding grounds and tenements in the Forests of Rossendale, Pendle and Trawden' to Thomas, Earl of Derby and James Stanley, Archdeacon of Richmond, for 21 years.[2]

Trouble was soon apparent when James Stanley's servants were obstructed in collecting rents by the forest tenants. Apparently previous leases by copy of court roll, granted without authority by the Steward, had been challenged by Stanley, and some tenants had actually been dispossessed from their holdings, thus provoking a confrontation.[3] In order to reconcile the tenants, the King instructed the Steward of Blackburnshire in July 1506 to make leases by copy, both of demesne and customary land, for terms of and not exceeding 12 years, nor above 40s rent per annum.[4]

However, the final Duchy decree of 12 March 1507 was far more favourable to the tenants. Holdings were granted to the tenants and their heirs for life or years, as they wished, by copy of court roll according to the custom of the manors. Fines at change of tenancy or death were fixed at one year's rent, just as the existing copyholders paid.[5] Rents also fixed in perpetuity by the surveyors.[6]

These rents all showed a noticeable increase on the old leases:

rents in Pendle forest rose by 39% from £86 12s 4d to £120 13s 4d and those in Trawden forest increased by 36% from £21 6s 8d to £29. In both forests, land previously not leased, the moiety of Rishton Thorns in Pendle and Emmott Moor in Trawden, were let for the first time. It should be noted, however, that substantial though these rent increases were, they were little in comparison with the Rossendale district, where rents rose by 61%.[7]

It is clear that the tenants were the chief beneficiaries of the disafforestation. In the first place, they gained security of tenure which was to last for a hundred years,[8] with fixed entry fines and rents. The Duchy secured an increase in rent returns, but by giving way on its original proposal to lease the forests in parcels for 12-year periods only, it surrendered its ability to revise fines and rents in line with market forces. In 1507, the Duchy officials were in no position to foresee the scale of inflation over the next century.[9] Nevertheless, Duchy officers could certainly not be described as businesslike.

The copyholders of Colne manor were in a similarly fortunate position. Their estates too were held by copy of court roll according to the custom of the manor, and were inheritable on payment of an entry fine of one year's customary rent.[10] In addition, rents were fixed at 4d an acre.[11] Thus the tenants of the forests and of the manor were not liable to arbitrary eviction, since their estates were inheritable. Furthermore, they were not in a position to be rack-rented, either by increasing entry fines or rents, since both were fixed. According to Tawney, such tenants were a minority of all customary tenants.[12] In real terms, they were increasingly better off during the sixteenth century, since rising prices of agricultural products were not accompanied by rising payments to the lord. In addition, tenants were free to improve their holdings, and indeed had every incentive to do so, since their security of tenure meant that it was they or their descendants who would ultimately reap the rewards of such improvements.[13]

The Duchy, however, made a number of attempts to increase its income. This was manifest in four different ways. First, the most usual way of increasing revenue was to lease additional property or rights. This could take the form of letting parcels of wasteland. For example, 90 acres of waste in Colne manor were leased to Lawrence Towneley Esquire in 1581 for an initial fine of £40 and a new rent of 32s 6d (though fines in the future were to be at the same level as other ancient copyholds).[14] On a much lesser scale, a rod of waste in Colne manor was leased to Richard Fenton in 1584, for an initial fine of £1 and a new rent of 1*d* per annum.[15]

Moreover, the Duchy might grant leases for new mills. The first example of this during our period was in 1542, when, for a rent of 13*s* 4*d* per annum, Lawrence Towneley Esquire of Barnside was granted permission to build a corn mill at New Carr in Pendle forest, and to take the soke of all the Crown tenants of the new hold for 40 years.[16] This decision followed a commission awarded to inquire whether if a new mill was built in Pendle, this would be prejudicial to the other Crown mills at Burnley, Padiham and Colne. Furthermore, this commission was also to inquire into the possibility of letting a new corn mill in Trawden forest.[17] Despite witnesses affirming that such a mill in Trawden would be of little loss to the other Crown mills, and the issue of another commission on this question in 1557,[18] it was not until 1565 that permission to build a mill in Trawden was finally given to Humphrey Farrer. He was to pay an annual rent of 5*s* for the mill, and a penny for the land on which it was to be built.[19] Later, permission to build a mill at Roughlee in Pendle forest was granted to Henry Towneley Esquire of Barnside, for a new rent of 2*s* per annum.[20] Clearly, by building new mills, the local gentry were responding to the opportunities created by rising local population. The Duchy saw the chance to increase its income, but, in comparison with the lessees, it only benefited financially to a relatively small extent.

At the end of the sixteenth century, the Duchy became particularly keen to lease rights to minerals, especially coal, in copyhold land. This was a departure from the earlier policy of granting exclusive rights to coal to the Crown farmers of the coal mines in the wastes, and forbidding anyone but the Crown farmer from exploiting coal in copyhold land. Though a number of leases were granted, they were usually at 5*s* or 10*s* rent per annum, a trivial sum in comparison with the potential value of a coal mine.[21] A more profitable policy would have been to demand a royalty, but this option was seldom taken up.[22] The right to exploit limestone was also leased during the period; in 1609 William Boswell gentleman obtained a licence to dig for limestone in the parishes of Burnley and Colne for 6*s* 8*d* new rent per annum.[23]

Secondly, the Duchy also made some attempt to obtain extra fines or increments on existing rents. In 1545, it was decreed that in return for a fine of £30, Fence in Pendle (originally a royal deer park) should be granted to the tenants on the same terms as the lands disafforested in 1507.[24] The Duchy claimed that Fence had not been specifically mentioned in the grants of 1507; it was thus exploiting a legal loophole. The matter was first raised as early as 1526, but the manorial jurors refuted the Duchy's case,[25] and apparently the Duchy did not pursue the matter again until 1544. No extra annual rent was demanded, for Fence lay within Sabden, West Close and Higham vaccaries, which had all been let in 1507. This policy also applied to mills and coal mines. Partly to recompense Lawrence Towneley for his expenses in building New Carr mill in 1542, and in return for an increase in rent of 6s 8d per annum, the Duchy granted the premises in 1546 by copy of court roll, where previously Towneley had been but a lessee for 40 years.[26] Similarly, 7s 6d increment per annum was obtained from a lease of coal mines in customary land in Great and Little Marsden in 1624–5.[27]

Thirdly, the Duchy was anxious to detect any illegal encroachments. A commission to detect such encroachments revealed three outhouses on Colne wastes and one house on Marsden waste in 1561.[28] These produced a new rent of 1s 3d per annum.[29] Earlier depositions the same year had revealed three of these encroachments,[30] but with four others the Duchy apparently took no action, for they are not recorded in the court rolls nor in the ministers' accounts. Similarly no action was apparently taken as a result of the encroachments discovered in 1579.[31] for several of these are referred to as encroachments not paying rent in depositions for a later commission in 1616.[32] This latter commission was probably issued to find out background information on the manorial wastes, preparatory to an offer to let them by copy, with liberty of enclosure.[33] Furthermore, when the Crown issued specific commissions to investigate individuals who had allegedly made encroachments, these not infrequently resulted in the disproval of the Crown's claims. This applied to a case in 1556 relating to Pendle forest,[34] and another three in 1584, also in Pendle forest.[35]

Fourthly, the Duchy made some attempt to prevent subdivision of holdings, on the assumption that small parcels of land, or 'quillets' as they were called, would be less likely to support a prosperous tenantry capable of paying rents consistently. In a decree of 1532,[36] it was noted that after the forests of Pendle, Trawden and Rossendale had been let by copy of court roll, these parcels of land had been severed 'into many small quillets to little value, to the deterioration of the inhabitants'. It was therefore ordered that no tenant was to bargain, let or surrender any parcel of their holdings for term of life, years or otherwise, unless these new tenants' lands were of the yearly value of 26s 8d above all charges. The penalty for disobedience was seizure of the holding by the Steward, but since no example of confiscation has been found in the manor court rolls, and since many small holdings are to be found in the rentals and court rolls, we must assume that this decree was not enforced.[37]

It is immediately apparent from an examination of the Duchy receivers' and ministers' accounts that all of these various revenue-raising devices were largely unsuccessful. Rent for Colne manor stood at £31 4s 0d in 1481–2,[38] and only produced £34 17s 3d in 1616–17,[39] which was an increase of just 12%. It then shot up to £84 3s 4d in 1618–19,[40] as a result of leasing the manorial wastes by copy for an annual rent, which was an increase of 141% in one year. This not only emphasises the abrupt nature of the increase in rent from letting the wastes, but also underlines the insignificant rent increases obtained for well over a hundred years previously.

In Pendle and Trawden forests, substantial increases in rent have already been noted as a result of letting the area by copy in 1507, but in the period to 1640 Trawden forest only yielded another 15s 1d rent and Pendle forest 22s annually in addition to the 1507 rents, and these increases came entirely from letting mills and coal mines.[41] Thus the Duchy was clearly failing to take advantage of the rising value of land and this is further seen in the amounts paid for land in sales and leases transacted between tenants.[42]

However, even where it could increase its rents from land, the Duchy was failing to do so. For example, the Parliamentary commissioners of 1651 found that 7 acres of meadow or pasture called the Vivar, formerly a fishpond and subsequently drained, had been granted in 1610 for 60 years, for the old customary rent of 2s 4d per annum. The commissioners claimed that it was worth £4 10s 0d upon improvement, besides the rent.[43] This was leasehold, not copyhold land, highly untypical of the area, but it illustrates that the Duchy was not exploiting its property fully where it had the opportunity to raise sizeable rents. The Duchy's freedom of action on copyhold land was severely circumscribed, since entry fines and rents were fixed by custom.

Throughout the Jacobean period, the Crown increasingly resorted to financial expedients to raise revenue.[44] The leasing of mineral rights has already been discussed.[45] Far greater significance must be attached to the copyhold dispute. This has already been described in detail by Tupling,[46] so we shall limit ourselves to a brief summary.

In 1607, the Duchy started proceedings against the tenants of the Blackburnshire forests for allegedly unlawful entry according to pretended titles, and prohibited the grant of further lands in these areas and the enrolment of transfers of land already made. The Stewards were informed that these lands were really assarts which could not be claimed as copyholds, either by custom or prescription, and they were ordered to call together the tenants to receive their suggestions for the perfection of their titles.[47]

The tenants' titles had never been questioned during the period from 1507 to 1607, and their lands were treated in the same way as the old copyholds, that is, as copyholds of inheritance paying fixed entry fines and rents.[48] Moreover, the Blackburnshire forests were not forests at all in the strictly legal sense, but rather were chases, and thus the law of assart and purpresture did not apply to them.[49] In any case, that the forests had been disafforested was explicitly stated in a commission of 1545.[50] Nevertheless, the ambiguity in the use of the term 'leases' in the 1507 commission[51] did not help the tenants' case, though the commission of 1545 also stated that copyholds of inheritance had been created.[52]

The tenants, no doubt bewildered by this legal chicanery, offered to pay twelve years' rent as a composition for the confirmation of their copyholds. Agreement was reached on this basis in 1608, in spite of an unsuccessful attempt by the Crown to increase the amount due to 20 years' rent.[53] The Duchy decree and Act of Parliament confirming the copyholds were both passed in 1609,[54] and the money was paid in three instalments in that year.[55]

Following soon after this composition for the forest lands was a commission to investigate whether further revenue could be raised from the manors by confirming the certainty of fines on those copyholds of inheritance where the fines were uncertain, or certain by reputation only. In addition, holdings enclosed from either the demesne or the wastes and commons and granted by copy were seen as illegal, and thus another potential area for a composition, in return for confirmation of tenure by Duchy decree and Act of Parliament.[56] The size of the composition was to be adjudicated according to the real value of the holdings.[57]

Another aspect of this second assault on the legality of the manorial tenures was the offer to lease the commons by copy and to permit their enclosure. This was not only a revenue-raising device, in that the Crown could expect an initial fine and subsequent rents and fines for the commons, but was also designed to induce the tenants to compound for their existing copyhold estates.[58]

The policy of attempting to lease the commons in Colne manor at improved rents was by no means new, for it was first raised in 1592. Then the tenants had apparently been willing to pay fairly small rents and fines proportionate to the size of their holdings so that the commons might forever lie open and unenclosed, for the decree of 1594 declared that the tenants saw the commons as their 'greatest stay of living', especially for the poor.[59] If the annual rents were subsequently demanded, they have not been recorded in the ministers' accounts nor in the court rolls.[60] In subsequent litigation concerning the cost of obtaining the decrees, Edward Marsden claimed in 1599 that being poor, he was not able to pay his fine to the Queen for his part of the wastes, and he had requested a longer time to pay up.[61]

Opposition was immediately apparent from the copyholders to this second composition demand. The Commissioners reported in July 1611 that having related the King's proposals to the tenants, and having expected that they would accept them, they found that the tenants were unwilling to deal with them then. The tenants stated that they preferred to consult with legal counsel first, but nevertheless claimed that they already had a better case for both their copyhold estates and customs, and also for the commons, than could be created by composition with the Crown. The commissioners, however, did report that some of the tenants inwardly desired a composition.[62] This dispute was protracted, for no fines are recorded in the Colne manor court rolls from September 1608 until July 1618;[63] the copyholders refused to pay the fines assessed by the Steward because they were arbitrary and assessed at a far greater rate than was the custom. They affirmed that they were very ready to pay their accustomed and ancient fines of one year's rent.[64]

Eventually, agreement was reached in 1618. The copyholders were to pay 40 years' rent (£1,050 9s 2d) for a composition fee to the Crown, in return for confirmation of the certainty of their copyhold estates and fines by Duchy decree and Act of Parliament. One half of the composition was to be paid at the passing of the decree, and the other half after ratification by Act of Parliament. In addition, the overdue fines, which amounted to £191 15s 4d, were to be paid after the passing of the decree. Furthermore, the copyholders agreed to pay $6\frac{1}{2}d$ for every acre of waste still unenclosed, in return for the granting of the wastes by copy of court roll according to the custom of the manor, with the liberty to enclose and improve them.[65]

It was subsequently agreed in February 1620, that since a good part of the commons and wastes were used as highways and coal pits, £4 5s 10d was to be deducted from the total rent to be paid to the Crown. Thus instead of £54 5s 10d being paid for the 2,004 acres, 2 rods and 20 falls of waste, only £50 per annum was to be levied. Fines were still fixed at one year's rent (6½d an acre), but the annual rents were reduced to 6d per acre. Individual disputes over the area of the waste to be allocated to each tenant were also dealt with. Lawrence Towneley Esquire of Barnside demanded that part of his allocation of the wastes should be reapportioned in other areas, but the Duchy refused to alter the allocation.[66]

The composition for the commons and wastes clearly conflicted with the interests of cottagers who had encroached on parts of the waste, and when the division of the commons was being allotted, the cottagers brought their case to the Duchy. It decreed in 1621 that five of the cottages should be held as copyhold of inheritance, paying annual nominal rents of 1d to the Crown and between 6d and 12d to Colne School, and entry fines of one year's rent (as the other copyholders did). In addition, 18 other cottages were granted as leases for three lives, for rents ranging from 1d to 3d to the Crown, and from 2d to 6d annually to the school. The inheritance of these last cottages was placed in the hands of feoffees of trust to the use of the school, who were not to displace the tenants, but were to make new leases upon 'reasonable' rents and fines (which the Duchy would set down if they could not agree amongst themselves).[67] The Duchy was certainly not rack-renting these tenants, for in 1651 the Parliamentary commissioners reported that substantial improvements could be obtained.[68] Furthermore, ten other cottages situated on portions of waste allotted to the copyholders were also protected in 1621, largely on generous terms.[69]

After the Duchy decree was passed, half of the composition payment (representing 20 years' rent) was paid,[70] but payment of the other half, due on the passing of an Act of Parliament, was delayed, since the necessary bill was not introduced until 1640. Due to the political difficulties of the period, the bill failed to become law, and was not passed until 1650. However, the money was not paid by the appointed time, and additional fines were exacted which amounted to a total payment equivalent to 32 years' rent, not 20 years', for the other half of the composition. At the Restoration, the Act of 1650 was declared illegal, but another Act

was eventually passed in 1662 which confirmed the estates and acquitted the tenants of any further payments of composition.[71]   •
The economic significance of these large payments for composition has not been studied in detail.[72] For the Pendle and Trawden tenants, the total composition amounted to about £1,448 and £348 respectively.[73] The Colne tenants were required to pay £525 4s 7d in 1618, the first half of their composition.[74] One should note that these large sums were demanded at short notice and that the payment was not spread out over a period of years to ameliorate the effects. Moreover, those tenants who had lands in both the forests and the manor had to pay towards both compositions. Furthermore, the Colne manor tenants had to find another £50 per annum for rent of the wastes.[75] However, it must be noted that many subtenants were paying higher rents than 12 or 20 years' rent to the Crown, and that the copyholders were able to transfer some of the burdens on to their subtenants. Hence no very significant upsurge in the numbers of sales and mortgages was recorded immediately after the composition payments.[76] Thus we should not over-exaggerate the difficulties which the copyholders faced.

Nevertheless, the size of the Pendle composition of 1609 may well have contributed to the social tension that produced the outbreak of witchcraft accusations in March 1612. Some of those brought to trial lived mainly by begging,[77] and the accusation of acts of witchcraft often centred around a curse following refusal of charity by a wealthier neighbour,[78] who no doubt had less to spare following the composition payment.

Similarly many in Colne manor must have experienced problems raising 20 years' rent immediately. Indeed, some of the copyholders fell into arrears with their fine and rent payments (the rents, one should remember, had been increased by leasing the commons). Some of those in arrears in 1621 were prominent gentry such as the Towneleys. Altogether, £18 6s 0d was claimed to be in arrears in January 1621.[79] The gentry figured prominently amongst those in arrears in 1627; Mrs. Anderton of Pendle Hall, Richard Towneley of Carr Esquire and Mr. Shuttleworth owed £3 0s 3d, £1 3s 6d and £22 18s 11½d respectively.[80] In 1633, it was stated that many of the copyhold tenants were in arrears, mainly for small sums of 1s or less, but these were to be written off, since too much rent had been collected, partly from the Pendle mills.[81]

The compositions must also be placed in the context of two other factors of great economic significance. First, it appears that the 1620s and 1630s was a period of local depression in the woollen cloth trade.[82] Secondly, the bad harvests of 1621–2 sent the price of corn rocketing skyward.[83] The conjunction of all these elements must have contributed to the demographic crisis of 1623, which seems to have been largely famine based.[84]

One should also note that the copyhold dispute may have had serious political consequences, in terms of the formation of the sides in the Civil War. Tupling convincingly argued that the Crown's action in this dispute was a significant factor alienating the tenants of the Honor of Clitheroe and increasing their Parliamentarian sympathies.[85]

Looking at the period as a whole, it seems that Duchy lordship in the sixteenth century was extremely benevolent.[86] The copyhold dispute of the early seventeenth century certainly provoked opposition and added to existing economic difficulties, but in the Crown's defence, two points ought to be made. First, in the light of the fact that receipts rose only slightly during the sixteenth century, the tenants were benefiting from inflation at the Crown's expense and it was likely that the Crown should attempt to redress the balance.[87] Secondly, since the legality of the copyholds in the forest areas and the certainty of entry fines in the manors had been called in question successfully, it is an example of the Crown's moderation that leases and arbitrary fines were not introduced, with the prospect of rapidly rising rents and fines, instead of confirming the fixed entry fines and rents (albeit for large compositions). Consistently, the Crown pursued a short-sighted, short-term economic strategy, preferring immediate financial gain to long-term advantage and seigneurial flexibility. Nevertheless, in comparison with some landlords, the Crown does appear moderate in its financial demands on its tenants,[88] with total Duchy revenue remaining fairly constant over the period from the mid-sixteenth century to 1642.[89]

NOTES

[1] See Chapter 1, p. 9; Shaw, *Royal forest of Lancaster*, p. 471; Tupling, *Economic history of Rossendale*, pp. 32–5

[2] Farrer, *Court rolls*, vol. 1, pp. 485–6. This is a transcription of P.R.O. D.L.12/1 fol. 58v. It is also cited by Shaw, *Royal forest of Lancaster*, p. 472

[3] Farrer, *Court rolls*, vol. 1, pp. 484–6 (transcription of P.R.O. D.L.12/1 fols. 57, 58v, 61). It is also cited by Shaw, *Royal forest of Lancaster*, p. 472, and by Tupling, *Economic history of Rossendale*, p. 43

[4] Farrer, *Court rolls*, vol. 1, pp. 484–5 (transcription of P.R.O. D.L.12/1

fol. 61v). It is also cited by Shaw, *Royal forest of Lancaster*, p. 472, and by Tupling, *Economic history of Rossendale*, p. 43

⁵ Farrer, *Court rolls*, vol. 1, pp. 235–6 (transcription of the decree of 12 March 1507 for Trawden forest, enrolled in the halmote of Colne)

⁶ Farrer, *Court rolls*, vol. 2, pp. 373–7 (transcription of B.L. Add. MSS 32103, fols. 136–9). There is also a copy in W.R.O. D/DZ A.4 'Honor of Clitheroe' volume, fols. 51–4v

⁷ *Ibid.* Total rent figures have been obtained by aggregating the separate old and new rents for each subdivision of the forests. See Tupling, *Economic history of Rossendale*, pp. 43–5

⁸ Shaw, *Royal forest of Lancaster*, p. 480; Tupling, *Economic history of Rossendale*, pp. 146–7. See below, p. 61

⁹ For price changes, see Bowden, 'Statistical appendix', *passim*

¹⁰ This was stated in the decree for disafforestation. Farrer, *Court rolls*, vol. 1, p. 236. See also the copyhold customs of the Honor of Clitheroe, printed in *ibid.*, vol. 1, pp. 478–81, especially customs 5, 8 and 10; this is a transcription of M.C.L. L1/38/3/2. The customs in 1402 are printed in Whitaker, *History of Whalley*, pp. 189–90, when estates were explicitly stated to be inheritable, though for a moderate or fair fine ('finem racionabilem'). As stated above, by 1507, fines were fixed at one year's customary rent

¹¹ Farrer, *Court rolls*, vol. 1, *passim*. New parcels of land on the waste were let at 4*d* an acre from at least the early fourteenth century, for an extent of Colne manor in 1323 shows that most parcels of rodland (improved from the waste) were let at exactly 4*d* an acre. Farrer, *Court rolls*, vol. 1, p. 483

¹² Tawney, *Agrarian problem*, p. 300. See also Kerridge, *Agrarian problems*, especially pp. 35–40

¹³ See Chapter 3, pp. 37–8

¹⁴ L.R.O. DDHCl3/5/6, Colne manor, 1st halmote, 16 Oct. 1582, recording a warrant of 20 Oct. 1581. See also P.R.O. D.L.29/84/1593, Colne manor (1583–4), when this appears for the first time in the surviving accounts

¹⁵ L.R.O. DDHCl3/67, Colne manor, 1st halmote, 13 Oct. 1584, recording a warrant of 24 May 1584. See also P.R.O. D.L.29/84/1594, Colne manor (1591–2), when this appears for the first time in the surviving accounts

¹⁶ P.R.O. D.L.5/7 fols. 322v–323v gives the date of this lease as 27 February 1542. It appears in the ministers' accounts for the first time in P.R.O. D.L.29/82/1575, Pendle forest (1543–4). See below, p. 59

¹⁷ P.R.O. D.L.3/40/R1

¹⁸ P.R.O. D.L.42/96 fol. 172v

¹⁹ Farrer, *Court rolls*, vol. 1, pp. 467–70. This appears in the surviving ministers' accounts for the first time in P.R.O. D.L.29/84/1590, Trawden forest (1569–70)

²⁰ P.R.O. D.L.29/86/1603, Pendle forest (1609–10), referring to a decree of 25 Dec. 1598

²¹ See Chapter 7, pp. 171–3

²² Somerville, *History of the Duchy of Lancaster*, p. 310. The only example found of a royalty being demanded on leases of coal mines in this area during the period 1500–1640 was the grant to Thomas Houghton gentleman

of a licence to search, mine and dig for lead, copper, sulphur and coal in the wastes and commons of the Hundreds of Blackburn, Lonsdale and Amounderness, and also in the copyhold and customary lands of the King's tenants there, for 21 years. This was given in Hilary Term 1609, and the rent was fixed at a third of the profits. P.R.O. IND 17596, p. 639

[23] P.R.O. D.L.29/86/1603 Colne manor (1609–10), granted in Michaelmas Term 1609 (IND 17596, p. 639)

[24] P.R.O. D.L.3/44/R9; D.L.5/7 fols. 277v–278v., printed in Farrer, *Court rolls*, vol. 2, pp. 181–5. Cited by Shaw, *Royal forest of Lancaster*, p. 477

[25] Farrer, *Court rolls*, vol. 2, pp. 75–6

[26] P.R.O. D.L.5/7 fols. 322v–323v. This appears for the first time in the surviving ministers' accounts in P.R.O. D.L.29/82/1576, Pendle forest (1545–6). See above, p. 58

[27] P.R.O. D.L.29/87/1615, Colne manor (1624–5). Half a year's rent was obtained in the previous year, D.L.29/87/1614, Colne manor (1623–4)

[28] P.R.O. D.L.44/33

[29] Farrer, *Court rolls*, vol. 1, p. 451. These appear in the surviving ministers' accounts for the first time in P.R.O. D.L.29/84/1589, Colne manor (1563–4)

[30] P.R.O. D.L.44/36

[31] P.R.O. D.L.44/285

[32] P.R.O. D.L.44/1009. The encroachments by James Whitehead, John Watson alias North, James Baldwin and John Wilson of Great Marsden are referred to in both P.R.O. D.L.44/285 and D.L.44/1009. There are others which probably refer to the same encroachment e.g. Hugh Walton's barn in Marsden in 1579 was probably the same as Henry Walton's in 1616

[33] Tupling, *Economic history of Rossendale*, p. 63. See below, p. 61

[34] P.R.O. D.L.3/61/R/1; printed in Fishwick, *Pleadings and depositions, Edward VI*, pp. 111–15; D.L.5/10 fol. 247v–248

[35] P.R.O. D.L.4/24/55, D.L.6/32, Crown v Richard Grimshaw P.R.O. D.L.4/24/54, D.L.6/32, Crown v Lawrence Towneley and Henry Blakey P.R.O. D.L.1/208/A14, D.L.6/32, Crown v Bernard Blakey

[36] P.R.O. D.L.1/8/R7; printed in Fishwick, *Pleadings and depositions, Henry VIII*, pp. 1–2; also Farrer, *Court rolls*, vol. 1, pp. 316–17, halmote at Colne for Trawden forest, 27 Oct. 1534

[37] See especially the rentals for Pendle and Trawden forests in 1608, printed in Farrer, *Court rolls*, vol. 2, pp. 402–4, and Farrer, *Court rolls*, vols. 1 and 2 (Trawden and Pendle forests), and L.R.O. DDHCl3 *passim*

[38] P.R.O. D.L.29/90/1651 Colne manor (1481–2)

[39] P.R.O. D.L.29/86/1609 Colne manor (1616–17)

[40] P.R.O. D.L.29/87/1610 Colne manor (1618–19)

[41] P.R.O. D.L.29/88/1629 Trawden forest and Pendle forest (1639–40)

[42] See Chapter 5, pp. 80–91

[43] P.R.O. E.317 Lancs.10, cf. Farrer, *Court rolls*, vol. 2, p. 447

[44] See, for example, Batho, 'Landlords in England. A. The Crown', pp. 268–76

[45] See above, p. 58

[46] Tupling, *Economic history of Rossendale*, chapter 5, especially pp. 145–60. See also Shaw, *Royal forest of Lancaster*, pp. 478–81

[47] Tupling, *Economic history of Rossendale*, pp. 148–9; Shaw, *Royal forest of Lancaster*, pp. 479–80; for other areas, see Batho, 'Landlords in England. A. The Crown', p. 270

[48] Tupling, *Economic history of Rossendale*, pp. 146–7

[49] Shaw, *Royal forest of Lancaster*, p. 479

[50] P.R.O. D.L.5/7, fol. 277v; printed in Farrer, *Court rolls*, vol. 2, pp. 181–4, especially p. 182. Cited by Shaw, *Royal forest of Lancaster*, pp. 477, 480

[51] Farrer, *Court rolls*, vol. 1, p. 235

[52] P.R.O. D.L.5/7, fol. 277v; printed in Farrer, *Court rolls*, vol. 2, pp. 181–4, especially p. 182. Cited by Shaw, *Royal forest of Lancaster*, p. 477

[53] P.R.O. D.L.5/19, fols. 395v, 400–1; D.L.44/777. See Tupling, *Economic history of Rossendale*, pp. 149–50 and Shaw, *Royal forest of Lancaster*, p. 480

[54] P.R.O. D.L.5/19, fols. 400–1; Statutes of the Realm, 7 James I (Private Acts No. 3)

[55] P.R.O. D.L.5/19, fol. 410v, D.L.44/777; S.P.14/44 fol. 15, S.P.14/61 fol. 106. See Tupling, *Economic history of Rossendale*, p. 150, and Shaw, *Royal forest of Lancaster*, p. 480

[56] P.R.O. S.P.14/61 fols. 103–5; Tupling, *Economic history of Rossendale*, pp. 150–1

[57] P.R.O. S.P.14/61 fol. 104. The suggested method for determining the size of the fine was to deduct the annual rent from the annual value of the land, and then double it. Thus, since the Colne copyholders were assessed at 40 years' rent for a composition, the commissioners must have calculated that the annual value of a Lancashire acre (rent 4*d* to the Crown) in Colne manor was 7*s* (i.e. 6*s* 8*d* above the rent). See Tupling, *Economic history of Rossendale*, pp. 151–2

[58] P.R.O. S.P.14/61, fols. 103, 105; S.P.14/64, fol. 50. See Tupling, *Economic history of Rossendale*, p. 152

[59] P.R.O. D.L.5/19, fols. 126–34; D.L.42/98, fol. 242v–244; D.L.44/498

[60] This casts some doubt on the reliability of the ministers' accounts as a total record of the financial relations between the Duchy and its tenants

[61] P.R.O. D.L.1/188/F8. See also D.L.1/181/F5

[62] P.R.O. S.P.14/64 fol. 50. See Tupling, *Economic history of Rossendale*, pp. 153–4

[63] No fines are recorded for Colne manor in L.R.O. DDHCl3/90, Colne manor, 2nd halmote, 9 Sept. 1608, to DDHCl3/100, Colne manor, 1st halmote, 21 Oct. 1617 inclusive. Fines reappear in DDHCl3/100, Colne manor, 2nd halmote, 8 July 1618, when the fines for the previously cited period are also recorded

[64] P.R.O. D.L.5/27, fol. 1315

[65] *Ibid.*, fols. 1316–25

[66] P.R.O. D.L.5/28, fol. 267–267v, revising the decree D.L.5/28, fol. 37–37v

[67] Farrer, *Court rolls*, vol. 2, pp. 443–7; L.R.O. DDHCl3/104, Colne manor, 2nd halmote, 21 May 1622; M.C.L. L1/47/3 fols. 24–7

[68] P.R.O. E.317 Lancs.12. It was then estimated that the rent from the cottages of 1*s* 9*d* to the Crown could be improved by £6 10*s* 2*d*

[69] L.R.O. DDHCl3/104, Colne manor, 2nd halmote, 21 May 1622, recording a Duchy decree of 20 Nov. 1621

[70] P.R.O. S.P.16/131 fol. 4; Tupling, *Economic history of Rossendale*, p. 155; Shaw, *Royal forest of Lancaster*, p. 481

[71] Tupling, *Economic history of Rossendale*, pp. 158–9) Shaw, *Royal forest of Lancaster*, p. 481

[72] Both Tupling and Cunliffe Shaw were essentially concerned with the legal rather than the economic aspects of the dispute.

[73] Calculated by multiplying the improved rents of 1507 by 12. See Farrer, *Court rolls*, vol. 2, pp. 373–7 for the rents of 1507, and P.R.O. S.P.14/44 fol. 15 for the total composition; cf. Tupling, *Economic history of Rossendale*, p. 150 note 8

[74] That is, half of the total payment of £1,050 9s 2d (40 years' rent) demanded. See P.R.O. D.L.5/27 fol. 1317

[75] See above, p. 63

[76] See Chapter 5, pp. 80–91

[77] Crossley, *Potts' discovery of witches*, B2v, C, Cv, F, R3v and R4 show that old Demdike, her granddaughter Alison Device and Elizabeth daughter of Old Chattox lived at least partly by begging

[78] *Ibid.*, G2, H3v–H4, O4, S. On the relationship between refusal of charity and witchcraft accusations, see Thomas, *Religion and the decline of magic*, pp. 553–6, 557–9 and Macfarlane, *Witchcraft in Tudor and Stuart England*, pp. 173–6, 196–8, 205–6

[79] L.R.O. DDKe 5/92

[80] L.R.O. DDKe 5/108

[81] P.R.O. D.L.44/1130

[82] See Chapter 6, pp. 127–38, 142–4

[83] See Chapter 2, p. 24

[84] See Chapter 2, pp. 22–5

[85] Tupling, 'Causes of the Civil War in Lancashire', pp. 17–20. This view is accepted by Manning in *English people and the English revolution*, pp. 130–1, 238–9, 260

[86] Somerville, *History of the Duchy of Lancaster*, pp. 305–8, 341–2; Batho, 'Landlords in England. A. The Crown', p. 267; Kerridge, 'Movement of rent', p. 30

[87] Tenants of other Duchy and Crown lands faced composition payments too, e.g. the Duchy of Lancaster's manor of Wakefield in Yorkshire paid a composition of 35 years' rent so that their fines upon admittance might be established by decree and Act of Parliament at 3 years' old rent (the tenants had claimed that they should only pay 1½ years' rent). P.R.O. S.P.14/61, fol. 106; Batho, 'Landlords in England. A. The Crown', pp. 269–71; Tupling, *Economic history of Rossendale*, pp. 135–45

[88] Ramsey, *Tudor economic problems*, pp. 42–3

[89] Batho, 'Landlords in England. A. The Crown', pp. 265–6; Dietz, *English government finance*, p. 26 points out that a rapid increase in Duchy revenue took place under Henry VII. However, from about the mid sixteenth century, Duchy revenue was fairly constant until 1642; *ibid.*, p. 138; Dietz, *English public finance*, p. 302. He does note, however, that as in 1618, the fines on the customary tenants might produce a sizeable increase in revenue

CHAPTER V

LANDHOLDING, WEALTH AND POVERTY

It will be shown in this chapter that the changing structure of landholding and distribution of wealth in Colne manor and the forests of Trawden and Pendle between 1500 and 1640 created conditions ripe for extensive rural industrialisation. Not only did land become increasingly scarce as population rose, but also holdings became fragmented to the point where supplementary income was essential for many, with or without land.

THE NATURE OF LANDHOLDING

Most of the land in this area was held 'by copy of court roll according to the custom of the manor', as was also the case in Rossendale.[1] In 1617, Colne manor consisted of just over 1,564 acres of cultivated land, and 2,200 acres of waste.[2] The only precise statement of the area of the forests was given in a map of the Honor of Clitheroe, drawn up between 1804 and 1810; the size of Trawden and Pendle forests amounted to just over 4,782 acres and 7,289 acres respectively.[3]

There was a small amount of freehold, leasehold and chantry land, which was concentrated particularly in Colne. Inquisitions post mortem and rentals suggest that the bulk of freehold land in Colne was held by the Towneleys of Royle. In Pendle forest, the Bannisters owned 120 acres of freehold at Parkhill in Barrowford, and the Towneleys of Barnside possessed 10 acres of freehold in Trawden forest.[4] Thus freehold land in this area was held largely by the gentry. In addition, there were 22 acres of chantry land (which was assigned to the use of the church of Colne after the dissolution of the chantries), and 7 acres of leasehold in Colne called the Vivar.[5] It appears, therefore, that most land in Colne, and virtually all of the forest land was held by copyhold tenure.

SUBDIVISION OF COPYHOLDS

The rentals point to a very high degree of subdivision of copyholds, though this varied over time and space, as can be seen from Table 5.1.[6]

Table 5.1 Numbers of tenants in Colne manor, and Trawden and Pendle forests, 1443–1617

Area	1443	1527	1539	1608	1617
Colne manor	(45)	51	—	—	102
Trawden forest	(11)	29	31	31	—
Pendle forest	(24)	100	100	115	—
(i) Barrowford and Roughlee	—	36	34	47	—
(ii) Rest of Pendle forest	—	64	66	68	—

It should be noted that the forests were not let by copy until 1507. Subsequently, the number of forest tenants increased substantially, as is apparent from the large numbers recorded in 1527. However, the main forest area where the number of copyholders continued to increase noticeably between 1527 and 1608 was north-east Pendle.[7] On the other hand, the number of tenants in Colne manor was only slightly larger in 1527 than it had been in the mid fifteenth century, but doubled in the next ninety years. Since the amount of land let by copy in 1608 or 1617 was virtually the same as it had been in 1527,[8] the increase in the number of copyholders implies considerable subdivision of holdings.

Rentals also exist for 1650 and 1662,[9] but these are not strictly comparable with earlier rentals, for three reasons. First, the 2,200 acres of commons in Colne manor were let by copy in 1618, and in addition, copyhold rights were granted to those who occupied cottages on the wastes.[10] As will be shown, it was now possible to be a copyholder simply by renting wasteland. Thus, the opportunities to lease land directly from the Duchy increased enormously. Secondly, the rentals for Colne manor in 1650 and 1662 were not drawn up in the same way as before, for in 1650 Colne manor was divided up into Colne township, Colne and Marsden, and in 1662 into Colne and Marsden.[11] A simple count of names might exaggerate the number of copyholders, for some may have held land in more than one sub-area. Thirdly, some later rentals include subtenants, who previously seem to have been excluded. This is certainly the case for Pendle and Trawden forests in 1650, though subtenants in Colne manor seem not to have been recorded in this rental.[12] In 1662, subtenants were included in all the rentals.[13]

Nevertheless, even allowing for these qualifications, it is clear that subdivision of holdings continued during the early seventeenth century. In 1650, there were 58 tenants in Barrowford and Roughlee (in Pendle forest) who held land directly from the Duchy, compared with 47 in 1608. The increase in the number of these tenants was even more noticeable in the rest of Pendle forest (68 in 1608; 97 in 1650). Trawden forest displayed more restrained tendencies towards subdivision during this period, for there were 36 tenants holding land directly from the Duchy in 1650, compared with 31 in 1608.[14] In Colne manor, comparison between the rentals for 1617 and 1650 is unjustified, for reasons already explained. Subdivision of holdings was also visible in Rossendale during our period.[15]

Merely noting the number of copyhold tenants gives no indication as to the size of holdings. Regrettably, it is only possible to analyse the size of copyholds in Colne manor, where land was let at $4d$ an acre (making it possible to convert a rent into an acreage), whereas land in the forests was let at varying amounts, but usually for rents of less than $4d$ an acre.[16]

Subdivision of holdings in Colne manor between 1527 and 1617 resulted in a disproportionate increase in the number of very small copyholds, upon which subsistence would have been virtually impossible without additional income. In 1527, for example, only 16% of holdings were of 5 (Lancashire) acres or less in size; by 1617, this proportion constituted nearly half (45%) of all tenancies.[17]

Rents paid by copyholders in north-east Pendle forest were far lower than in the rest of the forest or in Trawden forest, and due to subdivision, this difference in the level of rents increased over time. In 1527, average rent in north east Pendle was just $15s\ 1d$, compared with $28s\ 4d$ in the rest of Pendle and $21s\ 6d$ in Trawden; by 1608, the average rents were $11s\ 10d$, $26s\ 3d$ and $18s\ 9d$ respectively. Thus it is likely that holdings in north-east Pendle were far smaller than elsewhere in the forests (since we have no evidence that rents differed markedly from one area to another) which may have made them more susceptible to fragmentation, for reasons discussed below.

THE CAUSES OF THE SUBDIVISION OF HOLDINGS

The best evidence of contemporary awareness that the economic difficulties which faced copyholders were partly due to the subdivision of their holdings, is provided by a statement in 1604 by Sir Richard Molyneux. He claimed that there were not ten copyholders in Blackburn Hundred rich enough to enfranchise their copyholds, giving four reasons for his assertion. First, he pointed out that the forests of Rossendale, Pendle and Trawden were subdivided into smaller holdings than when they had been first let, 'either amongst coparceners or amongst younger children or by other sales whereby for the most part the copyholders there are grown poor'. Secondly, he noted that the poverty of the copyholders and inhabitants of the forests was also due to heavy expenses on 'enclosing, tilling and building', for the forests were very barren, unenclosed and without buildings when they were first let. Thirdly, he argued that 'within these few years, many particular persons have at excessive rates (assuring themselves of a good estate of inheritance) purchased several portions within the forests and so are now utterly unable to purchase the same anew'. Fourth, 'few or almost none of the copyholders stand seised in fee of their copyholds, but either their estates be for life or lives, or else there be one or more jointures out of their lands, or during the nonage of the heir younger children to be provided for, or surrenders are made to undertenants for lives or years', and therefore 'the heir in reversion will not be able to purchase it'.[18]

There were three essential reasons for the subdivision of holdings, namely inheritance customs, sales and mortgages, and subtenancies.

(a) *Inheritance customs*   An examination of the 255 available wills of male testators from this area between 1546 and 1640 indicates that inheritance practices with regard to the disposition of real estate were strongly biassed towards primogeniture. A total of 37 wills refer both to real estate and to more than one son; of these, no will has been found where a testator explicitly divided his lands equally between all his sons.[19] Examples of inheritance by younger sons are usually confined to testators with land in more than one place (where land, often in Yorkshire, is bequeathed to younger sons) or to small portions of land surrendered to younger sons, usually for a term of years, with reversion to the eldest son. However, partible inheritance was practised to a certain extent in the forests during the early sixteenth century, a period for which we do not possess wills.

It should be noted from the outset that a proper study of inheritance of land cannot be obtained from wills alone, for two reasons. First, some inheritance of land might occur during a copyholder's lifetime and before making a will. Thus, by way of justification for giving his eldest son only a small part of goods, James Hargreaves, a yeoman of Fence Yate in Pendle, mentioned in his will in 1591 that he had previously given his lands to his eldest son William, who had then sold them.[20] Semi-retirement might also occur, where a copyholder handed over control of part of the holding to his son. In 1551, John Emott surrendered his holding in Wycoller to his son James, but he reserved half the premises for his own use for life.[21] Such an arrangement would not normally lead to subdivision that was apparent in a rental; for example, three copyholders held land together with their sons, according to the rental for Colne manor in 1617, but their holdings are not recorded as subdivided.[22] Secondly, by the customs of the Honor of Clitheroe, if a copyholder died intestate, or had not made provision for inheritance by a previous surrender, a manorial jury would make an inquiry as to who was the rightful heir, and would enforce primogeniture inheritance.[23]

Turning to the inheritance of personal estate, the custom of the Province of York was that the wife was automatically entitled to one third, the children another third, and the testator was only able to dispose of the remaining third (the 'dead man's part') as he saw fit. If he had no children, his wife was to receive half of his personal estate automatically, or alternatively, if his wife had died, then any children were to receive half. It was not until 1692 that a testator in the Province of York could dispose of the whole of his personal estate as he chose.[24] The wills of testators from this area indicate that this custom was generally adhered to. Thus, although the eldest son might inherit the holding, younger sons and daughters had an unchallengeable right to a share in the personal estate.

In a similar way to real estate, personal estate was often bestowed on children during the father's lifetime, in the form of cash portions and dowries, before the making of a will. A good example of this is shown by the will of a yeoman, Roger Hartley of Trawden (1632). He stated that he had already given his sons Roger and Richard (who were in London) £40 and £19, and he then gave them £33 6s 8d and £60 respectively. He had bestowed dowries on two of his daughters at their marriages (£50 on Elizabeth and £80 on Alice) who now received £20 and 30s respectively. He bequeathed £80 and a chest to an unmarried daughter Janet, and after giving the wain gear, limestones and slatestones to his son and heir Robert, and loose timber and £1 to another son John, he bequeathed the rest of his personal estate to Robert and John, a third to the former and two-thirds to the latter.[25] This example shows a testator bestowing considerable sums on his children during his lifetime and also attempting to treat younger sons and daughters equally, by making the total portion of each child roughly the same.

Furthermore, a testator often stipulated that part of his holding should be devoted to the use of his younger children for a specified period after his death, particularly if his younger children were under-age, in order to provide them with portions. In 1610, a yeoman named Nicholas Stephenson of Goldshaw in Pendle left half his lands to feoffees to the use of John, his son and heir apparent, providing that John paid a total of £100 within ten years after his father's death (at the rate of £10 per annum), to his younger brother and four sisters. Nicholas bequeathed the other half to the feoffees to his wife's use, for her dower and for the education of his younger children, with the clause that if she died within the following fourteen years, the profits from this half of his lands were to be used for the benefit of his younger children. After this, the reversion was left to John. The goods were to be divided amongst his wife and children 'according to the custom of the country'.[26] If the heir was also under-age, a testator might leave his lands to the use of all his children until the heir came of age. In 1617, James Hartley, a yeoman of Winewall in Trawden, left his holding to feoffees to the use of his three children until his son and heir James was twenty-one, and if James paid £340 to his younger brother and sister, he was to receive the lands. To make matters more difficult for James (the heir), he was not to receive a share of the personal estate, for, after payment of debts, one third was left to his mother and two-thirds to his younger brother and sister.[27] Here is an example of an heir being doubly disadvantaged, not only having to provide portions for his siblings, but also denied a share in the personal estate of his father.

Sometimes the heir had further resources denied him by the obligation to support his widowed mother with lands and goods. It has already been noted that a widow was automatically entitled to a third of the personal estate of her husband by the custom of the Province of York, and she often obtained a further share by receiving some of the 'dead man's part'.[28] Furthermore, the widow of a copyholder was entitled to a share in her husband's lands which was fixed by custom at a quarter. This was stated in a declaration of the copyhold customs of the Honor of Clitheroe in 1668,[29] and although the customs of 1402 do not state explicitly the size of the widow's dower,[30] it is clear that this custom was established by at least the very early sixteenth century, and possibly earlier. For example, in 1513, a widow in Trawden successfully claimed a quarter of her husband's lands as dower.[31] Indeed, a copyholder might leave his widow with considerably more than a quarter of his holding for her dower; a third was by no means uncommon, and in some cases a half was reserved for the widow's use.[32] Although the rentals do not appear to classify widows' dowers as separate holdings, and hence this custom is not a reason for the subdivision of holdings apparent in the rentals, it nevertheless produced subdivision in practice.

The importance of the scale of provisions for both younger children and widows should not be underestimated. Howell has argued that these arrangements, representing a drain on the heir's resources, suggest a considerable blurring in the differences between unigeniture and partible inheritance. Spufford too has argued that portions of land and goods for the widow and younger children placed a considerable economic strain on the heir, and could help to promote subdivision of holdings, particularly following years of bad harvests.[33]

Indeed, the practice of primogeniture inevitably resulted in some subdivision of holdings, largely for demographic reasons. If a copyholder died without sons to succeed him and with more than one daughter, or alternatively, if he had no children but had more than one collateral heiress, the holding was held in common by the daughters or coheiresses, but could be subdivided by a writ of partition.[34] In 1539, Nicholas Hartley's holding in Beardshaw Booth in Trawden was inherited by his two married sisters, who immediately divided the lands between them.[35] In the 332 cases between 1507 and 1640 where the juries of Colne, Trawden and Pendle were asked to declare who was the rightful heir (after the death of a copyholder), only 28 (8%) involved inheritance by more than one heiress.[36]

However, such subdivision as did occur might be only temporary, for if an heiress married a copyholder, then the number of copyholds would be reduced. This also applied if an only daughter or collateral heiress inherited copyhold land and married a copyholder, but statistically this was not a significant group, for only 16 of the 332 cases of inheritance referred to above (5%) involved single heiresses. The rental for Pendle forest in 1608 is a good example of the marriage patterns of heiresses; nine copyholders held land *iure uxoris*, and only one of these had land himself in the same booth.[37] Thus, the overall effect of female inheritance seems to have contributed to subdivision of holdings.

A number of examples of the practice of partible inheritance can be found, particularly in the forest areas in the early sixteenth century, and this also led to subdivision of holdings. Tupling argued that the customary estates of the Honor of Clitheroe were 'practically as negotiable as freeholds' and that though primogeniture was sometimes practised, 'quite as frequently' a copyholder in Rossendale divided his lands between his children.[38] After the disafforestation in 1507, land was extremely abundant and copyholders could subdivide their lands between all their sons, whilst still bequeathing considerable holdings to each. For example, in 1514, James Hartley of Trawden surrendered half his lands to his son Roger and half to another son Henry.[39] Indeed, despite the King's prohibition in 1532 against letting land in small parcels in the forests of Blackburnshire,[40] the manorial authorites might enforce the practice of partible inheritance in cases where a dispute arose. Thus when a controversy occurred in 1537 between John and Geoffrey Hartley, the sons of Peter Hartley, with regard to a surrender to be made by their father of his lands in Wycoller in Trawden, the steward ordered Peter to surrender his lands to feoffees to Peter's use during his life, and afterwards to be split equally between his sons.[41]

Whilst partible inheritance was practised by some copyholders in the forests in the early sixteenth century, it soon became modified in the direction of primogeniture when land became more scarce.[42] Copyholders tended increasingly to give their eldest sons the bulk of the holding, whilst younger sons were allotted smaller portions, and often for the duration of their lives or a specified term of years only, with the reversion to the eldest son. In 1586, James Hartley of Trawden surrendered his holding in Beardshaw to a feoffee to his own use during his life, and after his death, half was bequeathed to his widow for her dower and then was left to his sons Richard and Bernard for their lives. The other half was given to the eldest son Roger for his life. Significantly, the remainder of all the premises was allotted to Roger's heirs.[43] In the manor of Colne, younger sons were very occasionally given portions of land. In 1534, John Hartley alias Birdee surrendered a messuage and 11 acres in Great Marsden to his sons James and Henry, on condition that he should occupy the premises during his life, followed by his wife if she survived him, after which the elder son James was to have the messuage and 6 acres, and the younger son Henry 5 acres. The remainder was left to the son who survived the other. In this case, only temporary subdivision resulted, and the matter was concluded rather more to the advantage of the elder son.[44]

Not all examples of partible inheritance would necessarily result in the subdivision of holdings apparent in the rentals. Some copyholders possessed land in more than one area, and divided it between their sons on geographical lines, especially where a copyholder owned lands in Yorkshire as well as Lancashire. In 1620, the yeoman Roger Folds of Trawden bequeathed his lands in Haworth and Oxenhope in Yorkshire to his four younger sons, whilst his eldest son received his holding in Trawden. This was subject to the proviso that his widow should retain half of the premises in Trawden for her life for the maintenance of his younger children, who included five daughters as well as four sons.[45] Copyholders who held land in more than one area in the Honor of Clitheroe might also divide their lands geographically. According to a Duchy lawsuit of 1548–51, Henry Nutter, the eldest son of Ellis Nutter, alleged that the inheritance to all his father's lands in New Laund and Reedley Hallows in Pendle rightfully belonged to him, but that his younger brother John had unlawfully dispossessed him of the premises in New Laund. Henry unsuccessfully disputed the validity of the will (which left the lands in New Laund to John) and appealed to the Duchy court against the decision of the manorial jury. The verdict does not appear to have survived, but Henry must have been unsuccessful, for John was admitted as tenant in 1552.[46]

In view of the high levels of illegitimacy prevailing in this area, it is especially important to investigate how inheritance customs affected illegitimate children. By canon, common and manorial law, a bastard had no automatic inheritance to land.[47] In practice, the situation was far from uniform. In 1601, Richard Hargreaves, a yeoman of Higham in Pendle, bequeathed his lands to his legitimate heirs (he had two legitimate sons and a daughter) and only if there were none alive at his death was his bastard son to inherit.[48] A yeoman, Lawrence Shaw of Colne, bequeathed his lands in Colne and Trawden in 1600 to feoffees to his own use during his life, and subsequently, first to the use of his stepfather, and then to his brother (the eldest son of his stepfather) rather than to his own illegitimate son, Lawrence England alias Shaw. Whoever inherited was to bring up his base son until the age of sixteen, when he was to be put to a trade. Lawrence junior was to receive £10 when he was twenty-one, which was a fairly insignificant portion for an only son of a copyholder with 31 acres.[49] On the other hand, Robert Smith, a yeoman of Roughlee in Pendle, left his lands in 1609 to his base son in preference to his legitimate daughter, though she was also given two-thirds of the personal estate, and the son was to pay £30 to her when she came of age.[50] It is certainly true that contemporaries were aware of the legal disabilities of bastardy, for a number of disputes brought before the Duchy court over title to land in this area, centred around the allegation that a legitimate relative of a copyholder had a better title to land than an illegitimate child of such a copyholder.[51]

With regard to the question of bastards' inheritance of personal estate, the example of the treatment of Lawrence England alias Shaw quoted above was certainly not unique. For example, in 1610, the clothier William Holt of Colne left only £5 to his 'supposed' illegitimate son William Holt, yet apparently he had no legitimate children or wife living. His inventory, including debts, was valued at £78 17s 2d, and he bequeathed more on his funeral expenses and to the poor (£6) than to his son.[52] However, when they came to bequeath their personal estate, many testators clearly felt obliged to treat their illegitimate offspring in a similar fashion to their legitimate children. In 1607, John Elliott, a yeoman of Alkincoats in Colne, left his copyhold lands to his son, and £40 to each of his daughters, one of whom was base born. Interestingly, if his son John were to die before coming of age, the inheritance of the lands was to descend to Grace, the legitimate daughter, but she was to pay £60 to her illegitimate sister Margaret. After miscellaneous bequests of goods, his wife and two daughters were given one-third of the personal estate each.[53] As a further example, in 1628, the husbandman Christopher Bulcock of Stony Edge in Pendle left £20 to his illegitimate son, which was a sum roughly equivalent to the amount received by each of the four legitimate children.[54] On balance, more illegitimate children seem to have been fairly endowed from testators' personal estates than were not, though one should not forget the plight of illegitimate children born to poor parents, for whom we do not possess wills.

Thus it seems that the effects of inheritance by coheiresses, and the practice of partible inheritance to a limited extent (notably in the forests in the early sixteenth century) contributed to subdivision of holdings. However, far more subdivision occurred, both temporary and permanent, due to inheritance customs than was apparent in the rentals. This was brought about through the arrangements made for semi-retirement, the widow's dower, bequests of land to younger children for specified periods, and partible inheritance on geographical lines. Inheritance practices concerning illegitimate children seem to have had little, if any, effect on the number of holdings.

(b) *Sales and mortgages*   A further important cause of subdivision of holdings lies in the extent of sales and mortgages of land, which became increasingly common from the 1590s, as can be seen from Graph 5.1.[55]

The first explicit example of a sale or mortgage recorded in the manor court rolls does not appear until 1543, though clearly this reflects a change in the procedure of registration, rather than the absence of sales and mortgages previously.[56] However, sales and mortgages did not become especially noticeable in the business of the halmotes until the 1590s, and though the total number of sales and mortgages fluctuated considerably from year to year, the upward trend is unmistakeable, particularly from the later 1610s.

Turning firstly to possible explanations for extreme short-term fluctuations, there seems to have been a clear relationship between times of hardship and peaks in the number of sales and mortgages recorded. The effects of the very bad harvests of 1594–7 can be seen in the rising number of sales and mortgages in 1596–1600. Similarly, the extremely deficient harvests of 1621–2 produced the same response in 1622–3.[57] It seems that bad harvests forced some tenants to mortgage or sell part or all of their holdings, in order to compensate for lost agricultural income and increased expenditure on food.[58]

Such sales and mortgages would not be recorded immediately in the court rolls, for two reasons. First, food would not usually become scarce following a bad harvest until the following spring or summer, and hence copyholders may not have resorted to mortgage or sale of land until then. Secondly, it was not necessary to register a transaction of land which had been made out of court until up to the third court following, which could be eighteen months away.[59] However, bad harvests are an insufficient explanation for the peaks in sales and mortgages. Even allowing for a 'lagged' response, it would be extremely difficult to justify correlating the bad harvest of 1586 with the peak in sales and mortgages in 1590–1. Also, harvests in the later 1620s were fairly good, yet there was a notable peak in the number of sales and mortgages in 1628.[60]

The composition paid by the forest tenants in 1609, whereby the

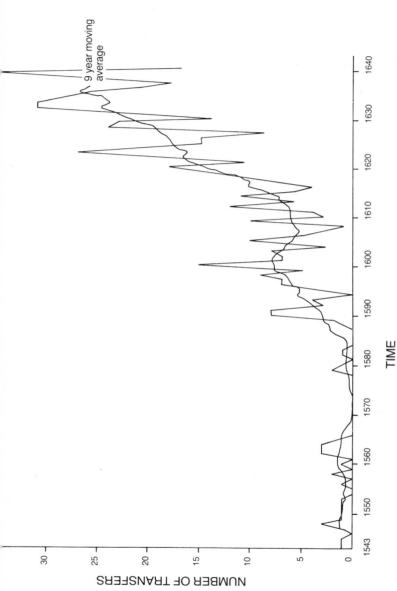

GRAPH 5.1   Transfers of land for money payment in Colne Manor and Trawden and Pendle Forests, 1543–1640

security of their copyholds was confirmed in return for payment of twelve years' rent, seems to have had a slight effect on the number of sales and mortgages registered, for eight were recorded in Trawden and Pendle forests in 1609, compared with only one both in 1607 and 1608, and three in 1610. On the other hand, the composition paid in 1618 by the tenants of Colne manor, which amounted to twenty years' rent and, in addition, a new rent of 6d an acre for the commons, does not seem to have affected the number of sales and mortgages recorded; the figures for 1616–21 were 1, 0, 1, 2, 6 and 2 respectively.[61] Large as these composition payments were, many of the copyholders' subtenants were paying far greater rents annually to the copyholders, who managed to transfer a proportion of their new burdens onto their subtenants. For example, forest subtenants who held a lease of land for three lives were required to pay six years' rent to the Crown as their share of the total composition of twelve years' rent demanded.[62]

From a longer-term perspective, however, the most important effect of the copyhold dispute in Colne manor was to stimulate the land market. The commons were let separately from the old copyhold land after 1618,[63] and thus it became possible to sell, mortgage or lease a portion of common alone. Prior to 1618, it was only possible to alienate rights to common along with copyhold land. Indeed, during the period from 1619 to 1640, at least 62 of 117 parcels of land in Colne manor transferred in perpetuity for cash payments were of waste alone.[64]

This had two important consequences for the structure of landholding, as can be seen from the rental for Colne manor in 1650. First, 34 copyhold tenancies (out of 125 in all) consisted of waste alone, and hence many copyholders seem to have been subsisting simply on marginal wasteland. In addition, a further 18 copyhold tenancies consisted of old copyhold land without waste. In all, 42% of copyhold tenancies in Colne manor in 1650 did not consist of the pre-1618 combination of old copyhold land and common.[65] Tupling, who noted a similar development in Rossendale, argued that these transfers of waste may have been attributable to the inability of some copyholders either to pay their share of the composition or to finance the enclosure of the portion of common allotted, or even that some may have had more common than they required.[66] In the Colne area, the first explanation seems the least probable, for, as already noted, the composition payment in 1618 did not produce an immediate upsurge in the numbers of sales and mortgages.

The effect of leasing the commons in Colne manor must have facilitated the acquisition of land by those not wealthy enough to purchase old copyhold land. The average price per acre of waste was just £3 6s 3d, compared with £19 1s 7d for old copyhold land sold during the period from 1619 to 1640.[67] Naturally, the poorer quality of waste was the major factor determining its lower value.

However, the substantial increase in the incidence of sales and mortgages, which is particularly apparent from the later 1610s, cannot be ascribed solely to the leasing of Colne manor wastes. If we compare the average annual number of transfers of land for money payment during the period from 1601 to 1620 and 1621 to 1640, it is clear that, whilst sales and mortgages rose in all areas, the most significant increase occurred in Colne manor and north-east Pendle. During these periods, the average number of transfers rose from 2·25 to 7·8 per annum in Colne manor, and from 1·6 to 6·5 in north-east Pendle; in the rest of Pendle forest, the increase was from 2·6 to 5·9, and in Trawden forest from 1·2 to just 1·45.[68] It seems that the most pronounced increase in sales and mortgages took place in areas most heavily hit by the depression in the kersey trade in the 1620s and 1630s.[69] The richest area, Trawden forest,[70] was hardly affected at all.

Clearly, sales and mortgages must have contributed to the subdivision of some holdings. Indeed, there was an increasing tendency in Colne manor for the sale or mortgage of very small plots of land; 17% of such transactions were for 3 acres or less between 1547 and 1579, compared with 52% during the period from 1580 to 1618.[71] However, multiplication of the total number of holdings through sale could only occur if the purchasers were not copyholders already. Some of the purchasers were landless younger sons, who used their cash portions to buy land. For example, Lawrence Emott, a younger son of Thomas Emott of Colne, bought land in Colne with £20 which had been given to him by his father.[72] Some purchasers were speculators intent on reselling the land at a profit. Thus Roger Hartley of Waterside bought land in Swinden from Gilbert Hartley for £54 4s 4d, only to resell it immediately for £60 to John Hartley.[73] Others were newcomers to the area, as in the case of the Shuttleworths, who were a gentry family from Smithills (near Bolton) who moved to Gawthorpe and who bought land from the Crankshaws in West Close, Hunterholme and Fence in Pendle forest, between 1582 and 1596.[74] However, the difficulty of positive identification of most purchasers makes generalisation impossible, but it is indisputable that sales and mortgages contributed to subdivision of many holdings.

(c) *Subtenants*   Since rents were usually drawn from those in legal possession of land and not from subtenants,[75] rentals do not normally include subtenants (though this does not seem to be true for sections of the rentals of 1650 and 1662).[76] Subtenants were not always recorded in the manor court rolls either, and it is particularly important to appreciate changes in the customs affecting registration of leases.

In 1402, the customs permitted subletting without surrender and fine in the manor court.[77] By 1668, the situation had changed significantly, for a copyholder then was not allowed to lease his lands for longer than a year and a day without surrender and fine.[78] A decisive change took place in the 1540s, for it was then that the halmote courts first began to record subtenancies by surrender and fine.[79] It seems that the transition from one custom to another was gradual, involving at least one intermediary stage, for it was alleged in two lawsuits in 1543 and 1553 that a copyholder might sublet his lands for periods of three years, without surrender.[80] Tupling noted the change regarding the registration of subtenancies in the mid-sixteenth century, and argued that it may have been attributable to the desire of the manorial authorities to profit from the growth of population and the increasing number of leases, by obtaining further entry fines.[81] This seems to be the most probable explanation, but it is also possible that the change was partly originated by the tenants, both copyholders and subtenants, in order to increase their security by having lease agreements recorded in the court rolls.

It is therefore possible to examine the nature and extent of leases for periods longer than a year and a day between 1545 and 1640. The number of leases recorded increased substantially over time. From 1545 to 1560, only 17 leases have been traced in the court rolls but during the next two decades, 60 leases were recorded. The number of leases increased considerably between 1581 and 1600, rising to a total of 108. In the early seventeenth century, the growth in the number of leases recorded continued; 132 leases were registered during the period from 1601 to 1620, and 174 between 1621 and 1640.[82]

Therefore, it can be seen that more tenants were turning to subletting part of their holdings. Most of these leases were granted for long periods; nearly half (45%) were for terms of at least one life (and often for three lives), and a further third (34%) were for periods of 21 years or longer.[83] Furthermore, it cannot be shown that the increase in the number of leases observed over time was due to a significant reduction in the length of the terms of the leases; in Colne manor, 25% of leases between 1548 and 1600 were for terms of 20 years or less, compared with 22% during the period from 1601 to 1640 (though in Pendle forest, the reverse occurred, since 14% of leases between 1545 and 1600 were for terms of 20 years or less, compared with 17% for the period from 1601 to 1640).[84]

Many of these leases were for small plots of land; nearly a third (30%) of leases were for parcels of land 2 (Lancashire) acres or less in size, and a further 18% were for plots of between 2 and 5 acres; only 6% of leases were for areas larger than 20 acres.[85] Leases of small parcels of land were especially noticeable in Colne and north-east Pendle, where 35% and 47% of leases were for 2 acres or less, compared with 17% in Trawden and 15% in the rest of Pendle.[86] There were also notable changes apparent over time; only 15% of leases were for plots of 2 acres or less in the period to 1580, compared with 36% subsequently. Leases of small parcels of this size were especially noticeable in Colne manor and north-east Pendle after 1580.[87]

In marked contrast to the low and stable level of copyhold rents to the Crown, rents paid by subtenants over and above the rent to the Crown were often extremely large. Indeed, this differential aspect to rent payment by copyholders and subtenants became even more apparent over time, for copyholders were finding it increasingly profitable to sublet land.[88] Graph 5.2 illustrates the levels of rents paid by subtenants to copyholders.[89] The data have been presented in the form of a scatter diagram because the wide range of rent possible at any one time makes the use of averages particularly dangerous. Some lessees clearly received their land on highly preferential terms, but at the other end of the scale, there were individuals paying enormous sums to copyholders, relative to the rents to the Crown; the most extreme example found was of a subtenant's rent which was 480 times the copyhold rent.[90]

The existence of preferential rents can be seen very clearly for all areas. One should not pay too much attention to the apparently large number of such rents for Colne manor between 1620 and 1640, since many of these leases were of waste only, and the most usual rent demanded for waste was just twice the copyhold rent.[91] Nevertheless, the majority of lessees seem to have paid economic rents. Whilst examples of very high rents can be found for all

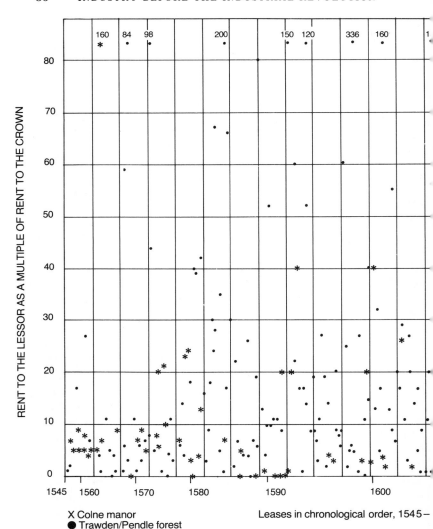

GRAPH 5.2   Levels of rent paid by subtenants in
Colne Manor and Trawden and Pendle Forests, 1545–1640

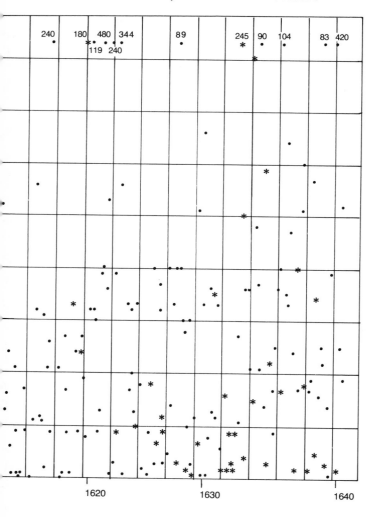

periods, the scatter of observations gradually increases over time, reflecting the rising value of land. Part of the explanation for this can be attributed to the effects of inflation and the desire of copyholders to maintain their standard of living by increasing the rents paid by their tenants. However, the levels of some non-preferential rents seem to have risen well in excess of inflation, and suggest chronic shortage of land and over-population.

An examination of individual rent payments may be misleading for three reasons. First, little information is usually given on the type and quality of land leased. Portions of waste leased in Colne manor in the 1620s and 1630s were usually at low rents, reflecting the poor quality of the land; individual plots of land were usually referred to in the standardised legal form, 'messuages, other buildings, lands, tenements, meadows and pastures', and so it is impossible to estimate the relative value of, for example, arable and meadow.

Secondly, it is not always possible to tell whether the lessor and lessee were related to each other, and therefore whether this kin relationship played a part in determining the level of rent. It is quite common to find examples of sons paying very high rents to their fathers. For example, John Hanson, the son and heir apparent of William Hanson, paid £20 annual rent to his father for a lease of a third of Emmott Moor in Trawden in 1637, whereas the rent to the Crown stood at only 6s 8d per annum.[92] Similarly, Geoffrey Shackleton paid £13 6s 8d annually to his father John, for a lease of 16 acres in Colne and 15 acres in Trawden in 1604, as against 10s 4d annually to the Crown.[93] On the other hand, and not surprisingly, it is possible to find examples of preferential rents between kin. In 1617, William Nutter junior of Goldshaw in Pendle leased land in Goldshaw to his younger brother Richard, who was to pay 1s to the Crown, and 1s additionally to him.[94] However, many preferential rents existed in cases where the lessor and lessee do not appear to be kin.

Thirdly, because the manor court rolls are only a partial record of land transactions, and rarely give us a complete picture of the agreement and motives of the parties concerned, it is extremely difficult to generalise about the economic position of lessors and lessees. Identification of individuals in an area with few surnames is an extremely hazardous exercise, and rather than attempting to link together land transactions by persons of the same name (who are very likely to be different individuals), it is more reliable to turn to sources where a complete picture of a man's lands is given.

Fortunately the rental for Pendle forest in 1650 gives subtenants as well as copyholders. Only 15 of the 188 tenants held both their own land and land as a subtenant, compared with 33 who held only as subtenants.[95] There is no reason to believe that this pattern was at all untypical, and thus it seems that the majority of subtenants holding land on terms longer than a year and a day held only the land which they leased, and did not hold their own copyhold land as well.

Unfortunately, neither the rentals nor the court rolls reveal any information on the extent of subletting for less than one year and a day, and we are forced to rely on occasional references in litigation and inventories. For example, in 1541, John Hanson alleged in a Duchy lawsuit that land at Wheathead in Pendle had been leased to him by Henry Baldwin in 1532 for one year, and then from year to year, but with the agreement that John and his wife should have security of tenure for their lives.[96] In another suit in 1593, it was alleged that John Cunliffe and James Hartley were both tenants at will who occupied land let for one year periods; the former held a little close in Colne and paid 13s 4d annually for it, whilst the latter occupied 2 acres for an annual rent of 20s.[97] Clearly these were very high rents for such small areas and short-term leases. Inventories also give occasional examples of this type of subletting. In 1630, it was recorded in the inventory of a husbandman, John Law of Reedley Hallows in Pendle, that he had taken a lease of half a meadow from Henry Jackson for a year.[98]

Lessors might wish to sublet land for less than a year and a day for a number of reasons. First, they could avoid paying an entry fine to the Crown.[99] Secondly, the shorter the lease, the greater were the opportunities for rack-renting tenants. Thirdly, tenants who let the property fall into decay or fall behind in their rent payments could be removed more easily.

It is certainly true that many subtenants, irrespective of the length of their lease, were subsisting on very small parcels of land. This is best illustrated by an examination of the presentments in the halmote courts under the Act of 31 Elizabeth (1589), which prohibited the use of a cottage for habitation if it had less than 4 acres of land attached to it, or the taking in of more than one family in a cottage as inmates.[100] These fines are particularly common in the 1590s and 1620s. For example, 13 individuals were presented in Colne manor court in September 1594 for keeping 43 inmates on their property, and in October 1621, 31 were presented in Pendle halmote under the inmates' statute.[101]

Indeed, we have evidence that subtenants were finding it increasingly difficult to pay their rents, particularly in the period 1622–4. From the mid-1610s, the juries began to present individuals for detinue of buildings and lands. Prior to 1615, this was extremely rare, though private suits for detinue were a common feature of the business of the courts. From 1615, however, the juries seem to have taken it upon themselves to present cases of detinue.[102] It seems that many of these cases must have been brought due to non-payment of rent by a subtenant. This is sometimes stated explicitly; John Emott was fined 4d in 1635 for detinue of a house from Roger Hartley of Colne and for non-payment of rent.[103] It is significant that fines for detinue were usually presented at the Easter rather than the Michaelmas halmote; 82% of such presentments occurred at the Easter court.[104] Rents were usually paid twice a year (Michaelmas and Easter), and clearly many subtenants would have found it harder to pay their Easter rents, since prices were generally higher and wage labour less available than in the period during and immediately following the harvest.[105]

Not surprisingly, the period 1622–4 stands out, for payment of rent at a time of high food prices (which followed bad harvests in 1621 and 1622) would have been particularly difficult.[106] There were only five presentments for detinue of buildings and land in Colne manor and in the forests of Trawden and Pendle in 1620, and four presentments were recorded in 1621. In 1622, however, the number of presentments increased to 17, and rose still further to 24 the next year. In 1624, the number of presentments fell to 13, still a substantial number, and it was not until 1625 that the situation returned to normal, with just five presentments. Moreover, fines for detinue remained at a significantly higher level after the crisis compared with the years immediately before it; the average number of presentments per annum between 1615 and 1621 was three, but during the period from 1625 to 1640 there was an annual average of eight presentments.[107] This strongly suggests that subtenants were facing increasing economic problems, which may have been associated with loss of income resulting from the depression in the kersey trade in the 1620s and 1630s.[108]

It is apparent, then, that a great deal of subletting of land occurred and that, at least judging from the numbers of leases recorded in the court rolls, the numbers of leases for periods longer than a year and a day increased substantially over time. Since many of these leases were for tiny plots of land, and since the majority of subtenants seem to have held no other lands, the actual proportion of smallholdings is likely to have been much higher than revealed by the rentals. Harrison is right to emphasise that the practice of subletting could alter greatly the distribution of land presented in a survey or rental,[109] but this is not necessarily an insuperable problem if further sources are utilised.

ENCROACHMENT ON THE WASTE

Scarcity of land is further suggested by evidence of numerous encroachments on the waste. Naturally, the leasing of the commons of Colne manor in 1618 conflicted with the interests of the cottagers who had illegally occupied small parcels of the waste. The subsequent agreement in 1621 gave the cottagers the security they desired. A total of five cottages were made copyhold of inheritance, and 18 were leased for life or lives, but the leases were to be renewable upon payment of reasonable rents and fines. All cottagers were to pay very small annual rents to the Crown and to Colne school. In addition, there were ten other cottages which stood on parts of the waste allotted to copyholders, but agreement was reached concerning those too, in return for annual rents of a few pence.[110]

In 1651, the parliamentary commissioners reviewed the rents paid by the cottagers of Colne manor, and estimated that cottages which were leased for an annual rent to the Crown of just 1d or 2d were actually worth rents ranging from 2s to 8s per annum. Furthermore, the commissioners calculated that five cottages which had been encroached recently should be valued at rents ranging from 4s to 30s per annum.[111] These improved rents were clearly put into effect, as can be seen from the rental of 1662.[112] Thus, cottagers who were direct tenants of the Duchy were well treated during our period and paid only nominal rents, in contrast to many subtenants, who usually paid extremely high rents to their copyholder–landlords (though of course they often leased better quality land than did the cottagers).

Successive Duchy commissions revealed a number of encroachments on Colne wastes, but, as we have shown, little was done to expel the offenders, or to raise new rents from them. The exception to this was in 1563, when new rents totalling 1s 3d were obtained from the holders of three houses encroached on Colne waste and one in Marsden. However, the commission of 1561 had also discovered four other alleged encroachments, but these produced no further action.[113] In later commissions, more encroachments were revealed. Seven encroachments were detected in Marsden in 1579,[114] and in 1616, 22 encroachments were discovered in Colne and Marsden, some of which had been in existence in 1579.[115] These encroachments usually each consisted of a house or cottage with a small portion of land; the largest plot recorded in the commissions was only half an acre.[116] Significantly, some of these plots were held by illegitimate persons. For example, John Watson alias North occupied a turf house on Great Marsden waste in 1579, which was still in existence in 1616, when there were also two other parcels of land occupied by bastards.[117] It is not at all surprising, in view of the disabilities which a bastard faced with regard to inheritance of land,[118] that some illegitimate persons had been forced to encroach portions of waste.

Encroachment was a necessary expedient for those without land or the resources to buy or lease it, and occurred on a significant scale in adjacent areas too. Tupling quoted many examples of encroachment in Rossendale during the sixteenth and early seventeenth centuries,[119] and, more recently, Porter has noted the widespread practice of encroachment in the forest of Bowland during this period.[120]

It is not surprising that the copyholders viewed with alarm the increasing number of encroachments on the waste, or that they were willing to disclose them to Duchy commissions. Rights to the waste were of crucial importance to all the copyholders and their subtenants, for they provided wood and turf for fuel, as well as pasture for stock, and any illegal encroachment was therefore against the interests of all the tenants. For this reason, manorial juries were also willing to detect and fine encroachers, but these fines seem to have been an ineffective deterrent, for the same individual was often presented for encroachment over a considerable period of time. For example, in August 1515, James Robinson was fined 4d for building three messuages on Marsden common. He obviously made no amendment, for he was fined again the following May, but at the increased rate of 3s 4d. Robinson was a persistent encroacher, for he was fined twice for encroachment at separate courts in 1520, and again in 1521.[121] He does not appear to have been a copyholder, for he is not mentioned in the court rolls as such, nor in the rental for 1527.[122] Other members of the Robinson family had previously been amerced for encroachments in Great Marsden.[123]

The period when fines for encroachment were most noticeable was in the 1500s and 1510s, partly due to the activities of the Robinsons, and the repeated efforts of the juries to bring them to order.[124] Thereafter, presentments for encroachment were occasionally made by the Colne jurors, as in 1537–8 (2 encroachments), 1566–7 (1), 1594 (3), 1623 (2) and 1625 (1).[125] The only recorded cases of encroachment presented by the juries for Trawden and Pendle forests were in Pendle halmote in 1623 and 1629.[126] These encroachments were usually of small plots of half an acre or less, as were those presented under the commissions.[127] However, in view of the large number of encroachments revealed both by Duchy commissions and by the settlement with the cottagers, 1618–21, it seems that the juries were becoming increasingly slack in presenting encroachments, and perhaps deliberately turned a blind eye in order to alleviate the effects of over-population. Those who were presented for encroachments were given only small fines even in the early seventeenth century, which was not a policy designed either to deter potential encroachers or to punish those who had encroached land.[128] As we have shown, the juries were not lethargic on similar issues; for instance, they rigorously enforced the Inmates Act of 1589.

THE DISTRIBUTION OF WEALTH

The most comprehensive sources for an examination of the distribution of wealth are the hearth tax of 1664 and the poll tax of 1660, but they fall slightly outside of our period. Under the hearth tax, heads of households were 'not chargeable' if they had an income from land of not more than £1 per annum, or if they had not more than £10 in lands or goods, or if they were exempt from the usual payments to the Church and to the poor on the grounds of poverty.[129] The proportion of households which did not pay the hearth tax was especially high in Colne, where 53% fell into this category. The two forests were relatively prosperous, since only a quarter of their households escaped taxation. Marsden lay between these extremes, with 38% of its households exempt from the tax.[130] As a whole, however, north-east Lancashire appears to have been far less poverty-stricken than the south east of the county, where many townships contained more than 40% of households exempt from the hearth tax.[131]

The poll tax of 1660[132] is more suitable than the hearth tax for delineating the distribution of wealth, since to utilise the hearth tax data for this purpose, we have to make the assumption that there was a positive correlation between the level of wealth of a household and the number of its hearths, which is not necessarily warranted for the north of England, where many prosperous yeomen lived in one-hearth houses.[133]

Table 5.2   Poll tax in the townships of Colne, Marsden and Foulridge, and in Trawden and Pendle forests, September 1660

	Colne		Marsden		Trawden forest		Pendle forest		Foulridge	
Amount	No.	%	No.	%	No.	%	No.	%	No.	%
Assessed on lands:										
£50 or over	6	5	4	3	4	7	2	1	0	0
£20 to <£50	5	5	5	3	12	19	17	9	3	4
£10 to <£20	10	9	19	12	6	10	27	13	4	6
£5 to <£10	17	15	24	15	7	11	29	14	10	14
<£5	64	58	107	67	33	53	127	63	49	70
Assessed on goods:										
£250	1	1	0	0	0	0	0	0	0	0
£200	2	2	0	0	0	0	0	0	0	0
£100	6	5	0	0	0	0	0	0	3	4
Other	0	0	0	0	0	0	0	0	1	2
Total	111	100	159	100	62	100	202	100	70	100

All except those on poor relief were liable to pay the poll tax.[134] The distribution of wealth is extremely revealing, for Trawden forest appears to have been by far the richest area, with a quarter of its tax-paying households rated on lands worth £20 or more, compared with 10% in Colne, not more than 10% in Pendle forest, and 6% in Marsden. At the other end of the scale, Trawden forest had the smallest proportion of households valued at less than £5 per annum –just 53% – compared with 58% in Colne, not less than 63% in Pendle forest, and 67% in Marsden.

It is instructive to contrast the evidence of the hearth and poll taxes of the 1660s with that of an early sixteenth-century subsidy roll. The subsidy roll of 1543[135] gives us a rough indication of the distribution of wealth of the upper and middle strata of society, for it taxed those who had an income from land of at least £1 per annum, or those with goods worth at least £1.[136]

The number of households taxed in this area in 1543 was far less than the number which took communion in 1563,[137] and even if we allow for the possibility of considerable population growth between 1543 and 1563, it is clear that many households must have escaped contributing to the subsidy in 1543. Nevertheless, allowing for the fact that the poorer households were excluded, it seems that the spectrum of wealth was greater in Colne and Marsden than in the forests. For example, 58% of Trawden taxpayers and 62% of those in Pendle were rated on goods assessed at just £1; in contrast, only 33% of taxpayers in Marsden and 44% of those in Colne fell into this category.[138] Furthermore, no taxpayer in either of the forests was rated on lands, but four people in Colne were assessed on lands (which ranged in annual value from £1 to £20), whilst in Marsden, another four taxpayers were rated on lands worth £2 and £3 per annum. Even at this early date, however, Trawden forest showed signs of later developments, for five taxpayers were assessed on goods worth £20 (by comparison, the richest taxpayer in Pendle was rated on only £5 in goods).[139] The small numbers of highly taxed persons in the forests in 1543 can be explained by the fact that these were areas of 'new' settlement, disafforested only in 1507,[140] and therefore copyhold families in the forests had had less time to build up their fortunes than had the copyholders of Colne manor, whilst the practice of partible inheritance by some of the forest tenants in the early sixteenth century[141] also militated against capital accumulation.

Thus, whilst it is true that the forests in particular were growing in wealth in the sixteenth and seventeenth centuries, relative to Colne manor, it would not be correct to argue, as Mary Brigg has done, that Pendle forest in the seventeenth century was 'industrious and prosperous'.[142] Her conclusion was based primarily on a study of wills and inventories, but it is essential to appreciate that these sources are socially selective, biassed towards the 'middling sort'.[143] It is hard to reconcile Brigg's hypothesis with the fact that 26% of Pendle households were exempt from the hearth tax in 1664 on the grounds of poverty[144] (a fact which she also notes),[145] or that not less than 63% of Pendle households not on poor relief in 1660 had an income of less than £5 per annum from their estates.[146]

POOR RELIEF

It is unfortunate that no accounts of overseers of the poor appear to have survived for this area during our period. However, we know from cases brought before Quarter Sessions that there were over 200 people on poor relief in 1662 in the town of Colne alone, who were said to constitute the largest part of the poor of Colne parish,[147] and a more detailed description in 1663 noted that there were 31 'impotent poor' and 199 persons who 'constantly beg' in the town of Colne.[148] These numbers are entirely consistent with the high levels of poverty in Colne suggested by the hearth tax of 1664. Whilst the disturbances of the civil wars and Interregnum may have exacerbated the scale of poverty, the extent of poverty in 1640 is unlikely to have been radically different from that prevailing at the Restoration.

In the absence of information on the numbers of the poor or the amounts of money raised as poor relief, one index of contemporaries' awareness of the problem of poverty and of their voluntary response to alleviate it, is their willingness to leave bequests of money for the use of the poor. Of 325 wills of testators from this area, 1546–1640, only 21 (6%) specifically made bequests to the poor, and three of these were simply for 'penny dole' to be distributed at the funeral, whilst another made a bequest to the poor of Pendleton.[149] The first recorded bequest to the poor was in 1572, when Gilbert Hartley of Swinden left a peck of meal to every poor householder in the town of Colne,[150] but subsequently all other recorded bequests in wills were of money. The first bequest of a specific sum of money was not recorded until November 1597, when the clothier Thomas Lacy alias College of Winewall in Trawden left £10 to the poor of Colne 'parish'.[151] In the following June, William Hargreaves of Wycoller in Trawden, also a clothier, left £26 13s 4d to the poor, the largest single bequest recorded).[152] The extremely deficient harvests of 1594–7 probably influenced their decisions to make these generous bequests. The next bequest on this scale did not occur until August 1623, when, at the height of the famine and mortality crisis of 1623–4, Lawrence Towneley Esquire of Barnside left £20 to the poor of Colne 'parish'.[153]

In addition to bequests of money, there is one example of a bequest of land for the use of the poor. It was recorded in 1601 that Alice Hartley, a widow of Laund in Pendle, had purchased property and land in Colne for £60, which she surrendered to feoffees who were to sublet the premises and use the rents for the relief of 'the needful poor born or living in the parish of Colne'. In 1601, half of this property produced an annual rent of £1 for the use of the poor.[154] However, this was the only recorded example of land left to the use of the poor between 1500 and 1640, and the next such bequest was not until 1660.[155]

Clearly some charity towards the poor existed on an informal level, in addition to the more formal and organised mechanisms of charity, the poor rates and bequests. For example, a number of those accused of witchcraft in 1612 lived by begging. Old Demdike, one of the leading witches, was a blind old woman aged about eighty, who had been a beggar for at least the previous twenty years. Her mendicant activities were no doubt facilitated by the fears of her magical powers, for it was alleged that no man escaped her if she was denied anything. However, her son-in-law John Device was so afraid of the spells of another leading witch, Old Chattox, that he agreed to pay Chattox a measure of meal annually, in return for a promise not to harm him or his goods. It seems that he had insufficient confidence in the magical powers of his mother-in-law to protect him! Indeed, the whole chain of witchcraft accusations in 1612 was sparked off by an incident where a pedlar had refused to give some pins to Old Demdike's granddaughter Alison Device, and had then suffered a stroke, which he attributed to Alison's doing. Alison too spent much of her time begging.[156] The witch trial of 1612 gives us a rare glimpse into the world of the very poor.

The manorial juries were especially concerned to reduce the level of begging, particularly by strangers to the neighbourhood. The Colne jurors fined ten persons in December 1585 for receiving 'foreign or strange beggars' into their houses, whilst in Pendle, there were 26 presentments for the same offence.[157] This appears to have been a peak period in presentments for harbouring beggars, for there were further fines in 1589–91.[158] Subsequently, the extent of vagabondage may have been disguised under presentments for keeping inmates.

CONCLUSION

It is apparent that both temporary and permanent subdivision of holdings occurred in the Colne area in the sixteenth and early seventeenth centuries in three main ways, namely inheritance arrangements, sales and mortgages, and leases. However, it is clear that sales and mortgages contributed far more to permanent subdivision of holdings than did infrequent division amongst coparceners, or the occasional example of partible inheritance.

Since holdings were virtually as negotiable as freeholds, we need to explain why most copyholders chose not to practice partible inheritance. Part of the answer must lie in contemporaries' awareness that excessive subdivision of land might produce holdings that were too small to be economically viable. This may be why partible inheritance became increasingly unusual in the forests. However, it is equally possible that copyholders may have felt that other opportunities existed for their younger sons, for example, in participation in industry. This would be particularly feasible for younger sons if provision were made for the payment of substantial cash portions, which could then be used for the purchase of a workshop, tools and raw materials, and possibly a small amount of land and livestock too. Thus the possibilities of earning a living, in part at least, from rural industry may have discouraged the practice of partible inheritance, since excessive subdivision of holdings would not enable younger children to be provided with generous portions.

At the same time, the structure of landholding must have led to considerable demand for supplementary income from groups other than younger sons of copyholders. Many eldest sons of copyholders would have welcomed additional income, since increasingly many inherited only small holdings, and yet were burdened with payment of sizeable portions to their siblings and widowed mothers. Furthermore, many subtenants were compelled to pay large rents to the copyholders for extremely small parcels of land, upon which subsistence would have been impossible without additional income. Above all, the landless and virtually landless would have had especial need of such employment or by-employment. If this picture is correct, we should expect to find evidence of participation in rural industry at all levels of society.[159]

We have also noted geographical variations in the structure of landholding and wealth, and in the degree of subdivision of holdings. Until the very early seventeenth century, the most noticeable subdivision of holdings occurred in Colne manor and, to a lesser extent, in north-east Pendle. It seems that from the outset, many holdings in these areas were extremely small, so that they were especially vulnerable to forces working towards subdivision. It is not surprising that these were areas which were especially heavily involved in industrial by-employments.[160] In Trawden forest and in the rest of Pendle forest by contrast, holdings were more substantial and therefore less susceptible to subdivision. However, here too, as in Colne manor and north-east Pendle forest, there was a strong demand for additional employment, particularly from younger and illegitimate sons, who for reasons of inheritance did not normally receive land from their parents.

NOTES

¹ Tupling, *Economic history of Rossendale*, pp. 72–3

² Farrer, *Court rolls*, vol. 2, p. 411. These acres were customary acres, three of which (at 7 yards to the rod) were equivalent to five statute acres; see Porter, 'Reclamation and settlement of Bowland', p. xi. There were several sizes of customary acre in Lancashire; see Smith, 'Lancashire long measure', *passim*. However, in the Colne area there are many references to the 7 yard rod, for example P.R.O. D.L.5/27 fol. 1318. All references to acres in this chapter are to Lancashire acres, unless otherwise stated

³ L.R.O. DDHCl3 Map 5

⁴ The inquisitions are found in P.R.O. D.L.7, *passim* (some are printed for the Jacobean period in Rylands, *Lancashire inquisitions, passim*). In 1616, Robert Bannister of Parkhill owned 4 messuages and 120 acres of freehold land, together with a corn mill and a fulling mill at Parkhill; Rylands, *ibid.*, vol. 2, pp. 29–30. In 1624, Lawrence Towneley, Esquire of Barnside possessed a messuage and 10 acres of freehold land in Trawden forest; *ibid.*, vol. 3, pp. 410–11. These seem to be the only examples of freehold land in the forests. In 1804, there were 243 acres, 2 rods and 20 falls of freehold land in Colne and 355 acres, 19 falls in Great Marsden. In Pendle forest, there were 133 acres, 3 rods and 33 falls of freehold land, all of which was in Barrowford. In Trawden forest, no freehold land at all was recorded. Clearly, some enfranchisement may have taken place since the early seventeenth century, but the relatively small amount of freehold land in this area in 1804 emphasises the unimportance of this type of tenure. See L.R.O. DDHCl3, Map 5. For further details of the medieval origins of the freehold land in this area, see Swain, 'Industry and economy', p. 115

⁵ Farrer, *Court rolls*, vol. 1, p. 385; the Vivar is the only example found of Duchy land on leasehold terms – see Chapter 4, p. 60

⁶ The figures for 1443 have been derived from Farrer, *Court rolls*, vol. 1, pp. 497–507. They have been placed in brackets because they are not strictly comparable with the rest, for two reasons; first, they include freeholders whose land is excluded from the subsequent rentals; secondly, the forests were not granted by copy until 1507. Those for 1527 and 1539 are from Farrer, *Court rolls*, vol. 2, pp. 377–81, 383–6. Sabden Hey and Ightenhill Park, not included in all rentals, have been excluded, as have the two mills in the Colne rental. 'Barrowford' includes Rishton Thorns. The most accurate rental for 1608, which has been used here, is found in P.R.O. D.L.5/19 fols. 396v., 399–400; other copies of this rental (L.R.O. DDKe 5/ 86; Farrer, *Court rolls*, vol. 2, pp. 402–4) contain omissions and inaccuracies. The two mills in Barrowford have been excluded from the total. The rental for Colne manor in 1617 is contained in P.R.O. D.L.5/27 fols. 1325–8

⁷ There is a list of the tenants in some of the forest booths and areas in 1507, in Farrer, *Court rolls*, vol. 2, pp. 373–7 (which is based on B.L. Add. MSS 32103 fols. 136–9). A full list of the tenants in Trawden forest in 1507 is not given, but there were well over 59 tenants in Pendle forest at this time (we have no information for Barrowford, or for some other small areas). Subdivision of holdings was noticeable in the rest of Pendle forest between

1527–1608 only in Higham, and to a lesser extent in Wheatley. The overall picture in the rest of Pendle was of far less subdivision than in the north east of the forest

  [8] See Chapter 4, pp. 56–60
  [9] For 1650; P.R.O. E.317 Lancs.8, m.12–23, 43, 47–66, 74. For 1662; Farrer, *Court rolls*, vol. 2, pp. 389–93, 425, 430, 439–54
  [10] See Chapter 4, pp. 62–3
  [11] P.R.O. E.317 Lancs.8, m.18–23; Farrer, *Court rolls*, vol. 2, pp. 440–3
  [12] P.R.O. E.317 Lancs.8, m.18–23, 52–66. Apparently there was only one subtenant in Trawden
  [13] Farrer, *Court rolls*, vol. 2, pp. 389–93, 440–3, 448–54. Subtenants are recorded in the Trawden rental (*ibid.*, pp. 389–90) where half-year rents are listed, but not in the full rental (*ibid.*, pp. 448–9)
  [14] For 1608, see Table 5.1. The number of tenants holding land from the Duchy has been calculated by excluding those who held land belonging to another, but including those holding land 'late of . . .' (which seem to be recent sales); P.R.O. E.317 Lancs.8, m.52–66
  [15] Tupling, *Economic history of Rossendale*, Chapters 3 and Appendix D, p. 235
  [16] See Chapter 4; Farrer, *Court rolls*, vols. 1 and 2 *passim*; L.R.O. DDHCl3, *passim*
  [17] For further details, see Swain, 'Industry and economy', Table 5.2, p. 119. For the size of the Lancashire acre, see note 2 above; for the location of the rentals, see note 6 above
  [18] W.R.O. D/DZ A.4 (Towneley MSS) fol. 56–56v
  [19] L.R.O. WGW *Supra* and *Infra*, *passim*; DRCh. *passim*. There are a few wills enrolled in the manor court rolls (DDHC13 *passim*) and individually in other collections (DDX 19/19, DDBd 60/2, DDBd 60/6). B.I., P.C.Y., *passim*
  [20] L.R.O. WCW *Supra*, will and inventory, 1591
  [21] Farrer, *Court rolls*, vol. 1, p. 388
  [22] P.R.O. D.L.5/27 fol. 1327 (Henry Walton, John Hartley and George Hartley all held land jointly with their sons)
  [23] There are many examples of this in the court rolls; Farrer, *Court rolls*, vols. 1 and 2, *passim*; L.R.O. DDHCl3, *passim*. In some cases, copyholders might make a will and yet make no bequest of their lands. For example, Christopher Baldwin of Wheathead in Pendle made no reference to his copyhold lands in his will (L.R.O. WCW *Supra*, will and inventory, 1594). Subsequently, his son and heir John inherited land (rent 16s 8d, L.R.O. DDHCl3/77, Pendle forest, 2nd halmote, 15 May 1595). Clearly, Baldwin intended primogeniture to take effect, for he mentioned two other sons, Alexander and Christopher, in his will, besides three daughters
  [24] Alexander, 'Custom of the Province of York', especially pp. 418–19, 428
  [25] L.R.O. WCW *Supra*, will and inventory, 1632. It is interesting to note that the total value of these bequests to younger children came to £195 16s 8d, which was more than the valuation of his inventory, and thus little would have been left for his sons Robert (his heir) or John
  [26] L.R.O. WCW *Supra*, will and inventory, 1610

[27] L.R.O. WCW *Supra* will, 1617

[28] This is quite common in the provisions made in the wills of testators from this area

[29] Farrer, *Court rolls*, vol. 1, p. 479

[30] Whitaker, *History of Whalley*, pp. 189–90, prints the customs of 1402

[31] Farrer, *Court rolls*, vol. 1, p. 256

[32] There are many examples of a widow receiving more than a quarter of her husband's holding as her dower; this was especially the case where there were children to support. For example, Thomas Shackleton of Trawden left half his lands to his wife for her life towards the maintenance of his younger children and in full satisfaction of her dower. L.R.O. WCW *Supra*, will and inventory, 1634

[33] Howell, 'Peasant inheritance customs in the Midlands', especially p. 146; Spufford, 'Peasant inheritance customs in Cambridgeshire', particularly pp. 157–60

[34] This is explained by Tupling, *Economic history of Rossendale*, pp. 75, 79–80

[35] Farrer, *Court rolls*, vol. 1, p. 337

[36] These 28 holdings split into 79. Farrer, *Court rolls*, vols. 1 and 2, *passim*; L.R.O. DDHCl3, *passim*

[37] P.R.O. D.L.5/19 fols. 399–400

[38] Tupling, *Economic history of Rossendale*, pp. 75–6

[39] Farrer, *Court rolls*, vol. 1, pp. 257–8

[40] See Chapter 4, pp. 49–60

[41] Farrer, *Court rolls*, vol. 1, pp. 323–5

[42] Tupling missed this development because he concentrated primarily on the period up to 1567, for which the court rolls are in print, and examined the subsequent court rolls relatively little. In addition, he did not have access to wills, which demonstrate clearly the predominance of primogeniture. Tupling, *Economic history of Rossendale*, Chapter 3

[43] L.R.O. DDHCl3/73, Trawden forest (at Colne), 2nd halmote, 12 May 1591

[44] Farrer, *Court rolls*, vol. 1, pp. 314–15

[45] B.I.P.C.Y. vol. 36, fol. 116

[46] P.R.O. D.L.3/57/N1; Farrer, *Court rolls*, vol. 2, pp. 204–5, 235

[47] Macfarlane, 'Illegitimacy and illegitimates in English history', p. 73

[48] L.R.O. WCW *Supra*, will and inventory, 1601

[49] L.R.O. DDHCl3/87, Colne manor, 2nd halmote, 11 July 1605

[50] L.R.O. WCW *Supra*, will and inventory, 1609. This is not a unique example; a husbandman named John Hargreaves of Whitley Booth in Pendle bequeathed the land which he rented from Peter Jennings and most of his personal estate to his base son, providing he kept John's legitimate daughter with meat, drink and apparel for the rest of her life. L.R.O. WCW *Supra*, will and inventory, 1627

[51] For example, see P.R.O. D.L.1/113/S9, D.L.4/21/18; D.L.1/198/L2, D.L.4/43/8. The most protracted dispute brought before the Duchy, concerning title to land at Greenfield, centred around alleged illegitimacy as a disqualification for inheritance; see P.R.O. D.L.3/30/B2, D.L.3/33/B2, D.L.3/34/H2, and many others (D.L.1, D.L.3 and D.L.4, *passim*)

[52] 'Supposed' may indicate that Holt challenged the paternity of the child; this may be why Holt's treatment of his son was not very generous. L.R.O. WCW *Supra*, will and inventory, 1610

[53] L.R.O. WCW *Supra*, will 1607, inventory 1610

[54] L.R.O. WCW *Supra*, will and inventory, 1628

[55] This graph includes all the examples of transfers of land for money payment registered in the halmotes of Colne manor and Trawden and Pendle forests to 1640, with certain excepted types of transfers. Explicit examples of marriage and testamentary agreements, and redemption of mortgages have been excluded. In addition, all leases (i.e. where an annual rent is mentioned) even if there was an initial payment too, have been excluded. We are thus left with sales and mortgages of land. These have been grouped together, since it is often impossible to distinguish them, particularly if the 'intent', recording the exact nature of the transaction, is not recorded in the court roll. Dates of the courts have been adjusted slightly, so that there are two courts per year, as was usual. Thus, if the Michaelmas court was delayed and held in January, February or March, it has been treated as if it took place in the previous year. Farrer, *Court rolls*, vols. 1 and 2, *passim*; L.R.O. DDHCl3, *passim*

[56] In Rossendale, the first explicit example of a sale occurred at this time too, in 1544. Tupling, *Economic history of Rossendale*, p. 91. This change in court registration procedure may have been connected with the change (also at this time) in the registration of leases; see below, p. 84

[57] For 'national' crop price data, see Bowden, 'Statistical appendix', pp. 815–21, 851–5; for local crop prices, see Swain, 'Industry and economy', pp. 334–6

[58] Margaret Spufford noted that the bad harvests of the 1590s had this effect in Cambridgeshire; Spufford, 'Peasant inheritance customs in Cambridgeshire', p. 163. One should note that by grouping together sales and mortgages, we have side-stepped Margaret Spufford's argument that it is not possible to correlate sales with bad harvests, since a man might stave off the immediate effects of a bad harvest by borrowing; *ibid.*, and Spufford, *Contrasting communities*, pp. 78–80

[59] For the customs relating to enrolment of land transactions, see Farrer, *Court rolls*, vol. 1, pp. 478–81, especially custom 3, p. 478

[60] The reasons for this peak are unclear, as are those for 1632–3 and 1639. Although the harvests of 1630 and 1637 were bad nationally, local harvests were fairly normal; see Swain, 'Industry and economy', pp. 335–6

[61] See Chapter 4, pp. 60–5

[62] P.R.O. D.L.44/777; L.R.O. DDTa 216, fol. 10. See below, pp. 85–91

[63] See Chapter 4, p. 62

[64] L.R.O. DDHCl3, *passim*. Not all the sales record the type of land, and so this figure should be treated as the minimum number of sales involving waste alone

[65] P.R.O. E.317 Lancs.8, m.18–23. The ten 'cottage rents' were for cottages on the waste, and have been included in the total of 34 copyhold tenancies which consisted of waste alone

[66] Tupling, *Economic history of Rossendale*, pp. 155–6

[67] Based on data extracted from L.R.O. DDHCl3, *passim*. Some

transfers do not record the precise amount of money paid; the calculations are based on 34 examples of the sale of waste, and 14 examples of the sale of old copyhold land without waste (in all cases where the price was explicitly stated)

[68] L.R.O. DDHCl3, *passim*

[69] See Chapter 6, pp. 127–38, 142–4

[70] See below, pp. 93–5

[71] Farrer, *Court rolls*, vol. 1, *passim*; L.R.O. DDHCl3, *passim*. The percentages are based on 24 and 32 examples respectively. It is impossible to pursue this development with regard to the forests, since the size of holdings is not usually stated

[72] B.I. P.C.Y. vol. 36, fol. 175. This was stated in the will of Thomas, dated 7 August 1612

[73] L.R.O. DDHCl3/79, Colne manor, 2nd halmote, 25 May 1597

[74] The Shuttleworths' purchases are enrolled in the following Pendle court rolls; L.R.O. DDHCl3/64, Pendle forest, 2nd halmote, 11 April 1582; DDHCl3/65, Pendle forest, 2nd halmote, 7 May 1583; DDHCl3/78, Pendle forest, 2nd halmote, 1 June 1596

[75] Tupling, *Economic history of Rossendale*, p. 84

[76] See above, pp. 71–2

[77] Whitaker, *History of Whalley*, p. 189

[78] Farrer, *Court rolls*, vol. 1, p. 479

[79] Farrer, *Court rolls*, vol. 1, p. 377; vol. 2, p. 181. In Rossendale, the first example of a subtenancy created by surrender and fine was in 1543; Tupling, *Economic history of Rossendale*, p. 87

[80] P.R.O. D.L.1/14/M1, D.L.1/34/R3

[81] Tupling, *Economic history of Rossendale*, p. 87

[82] Farrer, *Court rolls*, vols. 1 and 2, *passim*; L.R.O. DDHCl3, *passim*. The data include all transfers of land enrolled in the halmotes, where an annual rent is specifically mentioned. The data should not be regarded as a total record of all the leases of longer duration than a year and a day between 1545 and 1640, for two reasons. First, not all 'intents' (where lease arrangements are often described) are recorded in the court rolls. Secondly, leases where an initial payment of money was made, but no annual rent recorded or demanded, seem to be indistinguishable from mortgages, when the 'intent' is not given. For further details of the geographical distribution of the leases, see Swain, 'Industry and economy', Table 5.3, p. 142

[83] *Ibid.*; the size of the sample is 491 leases (this includes all those leases where the term was stated). For further details, see Swain, 'Industry and economy', Table 5.4, p. 144

[84] *Ibid.*; 13 out of 53 leases in Colne manor during the period from 1548 to 1600 were for terms of 20 years or less, compared with 13 out of 59 leases, 1601–40; in Pendle forest, 18 out of 128 leases, 1545–1600, were for 20 years or less, compared with 40 out of 234 during the period from 1601 to 1640

[85] *Ibid.*; the size of the sample is 122 leases (this includes all those leases where the size of the plot of land was stated). The period after 1618 for Colne manor is not strictly comparable with the period before it (since old copyhold land did not include rights to waste after 1618) and therefore has

been excluded. For further details, see Swain, 'Industry and economy', Table 5.5, p. 145

[86] *Ibid.*; in Colne between 1548 and 1618, 23 out of 65 leases were for 2 acres or less, and in north-east Pendle, 1572–1633, 8 out of 17 leases fell into this category; in contrast, only 1 out of 6 leases in Trawden forest, 1558–1639, was of 2 acres or less, and 5 out of 34 in the rest of Pendle forest, 1554–1633. Clearly the size of the Trawden forest sample is much too small, but those for the other areas are sufficiently large for a broad comparison to be made

[87] *Ibid.* A total of 5 out of 33 leases were for 2 acres or less in the period to 1580, compared with 32 out of 90 subsequently. However, 46% of leases after 1580 were for 2 acres or less in Colne manor (18 out of 39) and 50% in north-east Pendle (8 out of 16), compared with 16% in the rest of Pendle (5 out of 31) and 25% in Trawden (1 out of 4)

[88] The importance of the levels of rent paid by subtenants is a topic that has not been fully explored; for example, Tawney largely ignored the question in *The agrarian problem in the sixteenth century*

[89] Farrer, *Court rolls*, vols. 1 and 2, *passim*; L.R.O. DDHCl3, *passim*. The subtenant paid both a rent to the Crown (either directly or via the copyholder) and a rent to the copyholder on top of this; thus the 'rent to the lessor' represents the surplus paid by the subtenant over and above the rent to the Crown. To obtain the subtenant's total rent outlay, as a proportion of the rent to the Crown, it is necessary to add 1 to the multiple. These leases are those which involved the payment of an annual rent only, and not those which included an initial payment of money too (but this latter type of lease was not very common, constituting only 15% of 491 recorded leases). In addition, a small number of leases also required labour services (23 out of the 410 leases which did not demand an initial payment of money), usually 3 days' work in total during the year, and possibly a 'boon hen' as well. No attempt has been made to calculate the value of these extremely small labour services since there is insufficiently reliable data on the changing value of labour over time; however, this is of minimal importance, since invariably the labour services which were required were insignificant relative to the large rents paid to the copyholders

[90] P.R.O. DDHCl3/105, Pendle forest, 1st halmote, 24 October 1622. A house, barn and land at Blacko in Barrowford was leased for three lives by Lawrence Robinson to Thurstan Garstang, for an annual rent of £4, when the copyhold rent to the Crown was just 2d

[91] L.R.O. DDHCl3, *passim*

[92] L.R.O. DDHCl3/120, Trawden forest (at Colne), 1st halmote, 24 October 1637

[93] L.R.O. DDHCl3/86, Colne manor, 1st halmote, 26 January 1604

[94] L.R.O. DDHCl3/100, Pendle forest, 1st halmote, 20 October 1617

[95] P.R.O. E.317 Lancs.8, m.61–6. Subtenants are described as holding land of another; copyholders are described as holding their own land or land lately ('nuper') belonging to another

[96] P.R.O. D.L.3/37/B7

[97] P.R.O. D.L.1/161/P3

[98] L.R.O. WCW *Supra*, will and inventory, 1630

[99] Leases for terms longer than a year and a day required a surrender, and hence an entry fine, in the halmote; see above, p. 84

[100] 31 Eliz. c. 7

[101] L.R.O. DDHCl3/77, Colne manor, 1st halmote, 23 September 1594 (there were 17 presentments in all); DDHCl3/104, Pendle forest, 1st halmote, 25 October 1621 (in addition, 4 people were presented for receiving strangers or vagrants and one for receiving a pregnant woman into his house); DDHCl3, *passim*

[102] L.R.O. DDHCl3, *passim*. See Swain, 'Industry and economy', Graph 5.3, p. 153

[103] L.R.O. DDHCl3/117, Colne manor, 2nd halmote, 24 April 1635

[104] L.R.O. DDHCl3, *passim*; 168 out of 204 presentments for detinue occurred at the Easter halmote

[105] Everitt, 'Farm labourers', p. 434; Bowden, 'Agricultural prices, farm profits and rents', pp. 619–22

[106] For local crop prices, see Swain, 'Industry and economy', Table A.1, p. 335

[107] L.R.O. DDHCl3, *passim*; see Swain, 'Industry and economy', Graph 5.3, p. 153

[108] See Chapter 6, pp. 127–38, 142–4

[109] Harrison, 'Elizabethan village surveys', p. 89 and *passim*

[110] See Chapter 4, p. 63; L.R.O. DDHCl3/104, Colne manor, 2nd halmote, 21 May 1622; M.C.L. L1/47/3 fols. 24–7; Farrer, *Court rolls*, vol. 2, pp. 443–7. One should note that Farrer failed to transcribe the entries in the court roll relating to the 10 cottages which stood on parts of waste allotted to copyholders

[111] P.R.O. E.317 Lancs.12

[112] Farrer, *Court rolls*, vol. 2, p. 425

[113] See Chapter 4, p. 59

[114] P.R.O. D.L.44/285

[115] P.R.O. D.L.44/1009

[116] P.R.O. D.L.44/33, D.L.44/36, D.L.44/285, D.L.44/1009, *passim*. This same pattern was apparent in Rossendale; see Tupling, *Economic history of Rossendale*, pp. 64, 66

[117] P.R.O. D.L.44/285, D.L.44/1009. These were held by John Blakey alias Wilson and James Holgate alias Block

[118] See above, pp. 78–80

[119] Tupling, *Economic history of Rossendale*, pp. 57–68

[120] Porter, 'Reclamation and settlement of Bowland', Chapter 3

[121] Farrer, *Court rolls*, vol. 1, pp. 261, 266, 268–70, 273

[122] Robinson does not appear as a copyholder in the court rolls; Farrer, *Court rolls*, vol. 1, *passim*. Similarly his name is not amongst those of the Colne tenants in the rental for 1527; *ibid.*, pp. 380–1

[123] John Robinson was amerced twice in 1507 (*ibid.*, pp. 232–3). His widow was fined the following year (*ibid.*, p. 241), for encroachments at Grindlestone Hurst in Marsden. Nicholas Robinson was fined twice in 1510 for this offence (*ibid.*, pp. 248, 250)

[124] There were several other encroachments recorded during this period, apart from those of the Robinsons (*ibid.*, pp. 231, 238, 241, 248, 250, 260)

and a dispute with the Prior of Pontefract over his alleged encroachments (*ibid.*,   269–70;   P.R.O.   D.L.1/1/C14,   D.L.1/2/P8,   D.L.1/2/T12, D.L.3/12/P1, D.L.42/95/fols. 56, 71v.)

[125] Farrer, *Court rolls*, vol. 1, pp. 321, 329, 334; L.R.O. DDHCl3/49, Colne manor, 1st halmote, 5 November 1566 (this entry is omitted from Farrer, *Court rolls*, vol. 1, p. 470), DDHCl3/50, Colne manor, 1st halmote, 3 December 1567 (repeating the previous entry); DDHCl3/77, Colne manor, 1st halmote, 23 September 1594; DDHCl3/107, Colne manor, 2nd halmote, 10 May 1625

[126] L.R.O. DDHCl3/105, Pendle forest, 3rd halmote, 7 May 1623; DDHCl3/112, Pendle forest, 1st halmote, 22 October 1629

[127] This excludes the alleged encroachment of the Prior of Pontefract (which concerned 100 acres), for this case was less one of encroachment but rather disputed title of land

[128] For example, Henry Holgate was fined just 12d for building a barn or house at Waterside on land encroached on the highways and wastes of the King; L.R.O. DDHCl3/107, Colne manor, 2nd halmote, 10 May 1625

[129] 14 Charles II, c.10

[130] P.R.O. E.179/250/11, Part 3. In Colne, 103 out of 196 households were exempt from the hearth tax, compared with 61 out of 160 households in Marsden, 20 out of 79 households in Trawden forest and 79 out of 304 households in Pendle forest. In Foulridge, 25 out of 88 households (28%) were exempt. See Swain, 'Industry and economy', Table 5.7, p. 160

[131] Marshall, *Lancashire*, pp. 45–6

[132] P.R.O. E.179/250/4. The section for Pendle forest (m.63) is very slightly damaged where those assessed on lands worth less than £5 a year are listed

[133] Marshall, 'Study of local and regional "communities"', pp. 225–6. In any case, we have the additional problem of walled-up hearths; some deliberately walled up hearths to avoid paying tax, and though we possess a list of these (P.R.O. E.179/250/11, Part 7), the number of people with the same name makes it impossible to link these to their owners in E.179/250/ 11, part 3

[134] 12 Charles II c.9

[135] P.R.O. E.179/130/125

[136] Smith, *Land and politics*, p. 96. This subsidy return is far more comprehensive in its coverage of this area than the subsidy roll of 1524; for example, there are only 18 taxpayers listed in the Colne assessment for 1524, whereas in 1543 there are 50; P.R.O. E.179/130/87, E.179/130/125. Smith (*op. cit.*, pp. 96, 265–6) found a similar situation in the West Riding of Yorkshire

[137] In 1563, there were 315 households in Colne chapelry which took communion (see chapter 2, p. 17); in 1543, there were only 128 households taxed in Colne chapelry (excluding Barrowford, which formed part of the 37 taxed households in Pendle forest). P.R.O. E.179/130/125

[138] *Ibid.* In Trawden forest, 14 out of 24 taxpayers were assessed on movable goods worth £1, whilst in Pendle forest, the proportion was 23 out of 37; in Marsden, 12 taxpayers out of 36 were rated on goods assessed at £1, and in Colne, 22 out of 50 taxpayers were at this level

[139] *Ibid.* For further details, see Swain, 'Industry and economy', Table 5.11, p. 165

[140] See Chapter 4, pp. 56–7

[141] See above, pp. 73, 77

[142] Brigg, 'Forest of Pendle', Part 1, p. 65

[143] See Chapter 6, pp. 132–5

[144] See above, p. 93

[145] Brigg, 'Forest of Pendle', Part 2, p. 70

[146] See above, pp. 93–4

[147] L.R.O. QSP 230/3

[148] L.R.O. QSP 238/12

[149] The wills used are those listed in note 19

[150] L.R.O. DDHCl3/67, Colne manor, 2nd halmote, 20 April 1585. This is the first recorded bequest to the poor by a testator from this area; there is an earlier bequest of £2 to the poor of Colne parish by Robert Nowell of Read, who died in 1569; he also left £6 13s 4d to the poor of Burnley parish, besides numerous individual bequests. See Grosart, *Towneley Hall MSS*, pp. 84, 384 and *passim*

[151] B.I. P.C.Y. vol. 27, fol. 232

[152] B.I. P.C.Y. vol. 27, fol. 339

[153] B.I. P.C.Y. vol. 38, fol. 94. See Chapter 2, pp. 22–5

[154] L.R.O. DDHCl3/83, Colne manor, 1st halmote, 19 January 1601

[155] Bennett, *History of Marsden*, p. 85

[156] Crossley, *Potts' discovery of witches*, B2, B2v, C, Cv, E4, F, G2, O4, R3v, R4, S

[157] L.R.O. DDHCl3/68, Colne manor, 1st halmote, 7 December 1585; DDHCl3/68, Pendle forest, 1st halmote, 8 December 1585

[158] In June 1590, 16 people were fined in Colne for receiving strange beggars into their houses, and 3 people were amerced for this offence in Trawden forest; in May 1591, 5 people were similarly fined in Colne. L.R.O. DDHCl3/72, Colne manor and Trawden forest, 2nd halmotes, 2 June 1590; DDHCl3/73, Colne manor, 2nd halmote, 12 May 1591. In Pendle forest, 4 people were fined in April 1589 for receiving 'foreign beggars', 13 persons were amerced for this offence in June 1590, and one person was fined in December 1591. L.R.O. DDHCl3/71, Pendle forest, 3rd halmote, 11 April 1589; DDHCl3/72, Pendle forest, 2nd halmote, 3 June 1590; DDHCl3/74, Pendle forest, 1st halmote, 7 December 1591

[159] This is indeed the case for textile manufacture; see Chapter 6, pp. 118–22, 138–41

[160] For textiles, see Chapter 6, pp. 127–9, 138–41

CHAPTER VI

CLOTH MANUFACTURE

THE STRUCTURE OF THE CLOTH INDUSTRY

(a) *The types of cloth produced in the Colne area, 1500–1640* Colne was one of the most important clothing towns of Lancashire during this period. In 1640, the Royal Commission on the cloth industry reported that the Lancashire towns greatly involved in the cloth trade were Manchester, Rochdale, Colne, Bolton, Blackburn and Bury.[1] In 1604, Colne was included in a list of thirty clothing towns and villages in Lancashire, which allegedly made only friezes and Manchester cottons for export to France, by which it was claimed 10,000 people in Lancashire earned their livelihood.[2]

However, an examination of the types of cloth produced in the Colne area between 1500 and 1640 has failed to trace a single example of the manufacture of friezes or Manchester cottons. The cloth most commonly referred to was kersey, usually sold 'in the white' (i.e. undyed). White and grey kerseys from Colne were sold in London at least as early as 1565.[3] The inventories of testators from this area frequently record kerseys in stock or in the looms.[4] In addition, there are several lawsuits concerning kersey manufacture in this district.[5] Kerseys were also produced in Burnley, Padiham, Blackburn and Preston,[6] but this area appears to have been the limit of kersey manufacture in Lancashire. By contrast, no kerseys at all were included in the Manchester ulnage accounts, 1614–16.[7]

There are also occasional references in local inventories to coverlet yarn,[8] and the frequent recording of combs and combstocks, and the presence of coverlets and cushions in considerable numbers in some inventories,[9] suggests that these worsted cloths[10] were also made in this area, but, in contrast to kerseys, we have no evidence to suggest that they were produced for other than domestic and local use.

Similarly, a small number of inventories record linen yarn,[11] and one refers to possession of a linen wheel.[12] Some of the raw materials for linen manufacture were grown locally. John Shape of Wheatley Lane was fined 12d in 1622 for annoying his neighbours with hemp steeping in the water descending to Old Laund House.[13] However, only eleven (5%) *supra* inventories record flax or hemp, and always in small amounts.[14] The best evidence of the relative importance of woollen and linen cloth manufacture in the Colne area is provided by occupations recorded in the Quarter Sessions recognisance rolls. Of 21 weavers from Colne, Trawden and Pendle referred to between 1626 and 1642, all were described as woollen weavers. Linen manufacture appears to have been practised to a greater extent in the Burnley and Padiham areas, for of the 9 weavers from this district mentioned in the recognisance rolls during the same period, 7 were woollen and 2 linen weavers.[15] Similarly, of the 19 weavers buried in Burnley, 1653–60, 13 were woollen and 6 linen weavers.[16]

(b) *Kersey manufacture* Kerseys were a coarse woollen cloth, which, according to an Act of 1551, were required to be 18 yards in length and 1 yard wide, weighing 20 pounds in all.[17] Initially, the wool was prepared by oiling or greasing with butter. It was then ready for carding, which increased the cohesiveness of the wool by interlocking the fibres. This was done by working the wool between two cards of wire spikes. It was then spun into yarn on a spinning wheel, and woven on a narrow loom. After weaving, the cloth was taken to a fulling mill, where soap and fuller's earth were applied to remove the oil, and it was then beaten by water-powered hammers in order to felt the cloth. Then the nap of the cloth was raised with teasels, and the material was sheared to reduce all the projecting fibres to the same length. Subsequently it was laid out to dry and stretched back into shape on tenter bars.[18]

It is particularly important to appreciate the distribution of labour between these various processes of production. In 1588, the Vicar of Leeds wrote that the distribution of 60 kersey workers would be as follows: sorting and dressing 6, spinning and carding 40, weaving 8, shearing 6 (of whom 2 might be able to help the rest). The spinners were able to spin 20 stones of wool into yarn in a week, which would produce ten kerseys.[19] Thus an average of six people were involved in the manufacture of a kersey in a week. Heaton argued that since the wool was sold sorted, and since most kerseys were sold without shearing (fulling and possibly tentering too was done by the fuller), the small clothier could card, spin and weave a kersey in a week with the assistance of four workers.[20] However, this document was a draft of a scheme for setting up a clothmaking project at Skipton using full-time labour. As will be shown later, many households clearly divided their time between agriculture and industry, and few seem to have been involved in cloth production full-time all the year round.[21] Furthermore, intensity of production might vary between different branches of the textile industry, and we should not necessarily assume that there was a constant ratio of carders and spinners to weavers over time. Nevertheless, the Skipton scheme illustrates above all the numerical importance of carders and spinners in the industry.

(c) The units of production   An examination of inventories of testators from this area shows that the processes of carding or combing, spinning and weaving were often carried out under the same roof. Over one-third (36%) of clothmaking households in Colne chapelry and Roughlee participated in carding or combing, spinning and weaving, and nearly half (48%) were involved in both the spinning and weaving processes. Similarly, well over half (59%) of these cloth-producing households possessed both cards or combs and spinning wheels. On the other hand, 23% of such households were involved in weaving only.

Possession of looms was far more common amongst clothmaking households in Colne chapelry and Roughlee than it was in the rest of Pendle forest. In the former, 71% of clothmaking households possessed looms, compared with only 35% in the rest of Pendle forest where the structure of clothmaking was clearly different. Whilst only 18% of textile households were involved in all three processes of production, a further 62% had both cards or combs and spinning wheels.[22] Thus it is likely that the rest of Pendle forest was largely involved in the production of yarn which served looms in Colne chapelry and Roughlee.

Unfortunately, it is rarely stated precisely how many cards, combs or spinning wheels a household owned, whereas the number of looms is usually given. Of 90 supra inventories containing looms (where the number was stated), 58 (64%) possessed only one, and 26 (29%) had two looms. In 4 households (4%) there were three looms, and 2 (2%) possessed four looms.[23] There is no recorded example of a household owning more than four looms, and the overwhelming predominance of one- or two-loom households suggests that the units of production were small, with few households involved in cloth production on a sizeable scale. Proto-factory conditions clearly did not exist.

Thus it seems that the extent of clothiers' activities in the Colne area was similar to that in the kersey-producing district around Halifax, for Heaton found that they too operated on a small scale. Furthermore, Heaton also argued that there was a close connection between the labour supply required to make one kersey in a week (five people) and the normal size of the clothier's establishment (i.e. his family, including children, and possibly with the aid of an apprentice, or additional women to help with the spinning).[24] It is certainly true that many households were involved in all the major processes of production, but the existence of some households participating in only one or two of these processes, suggests that they must have been dependent on the labour of other households.

It is essential to establish which members of the household might be involved in the various processes of production. First, there is some dispute as to whether women and children might be involved in carding wool. Lowe argued, without any supporting evidence, that carding was apparently an unpleasant and arduous job which would not normally be done by women or children.[25] Mann suggested that if this were true, Lancashire must have been the only county in which women or children did not participate in carding, and claimed it would be much more true of combing.[26] For the Colne area, we have contemporary evidence that women were employed in carding wool. About six years before the great witch trial of 1612, Anne Whittle alias Old Chattox, one of the leading Pendle witches, was hired by the wife of James Robinson to card wool, despite being in her seventies and almost blind; she did so on a Friday, Saturday and the following Monday, until she made mischief by allegedly spoiling the ale, after drinking from it. Similarly Janet Booth of Padiham carded in the house of Edward Pearson of Padiham in 1612.[27] Lastly, in a largely fictional contemporary account of Pendle witchcraft, it was claimed that Mother Cuthbert and her two daughters lived in a little hovel at the foot of Pendle hill, and that the daughters both carded and spun wool for their living, and yet were very poor.[28] Although we have no direct contemporary evidence for it in this area, it may well be true that young children also carded wool.[29]

Spinning was clearly the province of female labour, as is evident in gentry accounts, where there are many examples of payments made to women for spinning.[30] In addition, the inventories of poor widows and spinsters often show the importance of spinning as a means of earning a livelihood. For example, Janet Hartley, a spinster of Laund in Pendle, died in 1616 leaving goods worth just £12 10s 8d, £5 5s 2d excluding debts. She owned no animals at all, but her goods included a spinning wheel and cards. In her will, Janet made a special bequest of the spinning wheel to her sister-in- law Dorothy.[31] It seems that children of both sexes were taught to spin from an early age. In 1634, the chief witness in the second Pendle witch trial, Edmund Robinson junior of Newchurch in Pendle, who was about ten years old, said that his mother had brought him up to spin wool, and also used him to fetch home her cattle.[32] Thus, if they had acquired the skills in childhood it is possible that some adult males were also engaged in spinning.[33]

A few examples of female weavers have been found,[34] and so it is not inconceivable that some weaving was performed by women as was the case in Yorkshire in the later fourteenth century.[35] Instruction in the art of weaving was also given from a fairly early age. According to a lawsuit of 1592, Edmund Crook as a child left his guardian and placed himself with a weaver, where he remained for a long time 'minding to frame himself to some occupation by means whereof he might the better in time to come relieve himself'.[36] Some houses had their own weaving shops or workshops in a separate room. William Bannister had his own weaving shop in the lower end of his house in Barrowford, according to a lawsuit of 1598.[37] Inventories rarely list goods room by room, so we cannot establish how usual it was to weave in a separate room, but occasionally we see glimpses of this. James Hartley of Winewall had a wool chamber in his house, which contained wool, feathers, woollen yarn and one piece in the looms. This appears to have been upstairs,[38] and thus the practice found by Barley in the West Riding of wealthier testators having their looms upstairs,[39] may well have applied to the Colne area too, for Hartley was a prosperous yeoman whose inventory was valued at about £217, including debts, at his death in 1632.

Thus, there was an overwhelming numerical importance of women and children in the local cloth industry. If we were to take an extreme position, and assume that no adult males participated in the carding and spinning processes, then the ratio of women and children working in these activities compared with males in weaving would be 5:1.[40] Even if we take a less extreme view, it is still obvious that the role of women's and children's labour in the family economy was crucial.

(d) *The organisation of production* We have established that textile
manufacture was carried out in the homes of the producers
themselves, and that often several of these processes were performed
under the same roof. But to what extent did Colne clothiers 'put out'
raw materials, wool or yarn, to be carded, spun or woven in other
households, paying wages for labour but continuing to own the
product?[41] The putting-out system has been found to have been
typical of many areas of Wiltshire and East Anglia.[42]

A Duchy lawsuit of 1575 is most illuminating on the system of
production in the Colne area. A clothier, Henry Parker of Colne
parish, said that he and his father were both makers and owners of
the white, grey and black kerseys which they sold, this being
corroborated by weavers and a carpenter.[43] Independent producers
were also in evidence in the 1630s. In a Duchy lawsuit of 1638,
clothiers stated that they had sold their cloths on a weekly basis to a
factor named Robert Walton of Marsden, some for ready money,
but mostly on trust. All sold their own cloth to Walton, and were
clearly not his employees.[44]

To the evidence which demonstrates the existence of independent
producers, we can add the lack of references to putting-out. There is
not a single explicit example found in the wills and inventories of
this district of a debt or credit showing that putting-out was
practised,[45] though wages were paid to specialists for finishing
cloth.[46] This is extremely convincing evidence that putting-out was
not present, for, although the proportion of debts and credits where
the nature of the transaction is clearly stated is small,[47] we would
expect to find occasional examples of wages paid for spinning or
weaving. In the West Riding by contrast, examples of such debts
may be found in wills and inventories.[48] Secondly, we have no
examples of 'wool at spinning' or 'yarn at weaving' in any of the
inventories of testators from this area,[49] although they too may be
found in the West Riding.[50]

Indeed, the various types of activity practised by men described
as clothiers is further testimony to the lack of specialisation in this
area. Firstly, 'clothier' might signify involvement as a wool brogger,
who bought and sold wool in large quantities, and who might also be
involved in the marketing of cloth as well. A clothier named
Lawrence Mitton of Great Marsden owned 44 stones of wool at his
death in 1558, and was also involved in the sale of warps and
kerseys, for he had two warps and twelve kerseys in stock; he
possessed cards and combs, but no spinning wheels or looms.[51]

Secondly, the term might by synonymous with chapman. Thus Robert Shaw, a clothier of Colne, alleged in a lawsuit of *c.*1571 that he made his living by buying cloth and driving packhorses loaded with kerseys and cottons to London and the East Anglian counties. He brought his action because a promised delivery of ten kerseys had been sold to another chapman who had offered a higher price.[52] Thirdly, a clothier might be personally involved in both the manufacturing and marketing of cloth. The clothiers Henry Rycroft of Colne and Henry Parker of Colne parish made their own kerseys and sold them both within and outside Lancashire, according to the lawsuit of 1575 cited above. Rycroft said that he was also involved in the finishing of his own and others' cloths in Yorkshire, which he then sold in London.[53] Lastly, in some cases, the term clothier was simply an alternative for weaver. In the manor court rolls of Colne, Henry Whittaker was described both as a clothier and a webster in 1586.[54]

The only local examples of putting-out which have been found relate to the gentry families of Shuttleworth of Smithills and Gawthorpe, and Walmsley of Dunkenhalgh. Both families had wool spun, woven and finished for them, but in very small quantities, and these cloths were probably designed for household consumption only.[55] These households presumably had access to better quality raw materials, and with the chance to choose the most skilled workers to make their cloths, they would be able to obtain better quality products than were available locally. However, these accounts relate to the Bolton, Burnley and Padiham areas; we do not possess gentry household accounts for Colne, Trawden or Pendle.

The conclusion that putting-out was not widely practised in the Lancashire woollen industry is not novel, for Lowe has noted its absence in the sixteenth century, and argued that this situation did not change until about the 1680s.[56] Lowe rightly criticised Bagley, who attempted to deduce the presence of a putting-out system on the basis of speculating on the nature of unspecified debts and credits in wills and inventories.[57]

The Colne area appears to be quite similar to two other areas of cloth production, namely the West Riding of Yorkshire and North Wales. Although examples of putting-out have been found for the West Riding, it seems that smaller clothiers predominated, particularly in the kersey-producing area around Halifax.[58] The best description of cloth production in Halifax is given in the preamble to the Halifax Act of 1555. It was stated that, due to the poor quality of the agricultural land, the population lived not by getting corn but by producing cloth. They were not wealthy enough to keep a horse to carry wool, nor to buy much wool at once, and therefore bought 1, 2, 3 or 4 stones from the wool driver in Halifax, made it into yarn or cloth, and then sold it in order to buy more wool.[59] In North Wales, the clothier with great quantities of capital and control over a large part of the manufacturing process was probably very rare, and in this respect North Wales was very similar to the West Riding and Lancashire.[60]

Instead of putting-out raw materials, cloth producers brought in extra labour, either when required, or on a semi-permanent basis as a servant or apprentice. The examples of women carding wool in the houses of others have already been given.[61] However, more permanent labour might be hired. A clothier named John Driver of Pasture in Pendle employed a wool weaver called Francis Hartley of Roughlee in 1628. He had bargained with Hartley to weave woollen cloth by the piece in his house, allowing him meat, drink and lodging.[62] Alternatively, an apprentice might be taken on to assist in weaving, as in the case of Edmund Crook previously given.[63] Although no examples have been discovered for this area of prosecutions in Quarter Sessions for infringements of the minimum seven-year apprenticeship for weavers stipulated by the Act of Artificers of 1563,[64] one should not necessarily assume that the regulations governing apprenticeship were therefore strictly observed.[65]

(e) *The sources of raw materials and cloth instruments* Given the absence of a putting-out system, the question remains of how the numerous independent clothmaking households were supplied with raw materials. Sheep were certainly kept in this area, but it is clear that their numbers were small, and consequently local wool supplies were insufficient to meet the demand from cloth manufacturers. Firstly, the evidence provided by the tithes of wool at Whalley Abbey in 1536 shows that Colne chapelry contributed 11 stones of wool, Pendle forest 12 stones and Trawden forest 10 stones.[66] On the assumption that these tithes represented a tenth of the wool produced, the inference is that there were between 1,540 and 2,310 sheep in Colne, Pendle and Trawden (since the Pennine sheep probably produced a fleece weighing from two to three pounds each).[67] Two stones of wool were needed to produce a kersey,[68] and thus the wool produced locally was capable of making only 165 kerseys per annum. These ought to be regarded as minimum figures, for some wool probably escaped tithe.

Secondly, the view that the number of sheep kept locally was small, is supported by analysis of inventories. Of 123 *supra* testators from Colne chapelry and Pendle forest who owned cards, combs or a spinning wheel, 1558–1640, 65 (53%) did not have any sheep at all. None of the 10 *infra* testators with these instruments possessed any sheep. On the other hand, there was a slightly stronger tendency for those owning sheep to be involved in cloth production, for of 96 inventories containing sheep, 58 (60%) possessed cards, combs or a spinning wheel. However, the median size of flocks was small, only 19·5 amongst male *supra* testators.[69]

Thus it is not surprising that we should find examples of wool being imported from elsewhere. In 1574, John Hargreaves of Goldshaw Booth in Pendle stated that forty years previously, he had drive a packhorse loaded with wool from Heptonstall parish in the West Riding to the house of Hugh Moore in Higham in Pendle.[70] Similarly, the clothiers John Hanson and Lawrence Hargreaves of 'Lancaster' (though their surnames suggest very strongly that they came from the Colne area), bought 30 stones of wool for £10 from the wife of John Hardy of Halifax in 1526–7.[71] The Yorkshire men apparently bought fine wool mostly from Lincolnshire, whilst selling their coarse wool to Rochdale clothiers.[72] This practice may have been followed in their dealings with Colne men.

The wool was distributed to the manufacturers by wool broggers. Their very existence is yet further proof of the absence of a putting-out system. Lawrence Mitton, a clothier of Great Marsden, was clearly engaged as a wool brogger at his death in 1558, for he had 44 stones of wool in stock, but possessed only twelve sheep and six lambs.[73] Mitton did not own spinning wheels or looms, in contrast to Henry Hargreaves of Colne, who possessed 38½ stones of wool (but no sheep), and, in addition, spinning wheels and two pairs of looms in 1622. These instruments were certainly in use, for Hargreaves also owned coarse yarn valued at 10s, a warpingwough, and eight pieces of cloth.[74]

These wool broggers performed an essential function in keeping the wool growers in touch with the producers. However, the government wished to restrain their activities, for it was believed that they were largely responsible for increasing wool prices.[75] For this reason, the Act of 1552 was passed, prohibiting the purchase of wool other than by manufacturers, Merchants of the Staple and Merchant Adventurers of Newcastle.[76] However, licences for the sale of wool were issued, and Halifax and Rochdale were exempted from the provisions of the 1552 Act, in 1555 and 1590.[77] The crucial role of wool broggers was fully appreciated by manufacturers, and when the licences for sale of wool were cancelled in 1576, a petition of poor inhabitants from Lancashire, Richmond, Westmorland, Cumberland and the Bishopric of Durham followed in 1577, requesting a licence for buying and selling wool, since the clothiers in this area were 'cottagers whose hability will not stretch neither to buy any substance of wools to maintain their work and labour, nor yet to fetch the same, the growth (of) wools being four or five score miles at the least distance'.[78] Dealers were permitted to operate again a few months later.[79]

In addition to wool, the availability of clothmaking instruments was also of major importance if those families who wished to participate in cloth production were to be able to do so. Lawrence Parker, a mercer of Colne, sold both cards and combs; he possessed $3\frac{1}{2}$ dozen cards, at 22d the dozen, and $1\frac{1}{2}$ dozen combs, at 8d the dozen, at his death in 1597.[80] Cards needed to be renewed frequently, since if the wires became split or hammer-headed, thick spinning resulted.[81]

Spinning wheels and looms might be bought from a carpenter. James Parker, a carpenter of Edge, had one pair of looms and bores in his house and shop, with other small pieces of wood, and also three spinning wheels valued at 2s in 1619.[82] Thus cards, combs and spinning wheels were all cheap instruments to buy. Looms were valued at far higher levels. Lowe claimed that looms were not expensive to build, and were often valued at only a few shillings, citing the example of a loom worth 2s 6d in 1593.[83] This appears to be an untypical example; certainly as far as the Colne area is concerned, the cheapest loom found for the period from 1558 to 1640 was valued at 5s in 1606,[84] and the most expensive was one worth 33s 4d in 1614.[85] Indeed, the average valuation of 67 looms in inventories from the Colne area between 1571 and 1640 was 17s 2d.[86] This demonstrates that looms were valuable instruments, certainly in comparison with cards, combs or spinning wheels.

Looms rose in money value from an average of 8s 4d in the 1570s to 23s 4d in the 1610s. This increase may be attributed to the effects of inflation, but the subsequent fall in the 1620s to an average of 17s 9d[87] can only be ascribed to contemporaries' perceptions of the declining economic usefulness of looms, a point to which we shall return in discussing the evidence for a textile depression in the 1620s and 1630s.[88]

Thus, taken together, cards, combs and spinning wheels were extremely cheap, and were well within the reach of even the poorest person. Looms were more expensive, but not prohibitively so.

(*f*) *The household economy*   The majority of *supra* testators in this area who possessed looms lived in the countryside, outside the township boundaries of Colne. Of 101 such testators, 1574–1640, 40 were found dwelling in Pendle forest, and 12 in Trawden forest. A further 20 lived in Great and Little Marsden, and 3 in Foulridge. The remaining 26 lived either in the township of Colne or its immediate environs (but only 5 of these can be positively identified as inhabitants of Colne township).[89] In any case, it is not justifiable to distinguish between 'rural' and 'urban' areas, for Colne was just a small market town, and many of its inhabitants were heavily involved in farming, as is apparent from an examination of inventories and rentals.[90]

Given, therefore, that there was no geographical division between areas of clothmaking and agriculture, we must ask to what extent households generated their income from both industry and agriculture?

Turning firstly to testators who were described as clothiers and weavers, it is immediately apparent that many in this group participated to a large extent in both clothmaking and pastoral agriculture. For example, Lawrence Blakey, a clothier of Blacko in Barrowford who died in 1574, was quite a wealthy man, for his personal estate was valued at £186 16s 8d, or £258 13s 8d if the debts and credits are included. He owned three pairs of looms, and wool and cloth valued at £38, indicating that he was heavily involved in clothmaking. He also possessed ten oxen, 25 cows, young beasts and calves, and three horses, and the valuation of his sheep at £11 suggests that he raised sheep in large numbers.[91] Similarly, the clothier Lawrence Mitton of Great Marsden was operating both as a wool brogger and a cloth factor, at his death in 1558. He owned 44 stones of wool and twelve kerseys, but was not involved in spinning or weaving himself. His inventory was valued at £78 9s 10d, or £148 19s 0d including debts owed to him. He also owned twelve cattle, two horses, a swine and poultry, as well as twelve sheep and six lambs.[92]

We find examples increasingly in the 1600s and 1610s, however, of men described as 'clothier' who owned few cattle or none at all. The inventory of a clothier named James Blakey of Emmott Lane Head (who died in 1604), is a good example of this; it was valued at £41, or about £106 including debts. Blakey owned one pair of looms, and had in stock kersey cloth worth £13 10s 0d. The only animals which he possessed were sheep worth 30s.[93] Similarly, William Holt, a clothier of Colne, owned personal estate worth just £15 6s 3d, or £78 17s 2d including debts and credits, at his death in 1610. His inventory included one pair of looms and two spinning wheels, besides wool, yarn and raw pieces and remnants of cloth. He owned just one horse, apart from poultry.[94] The significance of this greater division between agriculture and industry in the very early seventeenth century, will be discussed more fully in the next section.[95]

Those described as 'weaver' were also involved in pastoral agriculture as well as clothmaking, though to a lesser extent than the clothiers, at least before 1600. Robert Bulcock, a webster of Blacko, owned two pairs of looms as well as cards, combs and spinning wheels at his death in 1579. He also possessed a few cattle, worth just £6 13s 4d and one mare. His inventory was valued at £22 6s 0d, or £15 17s 0d including debts.[96] Even poorer weavers have been found amongst *infra* wills and inventories.[97] Henry Swain of Alkincoats was a woollen weaver whose goods were worth just £3 19s 4d in 1609, or £11 10s 4d including debts. He owned one pair of looms, and no animals at all.[98] Robert Hewitt of Colne was also a poor woollen webster. He owned cards, spinning wheels and one pair of looms at his death in 1604, but only one cow. His inventory was valued at £11 19s 10d, or £12 3s 10d including debts.[99]

It is more difficult to establish to what extent testators were involved in arable farming. Testators only occasionally mentioned real estate in their wills, but we cannot infer from this that many testators were without land, since provision for the inheritance of land may have been made before the will was drawn up, or alternatively testators may have intended that customary primogeniture inheritance should take place. Inventories, whilst listing crops, can give a misleading picture if we fail to take into account the season when the inventory was drawn up. Nevertheless, some of the above testators clearly derived part of their income from arable farming. The clothier Lawrence Blakey owned meal and corn valued at £24 and barley worth 53s 4d in March 1574, and husbandry tools valued at £3,[100] whilst the will of Lawrence Mitton indicates that he was a sub-tenant.[101] On the other hand, there is no evidence that James Blakey was involved in arable husbandry, for in January

1604, he owned neither crops nor husbandry tools.[102] The same was true of William Holt in February 1610.[103] The weaver Robert Bulcock possessed hay, corn and meal worth £2 18s 8d, as well as a harrow and iron tools in March 1579.[104] By contrast, Henry Swain possessed neither crops nor husbandry tools in August 1609,[105] whilst Robert Hewitt owned hay, meal and barley worth 25s, but no instruments for husbandry, in December 1604.[106] It is difficult to generalise from these examples. However, comparatively few of those testators for whom we possess inventories were described as cloth producers. Of 173 supra inventories of males from Colne chapelry and Pendle forest, 1558–1640, only 11 (6%) were described as a clothier, weaver or clothworker; this compares with 102 yeomen (59%) and 36 husbandmen (21%).[107] Many of these yeomen and husbandmen participated in cloth production; approximately half were involved in carding, combing and spinning, and the same proportion engaged in weaving in Colne chapelry and Roughlee. In the rest of Pendle forest, only one-fifth of the yeomen and one-quarter of the husbandmen possessed looms.[108]

Furthermore, craftsmen and tradesmen also participated in cloth manufacture, though not to the same extent as the yeomen and husbandmen. Of 17 supra inventories of such men, 5 possessed cards or combs, 8 spinning wheels and 5 looms.[109] Most earned their living by a combination of craft and agriculture, and therefore had less need of additional work by weaving, though their wives and children might increase the household's income by carding and spinning.[110]

Since it seems that the majority of testators involved in cloth production also participated in farming, though to a varying extent, it is interesting to test the hypothesis that cloth manufacture was largely a seasonal activity, following an inverse pattern to the seasonal demand for labour in agriculture. An analysis of 148 supra inventories which contained spinning wheels, looms or both, shows that 68 (46%) also listed yarn. However, if the inventories are divided by season, whilst 20 out of 58 inventories (34%) drawn up between May and June and between August and October inclusive contained yarn, the proportion for the remaining months rose to 48 out of 90 (53%).[111] This pattern suggests that, whilst clothmaking still continued in some households during haymaking and harvesting, production was at higher levels during the rest of the year. Our evidence broadly confirms the seasonal pattern in clothmaking found by Dickinson in his study of the cloth industry in the West

Riding during the eighteenth century,[112] and slightly modifies Mendels' hypothesis that weaving and spinning were winter activities, whilst agriculture was pursed for the rest of the year.[113] The conclusion that agriculture and industry were inextricably linked in many households supports the research done by Lowe on the sixteenth-century Lancashire textile industry, and by Heaton, Crump and Dickinson on the cloth industry in the West Riding.[114] Heaton found that the term 'yeoman' was often only an alias for 'clothier'.[115] Crump too noted the example of Christopher Hall of Bingley parish, who was described as a yeoman in his will and a clothier in the inventory.[116] Similarly, in Colne parish, John Hargreaves of Monkroyd was described as a yeoman in a will proved at Chester,[117] but as a clothier in a virtually identical will of the same date proved at York.[118] Clearly, the dividing line between classifying a person as clothier or yeoman was an extremely hazy one, and perhaps one should use the term 'yeoman-clothier', as Crump argued.[119]

Thus far, we have been discussing households which owned clothmaking instruments and produced the cloth themselves. However, there was another group of clothmakers who did not manufacture textiles for their own benefit, but who worked as paid employees in the households of others. This might take the form of an apprenticeship, or alternatively, service on a daily or longer-term, perhaps annual, basis.

In 1626, the wage for spinning a stone of wool for kerseys in north-east Lancashire was 2s 8d.[120] Since one spinner could work through half a stone of wool in a six-day working week this implies that the daily wage was just 2·67d.[121] Wages for spinning seem to have remained largely static during the period from the 1580s to the 1630s; for example, the rate for spinning one stone of wool for blankets remained at 2s.[122] The low level of payment for spinning presumably reflected the large amounts of female and child labour involved.[123]

Weaving was far more remunerative. Kersey weavers were paid at the rate of 3d a yard in the 1620s and 1630s, according to the accounts of the Walmsleys of Dunkenhalgh.[124] On the basis that one weaver could produce a kersey 18 yards in length in a six-day working week, this converts to a daily wage of 9d.[125] However, since these wage rates have been derived from gentry accounts, they are unlikely to be typical of weavers' wages generally, since the gentry could afford to hire the best weavers to make cloth for their own use, and probably rewarded higher standards of workmanship with higher wages. In the West Riding of Yorkshire, kersey weavers were paid 2s 1d weekly at most in 1588 and 1638.[126] Normal wage rates for adjacent north-east Lancashire are unlikely to have been very different.

Attempts to calculate the relative costs of raw materials, labour, credit and transportation in the price of a kersey are fraught with difficulties. We do not have sufficiently reliable information on the quality of the wool used, and hence its cost, the extent of hired as opposed to family labour, or the quality and price of a finished kersey. For example, in a lawsuit of 1575, George Folds said that he had sold raw kerseys for 20s, 26s 8d and 13s 4d 'according as they were of goodness'.[127] Clearly, with such wide variations possible, even in the quality of raw kerseys, an estimate of profit levels in kersey production becomes highly speculative. Nevertheless, if we take the price of wool, given an inventory of 1575, of 6s 8d a stone,[128] and since two stones of wool were required to produce a kersey,[129] we can see that labour earned 13s 4d, 6s 8d, or nothing at all, depending on which price for a raw kersey we choose. On the basis of five people producing one raw kersey in six days[130] daily remuneration each would be 2.67d, 5.3d or nothing. Such low rates of payment are fully consistent with the levels of poverty found amongst *infra* weavers, who produced cloth for their own benefit, but who did not possess significant agricultural assets.[131]

(g) *The finishing processes*   Although Colne had possessed a fulling mill from at least as early as 1295,[132] according to a claim made in a lawsuit of 1575, 'there neither now is nor of long time hath been any good fulling mills within three or four miles or more of the said parish of Colne', and therefore Colne kersey manufacturers 'were and of long time have been forced and constrained to their great charges to carry the said raw pieces into Heptonstall parish, being in Yorkshire and near adjoining to the aforesaid parish of Colne, to certain fulling mills . . .'[133] Witnesses claimed that 'great loss' would be sustained if local mills were used.[134] In 1617, it was alleged that the fulling mill at Colne had been previously decayed, but was now repaired again.[135] A fulling mill had also been built at Parkhill in Barrowford by this time, which was owned by Henry and Robert Bannister, according to an inquisition post mortem of 1616.[136]

Nevertheless, we should not exaggerate the problems of fulling in the Colne area. We have no evidence to suggest that the fulling mill rents were ever unpaid during the period 1529–1640, when Colne fulling mill (and the corn mill) were leased to the Towneley family.[137] Indeed, a clothier Henry Parker of Colne parish stated in the above case of 1575, that grey, black and white kerseys, made by him and his father, had been 'milled, scoured and thicked', and then sold within Lancashire (though he also claimed to have sold kerseys raw within Lancashire as well as raw and finished kerseys outside Lancashire).[138] It is probable that Colne cloth designed for the London or export market was finished at the superior Yorkshire mills, whilst those cloths intended for domestic or local use, were fulled in the Colne area.

After fulling, the cloth was then sheared. This might be done by the manufacturer on the premises. For example, a Colne man named John College, who was described as a clothworker, owned four pairs of clothworker's shears in 1639, but he was also involved in cloth production, for he had one piece in the looms.[139] Alternatively, a specialist shearer might be employed. Henry Whittaker, a yeoman of Great Marsden, was owed 45s at his death in 1606 by John Shackleton of Colne, out of which Henry owed him for dressing 14 yards of cloth.[140] Tentering was the next process to be undertaken, which was necessary to stretch the cloth after fulling, to enable it to recover its shape. An Act of Parliament was passed in 1597 which, in an attempt to curtail excessive stretching, prohibited the use of tenters.[141] Further consideration of this episode is given in the next section, when we look at the problems of marketing Lancashire cloth.[142] The ban was lifted in 1623, when an Act was passed permitting a limited amount of stretching.[143] John College was thus legally entitled to own his four pairs of tenters in 1639.[144]

Dyeing cloth might be performed at different points in the clothmaking process.[145] As already noted, many kerseys were sold 'in the white' (undyed).[146] Nevertheless, some cloth produced locally was dyed. John College possessed eight 'blue list kerseys' in 1639,[147] and Henry Parker claimed in 1575 to have sold black kerseys, as well as white and grey.[148] However, it is unclear at what stage dyeing was usually undertaken. The Shuttleworth accounts indicate that dyeing might be performed after milling and dressing,[149] but also both wool and yarn might be dyed.[150] Locally, Christopher Bulcock, a husbandman of Stony Edge in Barrowford owned both black and red wool in 1628.[151] Some buildings were set aside for dyeing purposes. A building, part of which was used for dyeing, was leased in 1636 for nine years by a Colne dyer named George Hutchinson to Stephen Morvell of Colne, for an initial payment of £5 14s 0d, and an annual rent of $\frac{1}{2}d$ (and 2d rent annually to the Duchy).[152]

(h) *Marketing*   Since most of the clothmakers in this area operated independently and on a small scale, there was an obvious need for middlemen, not only to supply raw materials, but also to market the cloth. The best example of such a middleman is given in a lawsuit of 1638. Robert Walton of Gibhill in Marsden was provided with £60 working capital by Henry Walton (it is unclear whether they were related), in order to operate as a cloth factor; the profits were to be shared equally between them, and Henry agreed to underwrite half of Robert's losses. As a result of this, many clothmakers claimed that they had sold cloths to Robert weekly, some for ready money, but mostly on trust. Previously, Robert had been a servant, of no great esteem amongst his neighbours, but the £60 increased his credit and enabled him to trade as a factor. However, when Robert fell heavily into debt, Henry refused to underwrite his losses, and claimed that Robert had been dismissed as his factor some time previously. Robert traded for nearly two years, from April 1635 until Christmas 1636, selling many of his cloths in Halifax.[153]

Other factors ventured further afield in selling kerseys. A clothier named Robert Shaw of Colne made his living by driving horses loaded with kerseys, cloths and cottons to London, Bury St Edmunds and other places in Suffolk, Essex, Cambridge and other shires, according to a lawsuit of c.1571.[154] Some took their own cloths to distant markets as well as those of others', and were thus directly involved in both production and marketing. For example, Henry Rycroft, a clothier of Colne, had his own cloths and those of others milled in Heptonstall in the West Riding, and afterwards sold them in London.[155]

The primary markets for Colne cloth seem to have centred on two areas: Yorkshire, especially the West Riding towns of Halifax and Heptonstall, where kerseys were also produced in large numbers,[156] and secondly, London and its environs. In a Chancery lawsuit of 1540, it was claimed that John Bannister of Haddershelf in the parish of Halifax had purchased cloth valued at £31 from Christopher Mitchell of Colne.[157] Wills and inventories illustrate some of these transactions with West Riding men. William Whittaker of Halifax owed £16 for cloth to William Holt, a clothier of Colne, in 1610.[158] Some Colne cloths were not only finished in Heptonstall, but were also sold there; James Staveley of Heptonstall owed £4 5s od for cloth to a yeoman James Parker of Wheatley Booth in Pendle in 1592.[159] Other cloth found its way to York, for in 1611, a yeoman named Robert Hodgson of Hunterholme in Pendle was owed £7 5s od for cloth by Henry Farrer, who had then sold it to a man named Dickinson of York.[160] Some cloth was certainly taken to London for sale. The examples of the Colne clothiers, Robert Shaw and Henry Rycroft, who were trading in London in the 1570s, have already been quoted.[161] Further evidence of Colne's involvement in the cloth trade with London has been found by an analysis of the lists of provincial clothmakers fined at Blackwell Hall for infringements of the clothing statutes;[162] of a total of 5,426 fines recorded in the Exchequer Memoranda Rolls between 1550 and 1585, only 264 (4·9%) came from Lancashire. Indeed, only three are identifiably from Colne, the earliest being in 1565.[163] Most of the Lancashire clothiers fined came from the south-east of the county, notably Manchester (112 fines) and Bolton (58 fines).[164] If we assume that the proportion of clothiers from a particularly county fined for putting up for sale defective cloths (compared with the total fined) is likely to reflect the geographical distribution of clothiers selling cloth at Blackwell Hall, these figures suggest that, although a considerable number of Lancashire clothiers were making the roughly 200 mile journey from Lancashire to London between 1550 and 1585, very few of these were from the Colne area.

Colne, however, continued to maintain its links with London. William Hargreaves, a clothier of Wycoller in Trawden, was owed £100, £9 13s od an £8 by three citizens of London at his death in 1598, presumably for cloth.[165] By the mid seventeenth century, some Colne clothiers had their own permanent factors in London. In 1649, Thomas Barcroft gentlemen had a factor in London called John Roberts, who came from Marsden. Roberts was allowed 6d by Barcroft for every kersey which he sold. On one occasion, Barcroft sent 22 kerseys which were valued at £55 and carried by a man named John Smith. Ten packs were sent on another occasion, but problems ensued when Roberts allegedly withheld £60 from Barcroft.[166] Clearly, it was not easy to maintain control over a factor at such a distance. Lawrence Smith was another factor in London working for a clothier from the Colne area, for he sold cloth on behalf of Mr. Ambrose Barcroft of Foulridge, and also bought wool for him in 1654.[167]

Many Lancashire kerseys were exported. A list of exports in 1594 included 30,000 pieces of 'new devised kerseys' from Lancashire,[168] which, as already indicated, must have originated in the north-east of the county.[169] Northern kerseys were exported largely to the Baltic, Germany, Hungary, the United Provinces and France.[170] The fortunes of this export trade will be discussed later when we examine change over time in cloth production.[171]

If one theme predominates in a study of Lancashire textiles during this period, it is that of the poor quality of the cloths manufactured, which was of crucial importance in determining and limiting the areas for marketing. Leake's criticisms of northern cloth in 1577 are well known; he highlighted in particular the use of flocks, chalk and false ointments, poor dyeing, and stretching and straining resulting in cloth shrinking when wet.[172] Colne clothiers were fined for various clothmaking offences at Blackwell Hall. In 1565, Harry Shaw forfeited 8s for putting up for sale a grey kersey which was flocked. In 1579, Harry Emott tried to sell a white kersey of insufficient length, and was fined 10s, whilst in 1580, Thomas Lacy was fined 10s for putting up for sale two white kerseys which were underweight.[173]

The issue of excessive stretching of northern cloths and kerseys was one which caused many complaints from foreign buyers. The government appreciated that, in the long run, this was likely to lead to a decline in the demand for English cloth overseas, and the Act of Parliament was passed in 1597 ordering the removal of all tenters on the north side of the Trent.[174] The French followed this up with an edict in 1600 that English cloth imported into France was to be confiscated if it had been tentered or stretched, made of two wools, rowed, cockled or stuffed with flocks.[175] Nevertheless, the Lancashire Justices were reported to be neglecting their duty in enforcing the statute,[176] for they realised that tentering was necessary in order to allow the cloth to recover its shape after fulling. For this reason, the Act was relaxed in 1601.[177] The Privy Council decreed, however, that no tenters were to be used for Lancashire kerseys which were sold as northern kerseys, other than the type used in Yorkshire. It was stated that kerseys and all cloth made in Lancashire, and sold under the name of Yorkshire cloth, were to be made as in Yorkshire, so that one should not hurt the other.[178] This clearly implies that Lancashire northern kerseys were seen to be of a lower standard to those made in Yorkshire. In May 1601, the statute was reimposed, due to confiscation of English cloth by the French on the grounds that imported cloths were shrinking after being immersed in water.[179] Two months later, James Hargreaves of Barrowford in Pendle was prosecuted at Quarter Sessions because he 'took out the pins outside his tenters and so allowed the lower bar to go at large, contrary to the order of the overseers'.[180] However, it seems that this Act was not rigorously enforced in Lancashire after 1601, just as it had not been enforced in the years before 1601.[181] The French lifted their ban on the import of English cloth stretched on tenters in 1606,[182] and an Act was passed in 1623 permitting a limited amount of stretching by tenters.[183] Nevertheless, this issue resurfaced in the 1630s, for Poland issued an edict in 1637 prohibiting the importation of stretched English cloth.[184] The poor quality of Lancashire kerseys was of fundamental importance in helping to precipitate the depression in kersey exports in the 1620s and 1630s, a theme to which we shall turn in the next section.[185]

CHANGE OVER TIME IN THE CLOTH INDUSTRY

(a) *Expansion and depression in the cloth industry, 1558–1640*   In the last section the structure of the cloth industry was examined from an essentially static perspective. We now turn to the dynamics of cloth production to see how the local textile industry changed over time.

An analysis of the presence of clothmaking instruments – cards, combs, spinning wheels and looms – in *supra* probate inventories of testators from this area, is extremely informative about the levels of cloth production and its geographical pattern.[186]

The most fundamental conclusion to be drawn from Table 6.1 is

Table 6.1   Clothmaking instruments in supra *inventories from Colne chapelry and Pendle forest, 1558–1640*

Area	Cards or combs		Spinning wheels		Looms	
	No.	%	No.	%	No.	%
Colne chapelry (excluding Barrowford)	50/118	42	63/120	53	58/117	50
North-east Pendle forest (Barrowford and Roughlee)	23/44	52	27/44	61	26/44	59
Rest of Pendle forest	30/57	53	29/56	52	12/56	21
Total	103/219	47	119/220	54	96/217	44

the exceptionally high incidence of clothmaking revealed, with 47% of testators owning cards or combs, 54% spinning wheels and 44% looms. Altogether, 70% of testators (155 out of 221 inventories) owned at least one of these instruments of textile production.[187] Secondly, it is extremely noticeable that, whilst the proportion of testators with cards, combs and spinning wheels was roughly similar in all three sub-areas, the proportion with looms was far higher in Colne chapelry and north-east Pendle forest than it was in the rest of Pendle forest.[188] The reasons for this stark contrast in the incidence of weaving between sub-areas within Pendle forest will be discussed later.[189] However, it was clearly necessary to extract the inventories from the rest of Pendle forest for an analysis of change over time in the incidence of weaving, since to include them in the total sample would be to aggregate the experience of two quite different areas, thereby producing a picture typical of neither area.

Table 6.2   Clothmaking instruments in supra inventories from Colne chapelry and Pendle forest, by sub-period, 1558–1640

| | Colne chapelry + Pendle forest | | | | Colne chapelry + Roughlee in Pendle | | Rest of Pendle | |
| | Cards or combs | | Spinning wheels | | Looms | | Looms | |
Period	No.	%	No.	%	No.	%	No.	%
1558–1600	25/61	41	27/61	44	23/46	50	3/14	21
1601–1620	55/94	59	63/95	66	37/68	54	3/25	12
1621–1640	23/64	36	29/64	45	24/47	51	6/17	35
Total	103/219	47	119/220	54	84/161	52	12/56	21

The proportion of *supra* testators with cards, combs and spinning wheels rose substantially in the period 1601–20, and then fell to roughly the pre-1600 level in the 1620s and 1630s. Similarly, the proportion with looms in Colne chapelry and Roughlee followed the same pattern, though the fluctuations were far less marked. We would not expect the proportion of testators with looms to fluctuate to the same extent as that with cards, combs and spinning wheels. Nevertheless, it should be noted that the extent of the fall in the proportion of Colne chapelry and Roughlee testators with looms in the 1620s and 1630s is hidden by an increase in the proportion of the sample from Trawden forest, most of whom possessed looms in this period. If the Trawden testators are removed, the fall in the proportion with looms from Colne chapelry and Roughlee is from 56% (1601–20) to 46% (1621–40).[190] The fluctuations in the proportion of testators with looms in the rest of Pendle forest followed a puzzling inverse pattern to the other areas in the sample. However, the small number of inventories available for this area for each sub-period, and the much lower level of weaving activity in this area compared with the incidence of looms in inventories from Colne chapelry and Roughlee (thus making random fluctuations in such a small sample more significant), suggest that these figures should not be relied upon too heavily.

A small number of *infra* inventories has also survived for the period from 1601 to 1621, and these confirm the importance of clothmaking in this area. Approximately a quarter of testators owned cards or combs, and nearly a half possessed spinning wheels. Just over a quarter of the inventories from Colne chapelry and Roughlee recorded looms.[191] It should be noted that some of these inventories belonged to poor women, who were not likely to own all instruments of cloth production, particularly not looms. If these are removed from the sample for Colne and north-east Pendle, over a third of the inventories contained looms.[192]

For comparative purposes, all of the *supra* and *infra* inventories from the adjacent chapelries of Burnley and Padiham (excluding Pendle forest) and from Whalley, Clitheroe and Downham have been examined. The *supra* sample from Burnley and Padiham suggests that the structure of clothmaking was similar to that of the rest of Pendle forest. Over a half of the inventories recorded cards, combs and spinning wheels, but less than a quarter listed looms.[193] In the *infra* sample, slightly over half of the inventories contained cards, combs and spinning wheels, but none recorded looms.[194]

The extent of clothmaking in the Ribble valley chapelries of Whalley, Clitheroe and Downham contrasts strongly with that in Colne, Newchurch in Pendle, Burnley and Padiham chapelries. Only 12% of *supra* testators owned cards or combs, 23% possessed spinning wheels and just 7% had looms.[195] None of the *infra* testators from this area owned cards, combs or looms, and 15% possessed spinning wheels.[196] Clearly, cloth production in the Ribble valley was at a very low level. Good arable land and a more labour-intensive economy removed the need for extensive dependence on textile by-employments.[197]

Putting north-east Lancashire in a wider geographical setting helps to emphasise the importance of the cloth industry in the local economy. For example, in a sample of 60 testators from the Bradford area of the West Riding of Yorkshire between 1600 and 1646, 10 possessed cards or combs (17%), 20 to 23 had spinning wheels (33% to 38%) and 19 owned looms (32%). In Devon, just 21 inventories out of 266 dated between 1531 and 1699 contained looms (8%). In Oxfordshire between 1550 and 1590, only 50 testators out of 259 (19%) possessed spinning wheels.[198] However, one caveat must be stressed. If putting-out were practised, cloth instruments would usually be found amongst the poorer sections of society, who tended not to leave inventories in great numbers.[199] We have already noted examples of putting-out from the Bradford wills and inventories.[200] Thus, the relative absence of cloth instruments in the Bradford area was probably due to the practice of putting-out, for we know that this was a flourishing cloth-producing area.[201]

The technique of discerning changes in the extent of textile production by calculating the proportion of inventories with clothmaking instruments has also been used by Mendels in a study of late seventeenth- and eighteenth-century Flanders. He found that a steadily increasing proportion of inventoried households owned spinning wheels and handlooms.[202] Similarly, Skipp noted that the percentage of inventoried households of below average wealth involved in carding and spinning in the forest of Arden increased from 33% (1530–69), to 60% (1570–1609), and to 62% (1610–49).[203]

(b) *Expansion and depression – evidence from inventory analysis* Whilst inventories represent a particularly informative source for the economic historian, it is necessary to examine possible pitfalls in their use, both in the foregoing analysis and in more general terms, in order to verify our conclusions.

First, we must remember that our analysis is based on a relatively small number of inventories. Clearly, when one is dealing with only 46 or 47 inventories (as in the case of the samples for the presence of looms in Colne chapelry and Roughlee, 1558–1600 and 1621–40), the reliability of statistics for percentage change is lessened, particularly when the small margin of change is noted. Indeed, the samples for looms in the rest of Pendle forest (14, 25 and 17 inventories respectively for the three main sub-periods) are much

too small as a basis for the calculation of percentage change.[204]
Nevertheless, the extremely large increases revealed in the samples
for the proportion of households with cards or combs and with
spinning wheels in the whole area 1601–20, compared with the
period 1558–1600 (an additional 18% and 22% of households
possessed these instruments) and the equally striking fall 1621–40
(23% and 21% respectively) are much too great to be accounted for
by random fluctations. Furthermore, these samples are sufficiently
large for us to be reasonably confident about the reliability of the
statistics produced for proportionate change.[205]

Secondly, a more telling criticism is that we cannot tell from the
mere presence of clothmaking instruments whether or not they were
being used, or had been employed in the recent past. One can state
with reasonable confidence that the absence of such tools in an
inventory suggests that cloth production was not being undertaken
in that household (though this does not discount the possibility that
some members of such households participated in cloth production
in other households). Nevertheless, we cannot deduce conclusively
from simply the presence of clothmaking instruments, whether they
were being used, or if they were being employed, how intensively
they were operated. One way around this problem is to note the
presence of yarn in households possessing looms. Of 95 *supra*
inventories containing looms, no less than 58 (61%) listed yarn.[206]
If we note the seasonal pattern to clothmaking discussed earlier,[207]
and also the fact that some households which were involved in
weaving woollen cloth would not necessarily possess yarn at the time
of the drawing up of the inventory,[208] then the inference is strong
that the vast majority of clothmaking instruments which were
recorded in inventories were being used. However, it must be
remembered that there is a lagged response to change in any
analysis based on inventories, since we have to wait for deaths before
such change becomes apparent, and therefore we ought to antedate
by a few years the changes which we have observed.[209]

Our argument is reinforced when we consider the durability of
cloth instruments. Cards, as discussed earlier required frequent
renewal if carding was to be done properly.[210] We have no evidence as
to how durable spinning wheels were, but looms might remain in use
for up to sixty years.[211] Nevertheless, whilst not being inordinately
expensive, looms represented a considerable capital outlay,[212] and
might therefore be disposed of by sale or loan if no longer required.
Thus a labourer, John Whitehead of Little Marsden, had a pair of

woollen looms recorded in his inventory in 1618, which stood in the house of John Duckworth of Lynroyd, and which were presumably there on loan.[213] Individual households clearly disposed of cloth instruments, or did not renew them when they became damaged or inherited by another household, if they were no longer required. Henry Mangnolls, a yeoman of Townhouse in Great Marsden, possessed cards, combs and spinning wheels valued at 13s 4d and two pairs of looms at his death in 1597. He was obviously involved in woollen cloth manufacture, for he owned yarn valued at 30s and seven kerseys and unshapen cloth.[214] In 1624, his son and heir John Mangnolls possessed no looms at all and only cards and spinning wheels worth 3s.[215] Indeed, the huge decline in the proportion of households with cards, combs and spinning wheels in the 1620s and 1630s[216] is the strongest evidence that households did not continue to possess cloth instruments when they were no longer needed, and by implication supports the hypothesis that the rise in the proportion of households owning clothmaking tools in the 1600s and 1610s reflects a genuine increase in the incidence of clothmaking activity, and was not simply because households always retained their instruments.

Thirdly, there are a number of problems inherent in any analysis of inventories, whether for the purposes described above or not. There are essentially three questions we must ask. In the first place, to what extent do the goods in inventories accurately reflect the wealth of the deceased? Second, are the inventories which have survived typical of those which were made? Last, do inventories consistently represent a cross-section of the community, or are they biassed towards a particular section of society?

First, it is essential to realise that inventories relate to personal estate and not to real estate. Whilst they record goods, leases of land, debts and credits, they do not record lands in entail,[217] and can therefore be misleading as a guide to total wealth.[218] Moreover, the debts and credits of a testator are not always listed in an inventory, or quite often credits owed to the deceased are recorded, but not the debts which he owed.[219] Thus it is necessary to include the debts and credits referred to in the will, to obtain a more accurate picture of the total value of the testator's personal estate.[220] Problems obviously arise if the will was drawn up a long time before the inventory (but this is uncommon),[221] or if the will has been lost, and the inventory does not record debts or credits, or credits only.[222] In any case, it is unclear whether many of these debts were recoverable[223] for the habit of classifying some debts as 'desperate', if they were unlikely to be repaid, was practised in some areas[224] but apparently not in the Colne district.

There is also the problem of to what extent goods were deliberately omitted from an inventory, or undervalued. It was alleged in a lawsuit of 1606 that much gold and silver had not been included in the inventories of the Hargreaves family of Higham in Pendle forest.[225] Similarly in 1633, the Duchy Court declared that the goods in the inventories of Lawrence and Richard Towneley were greatly under-valued, with many things omitted.[226] The motive for omission or undervaluation was obviously to minimise probate charges, but it is unlikely that this occurred on a significant scale in the recording of cloth instruments, since it would be easier to minimise the valuation of an inventory by omitting more expensive items (such as large stocks of money, livestock or crops). With regard to the reliability of prices, Bagley argues that there is little evidence that Lancashire executors deliberately under-estimated prices when assessing for probate, and claims that prices in inventories compare reasonably with retail prices in accounts, particularly when we make allowances for the wide variations in quality possible.[227]

The earliest surviving inventory from this area appears to be for 1558.[228] Wills and inventories for the period before 1541, when the district formed part of the diocese of Coventry and Lichfield, have unfortunately been lost.[229] Of the wills or inventories of testators from this area (which are catalogued in the indices for wills proved at Chester), 21 appear to have been mislaid, and 35 surviving wills do not have inventories with them.[230] Furthermore, the *infra* wills and inventories have survived in just a few cases, and only for the period 1601–21.[231] The inventories for those with 'bona notabilia' (i.e. personal estate valued at more than £5) in more than one diocese in the northern province, were proved in the Prerogative Court at York, but only those from the very late seventeenth century onwards have survived.[232] This is particularly disappointing, for as the Colne district bordered on Yorkshire, several people from this area with property in Yorkshire too had their wills proved before the Prerogative Court. For Colne chapelry and Pendle forest, 79 wills are extant 1597–1640 in the records of the Prerogative Court.[233] Thus whilst few inventories for the very poor have survived, those for many of the richer testators with property in Yorkshire as well as in Lancashire have not survived at all for our period, and therefore it seems that our sample of *supra* inventories represents the 'middling sort' of those who left inventories.

But to what extent do inventories fairly reflect the community as a whole? Since, by definition, inventories were drawn up just after death, they tend to represent the middle-aged and old. They are also representative mainly of males, for married women only made wills in exceptional circumstances, and thus the wills and inventories of women belong to widows and spinsters.[234] Inventories are also biassed against the very poor, for those with less than £5 in personal estate, were not obliged to make a will, and hence might leave no inventory.[235] We have already noted the small number of *infra* wills and inventories available, and conversely the absence of inventories for very rich testators whose wills were proved by the Prerogative Court of York. This bias towards the middle sections of a community has been noted for other areas.[236]

The *supra* sample of inventories gives the following occupational descriptions for males; of 173 inventories where the occupation was stated, 5 (2·9%) were described as gentry, 102 (59·0%) as yeomen, 36 (20·8%) as husbandmen, 8 (4·6%) as clothiers, 3 (1·7%) as weavers and clothworkers, 1 (0·6%) as labourer, and 18 (10·4%) as craftsmen and other occupations.[237] It is particularly clear when comparison is made with occupational information derived from parish registers and quarter sessions, that the yeomen are disproportionately over-represented and the husbandmen greatly under-represented.[238]

However, the groups represented in the *supra* sample changed over time, since price inflation[239] meant that increasingly, more testators would have had personal estate worth at least £40. This effect can be observed by noting the rising number of husbandmen's inventories available over time. During the period from 1558 to 1600, only 17% of males whose occupations were given were described as husbandmen; this proportion rose to 21% between 1601 and 1620, and increased to 24% during the period from 1621 until 1640.[240] This does not undermine our hypothesis that possession of cloth instruments amongst middling households became more common in the 1600s and 1610s, for we shall show that testators of all levels of personal estate were far more likely to possess these tools during this period.[241] Though *infra* testators were involved in cloth production to a considerable extent, they were less likely to own cards, combs, spinning wheels and looms than were *supra* testators in the 1600s and 1610s.[242] Thus it cannot be shown that the increase in the proportion of households with cloth instruments was due to poorer households 'swamping' the sample in the 1600s and 1610s. Moreover, the effect of inflation in changing the structure of the *supra* sample should not be exaggerated, for the above analysis of the proportion of inventories belonging to husbandmen does not support the notion that the character of the sample was changing significantly.

There is another aspect to consider in our analysis. We must not assume that a testator's position revealed by an inventory was necessarily typical of his economic activities during most of his life, or indeed that it represented the peak of his career.[243] Demographic variables, such as mean ages at death and at marriage, governed the length of time as head of the household and the period available for the accumulation of wealth, whilst the average size of the family and the stage of its life cycle, thereby altering the ratio of producers to dependents, clearly affected its economic fortunes. Inheritance customs too played a crucial part, for if the testator had retired or had recently bestowed substantial dowries or portions on his children, this would obviously reduce the level of his personal estate. The varying demands of the Crown as landlord, particularly with regard to the composition payments in the early seventeenth century, must have influenced the level of personal estate in the inventories of this period. Finally, agricultural factors, such as the relative productivity of one holding compared with another, whether the inventory had been drawn up immediately following or during a period of dearth or plenty, or one of animal disease, and above all the season (in particular, whether pre- or post-harvest or whether before or after sales of livestock), must have played an important part in determining the level of personal estate.

Thus, for all the above reasons, it would be dangerous to follow Lowe's methodology of dividing the inventories containing looms into 'lower', 'middle' and 'upper' class weavers and clothiers simply on the basis of the level of personal estate.[244] It would be equally dangerous to argue, as Brigg has done, that the wills and inventories of Pendle forest in the seventeenth century show that, in contrast to the picture presented by the witch trial of 1612, this was an 'industrious and prosperous community'.[245]

However, bearing in mind the reservations expressed above, it does seem justified to conclude that the incidence of clothmaking became more pronounced in the 1600s and 1610s and then fell back to its pre-1600 level in the 1620s and 1630s. Clothmaking was clearly a ubiquitous activity found amongst all levels of society. If we were tracing fluctuations in the incidence of a very small scale activity, then it would be impossible to do so from just over two hundred inventories. By contrast, we are measuring an activity which was common in all periods, but which became exceptionally pronounced in the 1600s and 1610s.

(c) *Other evidence*   There is other crucial evidence of a rise and decline in northern kersey production during this period. This is provided largely by export statistics for northern kerseys. Kerseys were also produced in other northern areas, notably in the Halifax area of the West Riding.[246] The importance of the export trade for the Halifax district can be illustrated by a statement in a lawsuit of 1638, where it was claimed by the keeper of the Halifax ulnage seals that 80,000 kerseys were manufactured annually in Yorkshire, of which 60,000 were for export via York, Hull, Newcastle, Chester, London and other ports.[247] We have no equivalent information for the Colne area, but as we have already shown, the Colne district seems to have been an adjunct of the Halifax area in terms of its reliance on West Riding supplies of raw materials and facilities for finishing cloth.[248] There is also much evidence that many Colne kerseys were sold in bulk in Halifax,[249] and thus it is extremely likely that some of these were exported together with other northern kerseys.[250]

Historians are generally agreed that the years immediately before the Cockayne Project of 1614 were prosperous ones for the cloth trade.[251] This certainly seems true of the northern kersey industry. Kerseys were cheap,[252] and were therefore in demand by a rising population at home, but it is in the sphere of exports that this expansion can best be measured. During the period from 1562 to 1580, an annual average of 2,983 kerseys were exported to the Baltic in English vessels, according to the Danish Sound records. This average rose to 12,645 kerseys between 1581 and 1600 (or 7,926 if the peak years of 1586–7 and 1598–1600 are excluded).[253] Data are available from English port books for the very early seventeenth century; the port book of Hull records a total of 39,470 northern kerseys exported in 1609,[254] and 46,017½ in 1614.[255]

We should certainly be aware of the deficiencies in the sources from which the data have been extracted. The Sound toll records are known to be particularly unreliable before 1618,[256] but, as Davis argues, whilst the data for any particular year cannot be relied upon, we may justifiably use these registers to illustrate the rate of change of cloth exports to the Baltic.[257] The port books seem a more reliable guide to exports for particular years, since the low duties on cloth and its bulk made smuggling unprofitable and difficult. Furthermore, there is no evidence during the period 1600–40 that the incidence of corruption in the customs service varied a great deal.[258] Thus, it seems indisputable that the export of northern kerseys increased significantly during the late sixteenth and very early seventeenth centuries, and it is highly likely that kerseys from the Colne area contributed to this expansion.

The evidence for a decline in northern kersey exports during the 1620s and 1630s is equally striking. According to the Sound toll records, English kersey exports to the Baltic in 1625 stood at 36,949; in 1635, they had fallen to just 17,966, and by 1646 to 6,069.[259] This same pattern is observable in the Hull port books, which show that 32,480 northern kerseys were exported to the Baltic in 1614, and only 13,742 in 1637. To a certain extent, Hull redirected its trade to the Low Countries, particularly Amsterdam, to compensate for the decline in the Baltic trade. Exports of northern kerseys from Hull to non-Baltic ports stood at 13,133 in 1614, but had risen to 20,613 in 1637.[260] Nevertheless, it is clear that this new area of increased trade did not compensate for the decline of the old, for Hull's total northern kersey exports before the Cockayne Project were far higher than subsequently.[261]

Much evidence of cloth depression is available in Lancashire. The situation in 1622 was extremely grave when the Bishop of Chester and J.P.s of Lancashire wrote to the Privy Council with the results of an investigation. They reported that, having called before them local clothiers in order to suggest reasons and remedies for the decay of the cloth trade, they 'do by them find a great decay of the said trade, and the poor brought into great extremity for want of work therein'.[262] Secondly, as we observed earlier, the noticeable fall which occurred in the 1620s in the valuation of looms in inventories of the Colne district also suggests that the demand for looms was falling. In the period 1611–20, looms were valued at an average of 23s 4d each, but in the following two decades were worth only 17s 9d and 19s 7d respectively.[263]

There is other evidence of bad trading conditions in the northern cloth trade. John Prowde, speaking on behalf of the Shrewsbury Drapers, claimed that even northern cloth, which was at least 10% cheaper than that of the Drapers', was 'at a stand' in 1621.[264] Indeed, in March 1622, whilst the number of broadcloths left unsold at Blackwell Hall was comparatively low, 5,159 pieces of northern cloth, presumably dozens and kerseys, were unsold.[265] In the Colne area, the bankruptcy of Robert Walton of Great Marsden, who operated as a cloth factor for two years 1635–6, but who accumulated debts of over £50, may have been due simply to bad business management, but the claim that Walton had sold cloths in Halifax for less than he paid for them, and the scale of his debts, suggests that he may have been experiencing difficulties in selling kerseys profitably at a time of depression in the cloth trade.[266]

It should always be remembered that we do not possess information as to what proportion of northern kerseys which were exported originated in the Colne area. Nevertheless, it does seem extremely likely that the fortunes of Colne's kerseys were inextricably tied to those of Halifax and the West Riding.

(d) *The causes of the expansion in clothmaking*   The expansion in cloth production in Colne chapelry and Pendle forest, apparent by the first two decades of the seventeenth century, can be attributed to three main causes: first population growth; secondly, inflation of food prices against a background of largely static money wages; thirdly, parcellation of copyholds and inheritance provisions generally.

We have shown that the population was rising throughout this area, and extremely rapidly in Colne chapelry in particular.[267] This must have increased the local demand for kerseys, whilst growth of population throughout England and a fall in the purchasing power of wages[268] provided further opportunities for the expansion of cloth production, especially of cheaper kinds. Overseas sales of kerseys were also increasing rapidly in the late sixteenth and very early seventeenth centuries, particularly in years of bad harvests at home, when kerseys were exported in huge quantities to pay for imports of Baltic corn.[269]

Although a rising demand for kerseys both at home and abroad provides a necessary precondition for expansion of production, it is not a sufficient explanation for such an expansion. A rising local population not only created additional demand for textiles, but also exacerbated the pressure on existing agricultural resources, and increased the need for further employment opportunities. It has been noted that the numbers of the landless and virtually landless seem to have risen substantially.[270] This was particularly significant in a period of rising prices, notably of cereals, whilst money wages remained largely static.[271] For households not producing a surplus of agricultural products for the market this was especially serious, since they could not take advantage of rising food prices, but were obliged to buy much of their food requirements in the market with wages that failed to keep pace with prices. For such households, cloth manufacture was an essential feature of the family economy, as can be seen from the large numbers of *infra* testators engaged in this activity.[272]

Furthermore, the size of copyholds was falling substantially in Colne manor in the sixteenth century and initial years of the seventeenth century, and subdivision of holdings was also noteworthy in Barrowford and Roughlee during this period, though not significantly in the rest of Pendle forest.[273] This not only reduced the cultivable acreage per holding and the number of cattle which could be pastured on the holding over the winter, but also limited the number of beasts which might be pastured on the commons over the summer, where the size of a herd was stinted according to the amount of 'inland' a copyholder held.[274] Thus small copyholders required additional employment in order to supplement insufficient income from land. For example, Edmund Crook stated in a lawsuit of 1592 that he had gone to the household of another to learn the trade of a weaver; Edmund was still in his 'teens, and could look forward to an inheritance of only five acres of land in Old Laund, and a fifth share in a lease of eight acres for nine years in Fence, in Pendle forest.[275]

Since inheritance arrangements in this area were strongly biassed towards primogeniture,[276] this left many younger sons without land, and with limited capital. Moreover, with a rapidly rising population, there were many more younger sons who required an economic 'niche'. Thus it is not surprising that we should find examples of some younger sons turning to clothmaking for their living. Twelve bequests of looms have been discovered from the wills proved at Chester and York. Significantly, they all relate to the period 1587–1624, which is further testimony to the particular importance with which testators regarded their looms during this period. Two of these twelve testators bequeathed their looms to only sons, but all three who clearly had younger sons bequeathed their looms to them, rather than to the eldest son. In addition, one made a bequest of a loom to a nephew, whilst another testator left his loom to a brother; in both cases, the recipients were younger sons (and where the testators were apparently childless).[277]

A second aspect to the inheritance question is that of illegitimacy. It was noted that illegitimacy in this area was high in all periods, but increased considerably in the early seventeenth century, compared with the late sixteenth.[278] By canon, common and manorial law, a bastard had no automatic right of inheritance to land, and though some testators made special provisions for their bastards, others pointedly did not.[279] Many bastards therefore turned to cloth production, in order to make a living. Of eight 'Prerogative' and *supra* testators from this area who were clearly illegitimate, three were described as clothiers and one as a webster.[280]

However, not all bastards involved in cloth production remained poor. Henry Hargreaves alias Hall or Sonkey was a clothier from Barrowford who was described in a lawsuit of 1652 as a 'very rich and able man in estate' who lent large sums of money at interest, including £200 on one occasion.[281] It is interesting to note that, of Colne, Newchurch in Pendle, Burnley and Padiham chapelries, the chapelry which had the highest illegitimacy ratio – Colne[282] – was also the area most involved in weaving.[283] Similarly, illegitimacy seems to have been higher in north-east Pendle in the early seventeenth century than it was in the rest of the forest,[284] which

Table 6.3   Cloth manufacture correlated with wealth in supra *wills and inventories of males from Colne chapelry and Pendle forest, 1558–1640*

| Period | Colne chapelry + Pendle forest | | | | Colne chapelry + Roughlee | | Rest of Pendle forest | |
| | Cards or combs | | Spinning wheels | | Looms | | Looms | |
	No.	%	No.	%	No.	%	No.	%
1558–1600								
Below median	11/26	42	12/26	46	8/20	40	0/6	0
Above median	13/27	48	12/27	44	11/20	55	2/6	33
Total	24/53	45	24/53	45	19/40	48	2/12	17
1601–1620								
Below median	25/43	58	31/43	72	18/30	60	2/12	17
Above median	27/43	63	28/43	65	16/31	52	1/12	8
Total	52/86	60	59/86	69	34/61	56	3/24	13
1621–1640								
Below median	8/28	29	12/28	43	9/20	45	2/7	29
Above median	12/28	43	14/28	50	12/21	57	4/8	50
Total	20/56	36	26/56	46	21/41	51	6/15	40

again reinforces the above conclusion, since north-east Pendle was far more involved in weaving than was the rest of the forest.

However, the hypothesis that the expansion in the cloth industry was due simply to the increasing proportion of households on low levels of income which were forced to turn to clothmaking to supplement insufficient agricultural income, is disproved by an analysis correlating possession of cloth instruments with levels of personal wealth. (Table 6.3).[285]

The samples for each sub-period have been divided into below and above median sections, in order to combat the problem of inflation. It is clear that, in the period to 1600, testators with wealth levels below and above the median were equally likely to be participating in carding, combing and spinning, though below median testators were less likely to be engaged in weaving. In the 1600s and 1610s, both groups increased their carding, combing and spinning activities by similar proportions, and below median testators from Colne chapelry and Roughlee increased their weaving activities to a slightly higher level than the above median testators (who remained at the same level as pre 1600 in the proportion with looms). Thus, both richer and less prosperous households showed an equal propensity to participate in carding, combing and spinning in the whole period to 1620.

In a pastoral economy, opportunities for employment of women and children in agriculture were far more restricted than in an arable area,[286] and thus it seems that wives and children from households of all wealth levels participated in clothmaking to keep themselves gainfully employed. When the population rose, particularly in the 1600s and 1610s, this had two effects on the average household. First, it increased the number of children and unmarried adults per household, and secondly, over the period of the life-cycle of the average household, there would be some children and unmarried adults present for a longer period. Therefore, all groups represented by inventories increased their involvement in carding, combing and spinning, but the motive for doing so must have been due more to economic necessity in less prosperous households than it was in the more wealthy ones. Less prosperous households in Colne chapelry and Roughlee also increased their involvement in weaving, in response to declining income and reduced employment opportunities for males caused by subdivision of holdings.[287]

We have found that there seems to have been a noticeable change in the economic position of persons described as clothiers, 1601–20, compared with previously. The three *supra* clothiers' inventories, which have survived for pre-1600, record 35, 21 and 12 cattle respectively.[288] Thus it was entirely possible to be described as a clothier in the sixteenth century, and yet generate a high proportion of income from agriculture. On the other hand, the five *supra* clothiers whose inventories have survived for the period 1601–20 possessed only 9, 6, 6, 0 and 0 cattle each.[289] Those described as clothiers in the 1600s and 1610s were therefore far less likely to be heavily involved in cattle-raising than were their predecessors. It is regrettable that we do not have more clothiers' inventories available where the number of cattle is stated. Any conclusion based on only eight inventories must, at best, be extremely tentative. Nevertheless, it does seem that 'meaner' clothiers predominated in the 1600s and 1610s, which is a finding in line with demographic, agricultural and landholding developments already described.

(*e*) *The causes of the depression in clothmaking* The reasons for the depression in the cloth industry in this area in the 1620s and 1630s seem to be entirely exogeneous. This was hinted at earlier when we noted the substantial decline in sales of kerseys overseas, especially in the Baltic.[290]

The Cranfield correspondence shows that whilst many northern kerseys were exported to Hungary in the early seventeenth century, problems were developing. These were partly due to political instability and war (or the threat of it) against the Turks, which disrupted trade, and also because Hungary, Silesia and adjoining countries were learning to copy English kerseys, which they found to be too highly priced for the poor quality offered.[291] Thus, we find that there was a switch to the Baltic, as the main market for northern kerseys. In 1609, 71% of all kerseys shipped from Hull were destined for Elbing.[292] However, the number of kerseys exported to the Baltic dropped off sharply in the 1620s and 1630s, and a redirection of some kersey exports to the United Provinces did not compensate for this.[293]

The disastrous consequences of the Cockayne Project of 1614–17 for the export trade in cloth have been long recognised.[294] The prohibition on the export of white cloths was extremely serious for areas such as Colne, which produced many undyed kerseys for the export market.[295] Also well documented are the disruption of trade caused by the Thirty Years' War, and the trade depression following 1620.[296] Supple argues that monetary manipulation on the Continent was the chief factor in this crisis, since it led to a virtual devaluation of foreign currencies and highly unfavourable terms of trade, pricing English cloth out of the market.[297] This, together with rival production of cloth overseas and high customs duties on textiles were the reasons advanced for the export crisis by John Ramsden, an Eastland merchant. He said in 1621 or 1622, that the trade in the export of northern kerseys and other northern cloths into the Eastland, was 'much to be decayed in all places; both as to the vent, much less than in former years, and as to the prices, much abated in all the parts beyond the sea'. He claimed that manufacture of kerseys in Danzig and other areas in Prussia and Silesia, had caused a severe reduction in the number of English kerseys sold in the Eastland. In addition, customs payments at home and abroad amounted to 7s per kersey, and since kerseys cost about 30s in England and could not be sold for more than 33s 9d in the Eastland, merchants were losing money on exports. Ramsden claimed that prices could not be increased due to the 'extraordinary rising' of foreign money, and the competition from native cloth. Previously, considerable profits had been made when kerseys had been sold for 47s 3d each.[298]

It is certainly true that English kerseys were more expensive for Poles to buy than the Silesian version; one estimate put English kersey between 20% and 25% dearer than the Silesian equivalent,[299] and another estimated that English cloth cost between 4½ florins and 6 florins per ell, in contrast to that of Danzig at 2 florins per ell.[300] This was despite attempts by the English to reduce the prices of their kerseys to make them more competitive. Thus, a kersey was priced at 8 rikdollars in 1615, but only 7 rikdollars in 1625.[301] Such price reductions may have reduced producers' as well as merchants' profits to the point where kersey manufacture was no longer viable.[302]

The more prosperous testators in the Colne area withstood the effects of depression far more easily than did the poorer, as can be seen from Table 6.3.[303] The proportion of *supra* testators of above median wealth in Colne chapelry and Roughlee who possessed looms was roughly similar in the 1620s and 1630s compared with the period 1601–20, though cards, combs and spinning wheels were found far less frequently in above median inventories from the whole area. However, the proportion of below median testators with cloth instruments fell dramatically, cards or combs from 58% to 29%, spinning wheels from 72% to 43%, and looms in Colne chapelry and Roughlee from 60% to 45%. In Trawden forest, which as we have shown was by far the most prosperous area,[304] the textile depression seems not to have hit these richer testators, for 55% owned cards or combs and spinning wheels and 73% had looms in the 1620s and 1630s.[305] The reasons for this divergence are by no means clear. Richer families may have found it easier to keep stocks of cloth on their hands for longer periods, or to wait longer for payment. Poorer households may have found it less easy to obtain credit than their richer neighbours at a time of depression in the cloth trade. Above all, more prosperous households would have been better able both to sustain production of cloth on a lower rate of return for their capital, and to sell occasionally at a loss. Indeed, it was suggested in a lawsuit of 1638 that a cloth factor from Great Marsden might have had to sell cloth in Halifax at a loss.[306] Clearly, reduced profit was of far greater significance to poorer families, for which cloth production was the sole or main source of income, than it was to families which had substantial interests in agriculture, and for which cloth production was no more than a useful by-employment.

It is in the light of the depression in the cloth trade that we should consider the effects of the bad harvests of 1621–2 and the crisis mortality of 1623.[307] The cloth depression must have exacerbated this crisis, since poorer families especially would have had need of additional income at a time of harvest failure. Moreover, it was precisely at this time that textile production would be even more depressed, due to the increased proportion of the family budget spent on food, which thereby reduced further the demand for textiles.[308] Furthermore, the payment of twenty years' rent, as half of the composition demanded by the Crown from Colne manor tenants in 1618 for confirmation of their copyholds and certainty of entry fines and customs, and the new annual rent of 6d per acre of common, must have contributed still further to the crisis.[309] It was the conjunction of three unfavourable elements – harvest failure, depression in the cloth industry, and the exactions of the Crown (but above all the first two), which led to famine conditions in 1623. Not surprisingly, many left the area, as is indicated by a substantial decline in the number of marriages celebrated in Colne chapelry.[310]

(*f*) *Other evidence of the extent of cloth production*   We have shown that *supra* inventories are typical only of the middling sections of society.[311] *Infra* inventories exist in very small numbers, but confirm the importance of clothmaking for the poor of Colne chapelry and

Pendle forest.[312] We have other evidence, however, of the extent of involvement in textile manufacture, which has been derived from an analysis of occupations given in Quarter Sessions recognisance rolls between 1626 and 1642.[313] For Colne chapelry and Pendle forest, 16% of occupations relate to cloth manufacture (with 10% described as weavers). Since this sample includes Pendle forest, where, with the exception of Barrowford and Roughlee, the incidence of weaving was less than in the rest of the area,[314] these figures may underestimate the proportion of the population primarily concerned with cloth manufacture in Colne chapelry and Roughlee. Furthermore, this sample has been drawn during a period of textile depression,[315] so the proportion of the population who would have been described as cloth producers in the 1600s and 1610s, would probably have been greater.

The fact that 16% of the sample should have been described as cloth producers primarily, reinforces the impression that woollen cloth manufacture was of considerable importance not just as a by-employment, but as the main source of income for many. Indeed, when we recall that many of the other occupations, notably yeomen and husbandmen, were also engaged in clothmaking to a significant extent,[316] the conclusion is inescapable that cloth production was practised, as a primary activity or as a by-employment, by a very large proportion of the population.

If we compare the occupational structure of Colne chapelry and Pendle forest, with that from Burnley and Padiham chapelries (excluding Pendle forest), the relative predominance in cloth production of the former, strongly suggested by *supra* and *infra* inventories, is again confirmed. Only 9% of the sample from Burnley and Padiham were described as cloth producers[317] (compared with 16% in Colne and Pendle).

However, we should beware of treating these samples as a necessarily accurate guide to occupational structure, for there seems to be a slight bias, first, in favour of higher status groups, particularly gentry and yeomen who were more likely to be accepted as pledges for the good behaviour of another, and secondly, towards poorer groups who were more likely to be prosecuted for offences relating to bastardy and felony.[318]

The best evidence which we have relating to occupational structure is from Burnley chapelry, and has been obtained from the parish registers from 1653 to 1660,[319] The registers for Colne, Newchurch and Padiham do not give occupations, except in rare cases.[320] The data confirm the hypothesis that the gentry and yeomen are slightly over-represented in the Quarter Sessions sample,[321] but suggest that the proportion described as cloth producers in the Quarter Sessions sample (9%) is reasonably accurate, for 10% are described as such in the burial register, and 11% in the baptism register. The Burnley register evidence further confirms the reliability of the Quarter Sessions sample for Colne and Pendle as a rough guide to the proportion described as clothmakers.

Comparison of this evidence with other Lancashire and Yorkshire Commonwealth parish registers indicates that specialisation in the cloth industry had not proceeded as far in this area as in some others. In the Rochdale marriage register, 1653–7, 30% of occupations related directly to textiles, as did 31% in the Middleton marriage register during the same period, and 35% in the Radcliffe baptism register 1656–9.[322] In Halifax, at least 48% of the occupations of men married 1654–7 were associated with the production of cloth.[323] This contrast is not surprising, for we have shown that many clothmakers were also involved in agriculture to a large extent,[324] and that putting-out had not yet developed in the Colne area.[325] These were factors likely to restrain occupational specialisation.

CONCLUSION

We have noted that the structure of the cloth industry in the Colne area altered very little during our period. There was no discernible technological change in the way cloth was manufactured, nor in the types of fabric produced. Heaton found that in the West Riding during the early seventeenth century, clothiers started to produce new types of kersey of greater length than before and of higher quality, mainly in response to foreign competition;[326] Colne may have been affected by this development too, but the documents leave no trace of it.[327] However, it is certainly true that there was no wholesale changeover to fustians or linens, a development which can be observed in other areas of Lancashire.[328] Colne's clothmaking links were firmly attached to the West Riding, and it is therefore not surprising that its textile history followed very closely that of Halifax, rather than the rest of Lancashire. Thus by 1720, a variety of worsted articles were being produced in the Colne area, including shalloons, ranters, perpets, tammies and serges,[329] which represented a diversification of cloth production along the lines followed in the West Riding.[330]

Furthermore, the economic organisation of the industry remained essentially the same, namely independent but small-scale producers who earned their livelihood by a combination of agriculture and industry, the putting-out system being noticeably absent. This structure was unlikely to change so long as producers had access to supplies of raw materials through wool broggers, and so long as the fixed and circulating capital required was small. Worsted manufacture was inherently more capitalistic due to the larger amount of capital required initially, and the higher element of risk.[331] The worsted manufacturers could afford to finance production on a scale large enough to make adoption of the putting-out system profitable, despite its inherent problems due to lack of supervision, greater transportation costs and the danger of embezzlement of materials by the workers. In 1717, the inventory of a worsted clothier William Roberts of Marsden shows that he was involved in putting-out on a wide scale, for he owned large amounts of wool out at spinning and had yarn in the hands of weavers, and was engaged in the manufacture of shalloons, tammies, serges and harateens.[332]

Change was certainly apparent, however, in the levels of production in the period before the Civil War. Output of northern kerseys rose until the mid-1610s as indicated by data for exports. In the Colne area, this was likely to have been due to expansion in breadth, that is by multiplying the units of production, rather than in depth, by increasing output per unit of production. This was achieved by population growth and by increasing the proportion of households involved in clothmaking. We have no information on output per household, but whilst it is possible that output rose per capita due to the increasing need for employment and by-employment, it is unlikely that such a change in intensity of production contributed as much to expanding output as did increasing the numbers of producers. Thus it appears that a considerable degree of 'proto-industrialisation' was possible in a traditional setting. Furthermore, the depression in the kersey trade in the 1620s and 1630s, induced largely by events overseas, illustrates that this expansion could be overturned quickly, with disastrous consequences for those dependent on income from cloth manufacture, particularly in years of harvest failure.

The reasons for the extraordinarily widespread incidence of clothmaking found in the Colne area seem to lie less in inheritance customs but rather in the nature of the pastoral economy itself. Seasonal unemployment or underemployment, and the shortage of agricultural wage labour in comparison with a more arable region, necessitated additional employment. This was made even more essential when population rose rapidly, holdings became subdivided, and the numbers of the landless and near-landless rose. It is true that a few examples of partible inheritance can be found, and that some testators chose to endow their younger sons with land for a specified period, with the reversion to the eldest son (especially when the heir was under twenty-one). Nevertheless, most testators followed the custom of primogeniture. Indeed, it could be argued that primogeniture helped to foster the development of the cloth industry in this area, since younger sons without land needed other sources of income. In turn, the existence of a widespread cloth industry, and the ease with which participation in it was possible with limited capital resources, perhaps militated against the need for partible inheritance, since younger sons might be adequately supported by textile production. Thus, the experience of the Colne area does not seem to support Joan Thirsk's argument that partible inheritance may have been an important element in helping to promote rural industry.[333]

NOTES

   [1] 'The Royal Commission on the cloth industry suggests remedies, 1640' in Thirsk and Cooper, *Seventeenth century economic documents*, pp. 249–50
   [2] B.L. Stowe MSS 132, fol. 150
   [3] See below, p. 126
   [4] L.R.O. WCW *Infra* and *Supra* inventories, *passim*
   [5] See especially P.R.O. D.L.1/213 Appendix No. 41; D.L.1/83/L6ab, D.L.4/17/54; P.L.6/18/202
   [6] Lowe, *Lancashire textile industry*, p. 4
   [7] Willan, 'Manchester clothiers', p. 176
   [8] For example, the inventory of the woollen webster Robert Hargreaves alias Ingham of Water Meetings in Pendle listed coverlet yarn valued at 8s. L.R.O. WCW *Supra*, will and inventory, 1613. However, only 4 of 221 *supra* inventories contained coverlet yarn; L.R.O. WCW *Supra* inventories, *passim*
   [9] L.R.O. WCW *Supra* inventories, *passim*. Of 103 *supra* testators from Colne chapelry and Pendle forest who possessed cards or combs between 1558 and 1640, 47 had cards only, 51 owned both cards and combs, and just 5 had combs only. Some testators owned combstocks, e.g. Christopher Robinson, a yeoman of Barley in Pendle; L.R.O. WCW *Supra*, will and inventory, 1621. Crump argued that, in the Bradford area, the presence of combs and combstocks in the early seventeenth century indicates the use of combed wool in weaving coverlets and cushions; Crump, 'Yeoman-clothier', p. 237
   [10] Bowden argues that coverlets seem to have been types of worsted. Bowden, *Wool trade*, p. 54. On the differences between cloth and worsted, see *ibid.*, pp. 41–3

[11] L.R.O. WCW *Supra* inventories, *passim*. Linen yarn was listed in only 7 of 221 *supra* inventories

[12] The inventory of John Mitchell of the town of Colne, linen draper, included both a spinning wheel and a linen wheel. L.R.O. WCW *Supra*, will and inventory, 1611

[13] L.R.O. DDHCl3/105, Pendle forest, 1st halmote, 24 Oct. 1622. Lowe noted that soaking flax caused an unpleasant stench and made water unfit for cattle to drink. Lowe, *Lancashire textile industry*, p. 43

[14] L.R.O. WCW *Supra* inventories, *passim*. The total number of inventories in the sample is 221

[15] L.R.O. QSB 1, *passim*

[16] L.R.O. P.R. 3027/1/2, *passim*

[17] 5 and 6 Edward VI c.6, quoted in Lowe, *Lancashire textile industry*, p. 5

[18] For further details, see Lowe, *Lancashire textile industry*, pp. 25–6, 35–8, 93

[19] *H. M. C. Kenyon MSS*, pp. 572–3; reprinted in Tawney and Power, *Tudor economic documents*, vol. 1, pp. 216–17

[20] Heaton, *Yorkshire woollen and worsted industries*, p. 96

[21] See below, pp. 118–21

[22] L.R.O. WCW *Supra* inventories, *passim*. There are 117 inventories in the sample for Colne chapelry and Roughlee, and 34 in that for the rest of Pendle forest; see Swain, 'Industry and economy', table 6.1, p. 177

[23] *Ibid.* Looms are usually referred to as a 'pair of looms', but this phrase should be interpreted as one loom, not two; see Lowe, *Lancashire textile industry*, pp. 101–2; Crump, 'Yeoman-clothier', p. 228

[24] Heaton, *Yorkshire woollen and worsted industries*, pp. 93, 96; see below, pp. 114–15

[25] Lowe, *Lancashire textile industry*, p. 26

[26] Mann, review of Lowe, p. 147. However, it is known that women participated in both carding and combing wool. See Baines, *Spinning wheels*, pp. 32–3

[27] Crossley, *Potts' discovery of witches*, E–E2, T

[28] 'The famous history of the Lancashire witches', printed in Harland and Wilkinson, *Lancashire legends*, p. 248

[29] Coleman, *Economy of England*, p. 76

[30] Harland, *Accounts of the Shuttleworths*, Part 1, pp. 51, 78, 82, 107, 110, 229

[31] L.R.O. WCW *Supra*, will and inventory, 1616

[32] C.S.P.D. Charles I, vol. 7, p. 141

[33] There are various examples of males being paid wages for spinning in the Walmsley accounts e.g. a man was paid 15s 4d for spinning two stones of best wool at 3s a stone, two stones of middle wool at 2s 8d a stone, and two stones of worst wool at 2s a stone, on 16 July 1629; L.R.O. DDPt 1. There are many other examples L.R.O. DDPt 1 *passim*; see also Harland, *Accounts of the Shuttleworths*, Part 1, p. 220; Part 2, pp. 246–7. However, it is possible that the men were not actually spinning themselves, but were receiving the wages on behalf of their wives

[34] These examples, however, refer to women weaving canvas cloth only. Harland, *Accounts of the Shuttleworths*, Part 1, pp. 51–3

[35] Heaton, *Yorkshire woollen and worsted industries*, p. 23

[36] P.R.O. D.L.1/156/C2

[37] P.R.O. D.L.1/209/B50

[38] L.R.O. WCW *Supra* inventory 1632. This room is placed between two rooms which are definitely upstairs; in addition, the other two chambers are upstairs

[39] Barley, *English farmhouse*, p. 175, referring to the Bradford area, 1615–42

[40] *H. M. C. Kenyon MSS*, p. 573

[41] On the subject of putting-out, see especially Coleman, *Industry in Tudor and Stuart England*, chapter 3, and Coleman, *Domestic system, passim*. See also Lipson, *History of the woollen and worsted industry*, chapter 2. One should note that there are various definitions of domestic system. For example, Lipson argued that there were two stages in the domestic system; first, where the influence of capital was negligible, as in the North of England in the seventeenth century; secondly, where the influence of capital was considerable, as in the West Country during the same period; *ibid.*, p. 40. However, he argued that the domestic system was where the materials were not owned by the workers but by the employers, who united all different branches of the industry under a single control; *ibid.*, p. 36. Coleman followed this latter definition, and argued that the two crucial features of the domestic system were that most or all of the major processes of production were carried out in the houses of the workers themselves, and that the workers did not own the raw materials or semi-finished goods; Coleman, *Domestic system*, p. 3. Other writers have accepted, uncritically, the notion that the domestic system and the putting-out system were one and the same, e.g. Ramsay, *Wiltshire woollen industry*, p. 6. Wild, by contrast, argues that the term 'domestic system' simply implies that production was carried out in the homes of the manufacturers, and that there were various types of 'domestic system' ranging from 'putting-out' to a 'small clothier system'; Wild, 'Yorkshire wool textile industry', p. 201. Wild's definition seems to be the most logical

[42] Coleman, *Industry in Tudor and Stuart England*, p. 27; Ramsay, *Wiltshire woollen industry, passim*

[43] P.R.O. D.L.4/17/54

[44] P.R.O. D.L.4/94/49

[45] L.R.O. WCW *Supra* and *Infra*, wills and inventories, *passim*

[46] See below pp. 122–4

[47] In a sample of 1,000 debts and credits in wills and inventories from Colne chapelry, 1553–1609, the nature of only 69 were specified (6.9%). L.R.O. WCW *Supra*, wills and inventories, *passim*

[48] Preston, *Crosley wills*, pp. 13–14

[49] L.R.O. WCW *Supra* and *Infra*, wills and inventories, *passim*

[50] Norcliffe, 'Inventory of John Pawson', p. 164

[51] L.R.O. WCW *Supra*, will and inventory, 1558. Lowe incorrectly states that Mitton was directly involved in spinning (Lowe, *Lancashire textile industry*, p. 26), but there are no spinning wheels recorded in his inventory

[52] P.R.O. D.L.1/213 Appendix No. 41

[53] P.R.O. D.L.4/17/54

54 L.R.O. DDHCl3/69, Colne manor, 1st halmote, 25 October, 1586
55 Harland, *Accounts of the Shuttleworths*, Parts 1 and 2, *passim*. L.R.O. DDPt1, *passim*
56 Lowe, *Lancashire textile industry*, pp. 20–3, 26–7, 31–3, 40–2, 99–100.

King too failed to discover any evidence of large scale putting-out in the Rossendale textile industry during the period from 1650 to 1715; King, 'Economic and demographic development of Rossendale', p. 119. Brigg, however, implies that putting-out existed in Pendle by the seventeenth century, but gives no evidence for her claim; Brigg 'Forest of Pendle', Part 1, p. 89
57 Bagley, 'Matthew Markland', pp. 61–8. See Lowe's criticisms of Bagley in *Lancashire textile industry*, pp. 31–3
58 For examples of putting-out in the Bradford area, see above; p. 113. Smaller clothiers predominated in the Halifax area – see Heaton, *Yorkshire woollen and worsted industries*, p. 93 and above; p. 111
59 Statutes of the Realm, 2 and 3 Philip and Mary c.13, printed in Tawney and Power, *Tudor economic documents*, vol. 1, pp. 187–8. See comments by Heaton, *Yorkshire woollen and worsted industries*, pp. 94–5
60 Mendenhall, *Shrewsbury drapers*, pp. 10–11, 211–12
61 See above, p. 111
62 L.R.O. QSB 1/49/36
63 See above, p. 112
64 5 Elizabeth c.4 (1563) clause 24; printed in Tawney and Power, *Tudor economic documents*, vol. 1, p. 347; Tait, *Lancashire Quarter Sessionrs records*, *passim*; L.R.O. QSB 1, *passim*
65 Lowe, *Lancashire textile industry*, pp. 84–5. See also Heaton, *Yorkshire woollen and worsted industries*, pp. 102–7
66 Farrer, *Court rolls*, vol. 3, pp. 408–13
67 Bowden, *Wool trade*, p. 37
68 *H. M. C. Kenyon MSS*, p. 573
69 See Chapter 3, p. 48
70 P.R.O. D.L.4/15/4 m.5
71 P.R.O. C.1/639/43
72 *H. M. C. Kenyon MSS*, p. 573
73 L.R.O. WCW *Supra*, will and inventory, 1558
74 L.R.O. WCW *Supra*, will and inventory, 1622
75 Bowden, *Wool trade*, p. 136
76 5 and 6 Edward VI c.7. For further details, see Bowden, *Wool trade*, 115–18 and ff; Lowe, *Lancashire textile industry*, p. 22; Heaton, *Yorkshire woollen and worsted industries*, p. 120
77 The Halifax Act of 1555 (2 and 3 Philip and Mary c.13) is printed in Tawney and Power, *Tudor economic documents*, vol. 1, pp. 187–8; for Rochdale, see A.P.C. vol. 19, pp. 370–1. See Bowden, *Wool trade*, p. 120; Lowe, *Lancashire textile industry*, p. 22; Heaton, *Yorkshire woollen and worsted industries*, pp. 120–2
78 P.R.O. S.P.12/117 fol. 90. (Oct. ? 1577). Cited by Lowe, *Lancashire textile industry*, p. 23; Heaton, *Yorkshire woollen and worsted industries*, pp. 121–2; Bowden, *Wool trade*, p. 142, note 1; also Wadsworth and Mann, *Cotton trade and industrial Lancashire*, p. 7

79 Bowden, *Wool trade*, p. 141
80 L.R.O. WCW *Supra* inventory, 1597
81 Dickinson, 'West Riding woollen and worsted industries', p. 59
82 L.R.O. WCW *Supra*, will 1618, inventory 1619
83 Lowe, *Lancashire textile industry*, p. 28
84 This belonged to the yeoman Henry Whittaker of Great Marsden. L.R.O. WCW *Supra*, will and inventory, 1606
85 This belonged to the yeoman Richard Walton of Great Marsden. L.R.O. WCW *Supra*, will and inventory, 1614
86 L.R.O. WCW *Infra* and *Supra* inventories, *passim*
87 *Ibid.* The average valuations of looms were as follows (bracketed figures indicate the size of the sample): 1571–80 (3) 8s 4d; 1581–90 (4) 10s 10d; 1591–1600 (12) 15s 4d; 1601–10 (16) 15s 0d; 1611–20 (12) 23s 4d; 1621–30 (9) 17s 9d; 1631–40 (11) 19s 7d. The average valuation of these 67 inventories was 17s 2d. See Swain, 'Industry and economy', Table 6.2, p. 193
88 See below, p. 137. There is no evidence of any technological improvements which might have affected the valuation of looms
89 L.R.O. WCW *Supra* inventories, *passim*
90 See Chapter 1, p. 4
91 L.R.O. WCW *Supra*, will and inventory, 1574
92 L.R.O. WCW *Supra*, will and inventory, 1558
93 L.R.O. WCW *Supra*, will and inventory, 1604
94 L.R.O. WCW *Supra*, will and inventory, 1610
95 See below pp. 141–2
96 L.R.O. DRCh inventory, 1579
97 Lowe seems not to have examined *Infra* wills and inventories, or the disputed cases in DRCh. The poorest woollen weaver whom Lowe found was Edward Butterworth of Rochdale, who died in 1598 with goods worth under £17. Lowe, *Lancashire textile industry*, p. 42
98 L.R.O. WCW *Infra*, will and inventory, 1609
99 L.R.O. WCW *Infra*, will and inventory, 1604
100 L.R.O. WCW *Supra*, will and inventory, 1574
101 L.R.O. WCW *Supra*, will and inventory, 1558
102 L.R.O. WCW *Supra*, will and inventory, 1604
103 L.R.O. WCW *Supra*, will and inventory, 1610
104 L.R.O. DRCh inventory, 1579
105 L.R.O. WCW *Infra*, will and inventory, 1609
106 L.R.O. WCW *Infra*, will and inventory, 1604
107 L.R.O. WCW *Supra* inventories, *passim*
108 *Ibid.* Pendle forest (excluding Barrowford and Roughlee) has been distinguished from the rest of the area, since weaving activity was far less developed; see below, pp. 127–8. In the following data, bracketed figures indicate the size of the sample. In Colne chapelry and Roughlee, 51% of the yeomen owned cards or combs (75), 57% had spinning wheels (75), and 53% possessed looms (73); of the husbandmen from this area, 62% had cards or combs (21), 71% owned spinning wheels (21), and 52% had looms (21). In the rest of Pendle forest, 52% of the yeomen owned cards or combs (27), 50% had spinning wheels (26), and 19% possessed looms (26); 67% of the husbandmen had cards or combs (12), 50% owned spinning wheels (12), and

25% possessed looms (12). The size of the samples vary slightly due to the inclusion of a small number of damaged inventories. For further details, see Swain, 'Industry and economy', Table 6.3, p. 198

[109] L.R.O. WCW *Supra* inventories, *passim*

[110] For the involvement of building craftsmen in other business activities and in agriculture, see Woodward, 'Wage rates and living standards', especially pp. 39–42

[111] L.R.O. WCW *Supra* inventories, *passim*

[112] Dickinson, 'West Riding woollen and worsted industries', pp. 124–5, 239–40. He found that there were two boom periods of intense output, from late June to early August (just after the hay harvest), and from 30 December to March. These conclusions are based on the Day Book of a shalloon merchant, June 1750–March 1751. The textile workers participated in harvesting in the autumn

[113] Mendels, 'Agriculture and peasant industry', p. 165

[114] Lowe, *Lancashire textile industry*, p. 27 and *passim*; Heaton, *Yorkshire woollen and worsted industries*, pp. 93, 203 and *passim*; Crump, 'Yeoman-clothier', *passim*; Dickinson, 'West Riding woollen and worsted industries', pp. 97–8 and *passim*

[115] Heaton, *Yorkshire woollen and worsted industries*, p. 93

[116] Crump, 'Yeoman-clothier', p. 229

[117] L.R.O. WCW *Supra*, will and inventory, 1604 of John Hargreaves of Monkroyd in Colne parish, yeoman

[118] B.I., P.C.Y., vol. 29, fol. 407, will of John Hargreaves alias Driver of Monkroyd in Colne parish, clothier. This is an identical will to the one proved at Chester, with the exception of the 'alias Driver' addition, and the different occupation

[119] Crump, 'Yeoman-clothier', title and pp. 219, 229

[120] L.R.O. DDPt 1

[121] It was stated in 1588 that 40 kersey spinners could spin 20 stones of wool in a week. *H. M. C. Kenyon MSS*, p. 573

[122] The wage for spinning a stone of wool for blankets was 2*s* in 1587 and 1617; Harland, *Accounts of the Shuttleworths*, Part 1, pp. 39, 220. It remained at 2*s*, according to references in accounts in 1626, 1627 and 1631; L.R.O. DDPt 1

[123] Heaton, *Yorkshire woollen and worsted industries*, p. 116

[124] L.R.O. DDPt 1 *passim*

[125] One kersey per week was alleged to be the usual output of a weaver, according to a lawsuit of 1638. P.R.O. E.134 14 Charles I. Michaelmas No. 21 York, cited by Heaton, *Yorkshire woollen and worsted industries*, p. 115. If, on the other hand, a weaver produced 1¼ kerseys in a week, as implied in the document of 1588 (*H. M. C. Kenyon MSS*, p. 573), this would produce a daily wage of 11¼*d* (assuming a six-day working week)

[126] *H. M. C. Kenyon MSS*, p. 573; P.R.O. E.134 14 Charles I Michaelmas No. 21 York, quoted by Heaton, *Yorkshire woollen and worsted industries*, pp. 115–16

[127] P.R.O. D.L.4/17/54

[128] L.R.O. WCW *Supra*, will and inventory, 1575, of James Smith yeoman of Edge in Colne

[129] *H. M. C. Kenyon MSS*, p. 573
[130] *Ibid.*, and Heaton, *Yorkshire woollen and worsted industries*, p. 96
[131] See above, pp. 119–20
[132] See Chapter 1, p. 4
[133] P.R.O. D.L.1/83/L6a
[134] P.R.O. D.L.4/17/54 m.22, 26, 29–30, 32
[135] P.R.O. D.L.4/65/25 m.6
[136] Rylands, *Lancashire inquisitions*, vol. 2, p. 29
[137] P.R.O. D.L.29/81/1562 to D.L.29/88/1629 (ministers' accounts for the manor of Colne, 1529–1640)
[138] P.R.O. D.L.4/17/54 m.5–6
[139] L.R.O. WCW *Supra* inventory 1639
[140] L.R.O. WCW *Supra*, will and inventory, 1606
[141] 39 Elizabeth c.20. The Lancashire J.P.s obstructed its implementation – see A.P.C. vol. 30, pp. 602–4 (24 August 1600) and P.R.O. S.P.12/279 fol. 177 (May 1601)
[142] See below, pp. 126–7
[143] 21 James I c.18; quoted by Heaton, *Yorkshire woollen and worsted industries*, p. 143
[144] L.R.O. WCW *Supra* inventory 1639
[145] Lowe, *Lancashire textile industry*, p. 35. Lowe points out that dyeing might be performed either before or after weaving
[146] Heaton, *Yorkshire woollen and worsted industries*, p. 109. See above p. 108
[147] L.R.O. WCW *Supra* inventory 1639
[148] P.R.O. D.L.4/17/54 m.5–6
[149] Harland, *Accounts of the Shuttleworths*, Part 2, pp. 235, 248
[150] Wool could be dyed – Harland, *Accounts of the Shuttleworths*, Part 1, p. 110. Yarn might also be dyed; *ibid.*, p. 39
[151] L.R.O. WCW *Supra*, will and inventory, 1628
[152] L.R.O. DDHCl3/119, Colne manor, 1st halmote, 25 October 1636
[153] P.R.O. D.L.4/94/49
[154] P.R.O. D.L.1/213/Appendix, No. 41
[155] P.R.O. D.L.4/17/54 m.2
[156] Heaton, *Yorkshire woollen and worsted industries*, pp. 80, 150
[157] P.R.O. C.1/1034/41–45
[158] L.R.O. WCW *Supra*, will and inventory, 1610, of William Holt of Colne, clothier
[159] L.R.O. WCW *Supra*, will and inventory, 1592, of James Parker of Whitleyhey Booth in Pendle, yeoman
[160] L.R.O. WCW *Supra*, will and inventory, 1611, of Robert Hodgson of Hunterholme in Pendle, yeoman
[161] See above p. 124
[162] These are found in P.R.O. E.159. The list for 1561–2 has been printed; See Ramsay, 'Distribution of the cloth industry', *passim*. M. L. Zell has compiled a table of all the available lists of the period, 1550–1585 (this method of recording then appears to have fallen into abeyance); Zell, 'Exchequer lists of provincial clothmakers', *passim*. I am grateful to Mr. David Lidington of Sidney Sussex College, Cambridge, for drawing my attention to this list

[163] The total of 5,426 does not include E.159/3/32 Easter 31 (1552–3) where 24 fines are recorded, but locations are not given. The three Colne clothiers fined were:

P.R.O. E.159/355 Trinity 206 (1564–5). Harry Shaw of Colne, clothier, was fined 8s on 24 August 1565 for having a flocked grey kersey for sale

P.R.O. E.159/378 Hilary 201 (1578–9). Harry Emott of Colne, clothier, was fined 10s on 28 March 1579 for having for sale a white kersey of insufficient length

P.R.O. E.159/380 Hilary 134 (1579–80). Thomas Lacy of Colne (written 'Toulne' but almost certainly Colne) clothier, was fined 10s on 30 January 1580 for having for sale two white kerseys which were underweight by two pounds

In addition, there was one from the Burnley area:

P.R.O. E.159/380 Hilary 134 (1579–80) William Barcroft of Burnley parish, clothier, was fined 10s on 22 April 1580 for having for sale two kerseys which were underweight by two pounds

There were two other clothiers fined for offences involving kerseys, but their origin is not stated:

P.R.O. E.159/350 Hilary 331 (1560–1) Thomas Knight

P.R.O. E.159/370 Hilary 292 (1573–4) Richard Ingham

[164] Hamlets in the parishes of Bolton and Deane (e.g. Horwich, Deane, Hulton) have been included under 'Bolton'. Also 27 fines have unspecified locations in Lancashire and a small number of other fines are unclear – e.g. 'Binton' may be 'Bolton'. Thus the true proportion of Manchester and Bolton fines was probably greater

[165] B.I. P.C.Y., vol. 27, fol. 338

[166] P.R.O. P.L.6/18/202

[167] L.R.O. DDB 61/1–3

[168] P.R.O. S.P.12/250 fol. 147–147v (1594?)

[169] See above, p. 108

[170] For the exports of northern kerseys from Hull in 1609, see Zins, England and the Baltic, p. 176. On the subject of English kersey exports to eastern Europe, especially Hungary, see Endrei, 'English kersey in eastern Europe', passim

[171] See below, pp. 136–8

[172] Tawney and Power, Tudor economic documents, vol. 3, pp. 214, 216–18

[173] See above, note 163

[174] 39 Elizabeth c.20

[175] A.P.C. vol. 30, pp. 602–4 (24 August 1600), refers to this edict

[176] A.P.C. vol. 30, pp. 602–4 (24 August 1600); P.R.O. S.P.12/279, fol. 177–177v (May 1601)

[177] A.P.C. vol. 31, pp. 78–9 (4 January 1601)

[178] Ibid.

[179] A.P.C. vol. 31, pp. 387–9 (31 May 1601); P.R.O. S.P.12/279 fol. 177–177v (May 1601)

[180] Tait, Lancashire Quarter Sessions records, p. 106. For the order that the lower bars of tenters should be taken away, see ibid., p. 104

[181] Lowe, Lancashire textile industry, p. 94

[182] Mendenhall, Shrewsbury drapers, p. 139

[183] 21 James I c.18; see Heaton, *Yorkshire woollen and worsted industries*, pp. 143–4

[184] Fedorowicz, *England's Baltic trade*, pp. 220, 238–40

[185] See below, pp. 142–3

[186] L.R.O. WCW *Supra* inventories, *passim*. As before, the inclusion of a few damaged inventories explains the variation in the size of the samples used

[187] *Ibid.* Brigg noted that of her sample of 123 Pendle forest inventories from the seventeenth century, 93 possessed cards, combs and spinning wheels, and 45 owned one or two looms as well; Brigg, 'Forest of Pendle', Part 1, pp. 68, 90

[188] Brigg also noted that weaving in Pendle forest in the seventeenth century was extensively developed in Roughlee and Barrowford Booths, with half of the testators owning looms living in these two areas. Brigg, 'Forest of Pendle', Part 1, p. 93

[189] See below, pp. 129, 139–41

[190] L.R.O. WCW *Supra* inventories, *passim*. In the period to 1600, 50% of testators (19 out of 38 inventories) from Colne chapelry and Roughlee (excluding Trawden forest) possessed looms; this proportion rose to 56% (37 out of 66 inventories) in the period 1601–20, but fell to 46% (17 out of 37 inventories) in the period from 1621 to 1640. For the high incidence of weaving in Trawden in the 1620s and 1630s, see below, pp. 143–4

[191] L.R.O. WCW *Infra* inventories, *passim*. Of a total of 21 inventories, 5 owned cards or combs (24%) and 10 had spinning wheels (48%). In the 19 inventories from Colne chapelry and Roughlee, 5 contained looms (26%). Neither of the inventories from the rest of Pendle forest recorded looms

[192] Of the 13 male testators from this area, 5 owned looms (38%); 3 were actually described as websters

[193] L.R.O. WCW *Supra* inventories, *passim*. These inventories are drawn from the period 1560–1640; 57% (78 out of 136) contained cards or combs, 60% (82 out of 137) listed spinning wheels, and 23% (32 out of 137) recorded looms. For further details, see Swain, 'Industry and economy', pp. 219–20

[194] L.R.O. WCW *Infra* inventories, *passim*. These inventories cover the period from 1600 to 1620; 53% (9 out of 17) listed cards or combs and spinning wheels

[195] L.R.O. WCW *Supra* inventories, *passim*. These inventories are drawn from the period from 1549–1640; of 123 inventories, 15 contained cards or combs, 28 listed spinning wheels and 8 recorded looms. For further details, see Swain, 'Industry and economy', pp. 220–1

[196] L.R.O. WCW *Infra* inventories, *passim*. These inventories cover the period from 1591–1620; amongst the 13 inventories, only 2 contained instruments of cloth production (spinning wheels)

[197] On land use in this area, see Rodgers, 'Land use in Tudor Lancashire', pp. 82–3, 85, 88–9, 94–5. Rodgers found that this area was a district with a high proportion of arable land. The fact that arable farming is more labour-intensive than pastoral is well known; see chapter 3, p. 50

[198] Preston, *Crosley wills*, *passim* (in three inventories, it is unclear whether the wheel referred to was a spinning wheel); Cash, *Devon inventories*, p. xxii;

Havinden, *Oxfordshire inventories*, p. 27. As a further example, over a third of 166 Bedfordshire inventories for the period from 1617 to 1619 contained spinning wheels, but only 7 (4%) listed looms; Emmison, *Jacobean household inventories*, pp. 33, 37

[199] Havinden, *Oxfordshire inventories*, p. 2 and Vaisey, *Lichfield inventories*, p. 1. Both point out that the poor are not adequately represented in a sample of inventories

[200] See above, p. 113

[201] In 1638, estimates for the proportion of the population of the parishes of Halifax, Bradford, Keighley and Bingley who lived entirely by clothmaking varied from a half to a quarter, but a third was the proportion most often cited. P.R.O. E.134 14 Charles I, Michaelmas No. 21, York

[202] Mendels, 'Agriculture and peasant industry', pp. 161–4

[203] Skipp, *Crisis and development*, pp. 57–8

[204] See Table 6.2

[205] *Ibid.* (61 to 95 inventories)

[206] L.R.O. WCW *Supra* inventories, *passim*

[207] See above, pp. 120–1

[208] The imminent death of the testator may have caused a disruption in cloth production, particularly if he was responsible for weaving. In any case, even households which were heavily involved in weaving would not necessarily have yarn all the time

[209] Overton, 'Agricultural change in Norfolk and Suffolk', p. 132

[210] See above, p. 117

[211] Mendels, 'Proto-industrialisation: the first phase', p. 243

[212] See above, pp. 117–18

[213] L.R.O. WCW *Supra*, will and inventory, 1618

[214] L.R.O. DRCh inventory 1597 (will WCW *Supra*, 1597). The valuation of the wheels, cards and combs at 13s 4d suggests that Mangnolls owned a large number, for these instruments were very cheap. See above, p. 117

[215] L.R.O. WCW *Supra*, will 1612, inventory 1624

[216] See Table 6.2

[217] Batho, 'Landlords in England. B. Noblemen, gentlemen and yeomen', p. 278

[218] Willan, *The inland trade*, p. 59

[219] Of 224 usable *supra* inventories from Colne chapelry and Pendle forest, 1558–1640, only 47 (21%) included both credits and debts; (a credit is defined as a 'debt' owed to the testator, and a debt as one the testator owed to another). Those who had credits only numbered 88 (39%); 13 (6%) had debts only, and 76 (34%) had neither credits nor debts listed. If the credits and debts in the will are included too, a further 36 testators had credits listed in the will but not in the inventory, and 39 had debts listed in the will but not in the inventory. L.R.O. WCW *Supra*, wills and inventories, *passim*. See Chapter 8, pp. 189–92

[220] This point has been made by Willan, *Elizabethan Manchester*, p. 84

[221] *Ibid.*, p. 84. Of 180 *Supra* inventories where the date of appraisal is clear, and where there is an accompanying dated will, in 104 cases (58%), the time gap between will and inventory was less than a month, and in only 42 cases (23%) was the time gap more than three months. Of these 42 cases,

in only 19 (11%) was the time gap a year or more. L.R.O. WCW *Supra*, wills and inventories, *passim*

[222] In 36 cases where an undamaged inventory is available, the will has either not survived or is too damaged for use. Of these inventories, 12 listed both credits and debts, 17 recorded credits only, 4 debts only, and 3 neither credits nor debts. L.R.O. WCW *Supra* inventories, *passim*

[223] Willan, *Elizabethan Manchester*, p. 84

[224] Cash, *Devon inventories*, p. xxiv

[225] P.R.O. D.L.4/51/47 m.5

[226] P.R.O. D.L.5/31 fol. 389v

[227] Bagley, 'Matthew Markland', pp. 57–8

[228] L.R.O. WCW *Supra*, will and inventory of Lawrence Mitton of Great Marsden, clothier, 1558

[229] Camp, *Wills and their whereabouts*, p. 59

[230] L.R.O. WCW *Supra* and *Infra*, wills and inventories, *passim*. R.S.L.C. vols. 2 (1879), 4 (1881), 33 (1896), 43 (1902), 52 (1906)

[231] L.R.O. WCW *Infra*, wills and inventories of testators from Colne chapelry and Pendle forest, 1601–21, *passim*. See index in R.S.L.C. vol. 52 (1906)

[232] Camp, *Wills and their whereabouts*, pp. 153–4

[233] There is a manuscript index of Lancashire wills proved at York (compiled from the indexes of the Yorkshire Archaeological Society Record Series) at the Lancashire Record Office. For the original indexes, see Y.A.S.R.S. vols. 24, 26, 28, 32, 35

[234] Camp, *Wills and their whereabouts*, introduction, p. xiii

[235] Havinden, *Oxfordshire inventories*, p. 2; Vaisey, *Lichfield inventories*, p. 1. See also Willan, *The inland trade*, p. 71

[236] Havinden, *Oxfordshire inventories*, pp. 2–3; Vaisey, *Lichfield inventories*, p. 1

[237] L.R.O. WCW *Supra* inventories, *passim*

[238] See Swain, 'Industry and economy', pp. 253, 256

[239] For a discussion of local price movements, see *ibid.*, pp. 334–41

[240] L.R.O. WCW *Supra* inventories, *passim*. The size of the samples were as follows: between 1558 and 1600, 8 of the 46 inventories belonged to husbandmen; from 1601 to 1620, there were 16 husbandmen's inventories out of a total of 78; between 1621 and 1640, husbandmen represented 12 out of 49 inventories

[241] See below, pp. 140–1

[242] See above, p. 129

[243] Marshall, 'Agrarian wealth and social structure', p. 504. See also Willan, *The inland trade*, p. 59

[244] Lowe, *Lancashire textile industry*, pp. 26–35

[245] Brigg, 'Forest of Pendle', Part 1, p. 65

[246] Heaton, *Yorkshire woollen and worsted industries*, p. 95

[247] *Ibid.*, p. 150

[248] See above, pp. 116, 122–3

[249] See above, pp. 124–5

[250] In a lawsuit of 1638, Robert Sandes of Heptonstall stated that kerseys 18 yards long and 20 pounds in weight were sold for export and made by

clothiers of Lancashire, Heptonstall parish and other places; P.R.O. E.134 14 Charles I, Michaelmas No. 21, York. In *c.*1594, 30,000 Lancashire 'new devised kerseys' were exported; see above, p. 125–6

[251] Supple, *Commercial crisis and change*, pp. 28–9

[252] The northern kersey was valued at only 3*s* or 4*s* a yard in 1638, compared with the cloth produced in Suffolk and the West Country at 12*s*, 20*s* or 26*s*, a yard (and which used the same type of wool); Heaton, *Yorkshire woollen and worsted industries*, p. 206

[253] Averages based on statistics in Zins, *England and the Baltic*, pp. 184–5. One should note that statistics for the period 1570–3 inclusive are not available

[254] P.R.O. E.190/312/6. A slightly different total of 39,142 kerseys is given in Zins, *England and the Baltic*, p. 176, whilst Hall, in 'Trade of Newcastle', p. 283, gives a figure of 39,079. However, our total has been rechecked against the port book

[255] P.R.O. E.190/313/8. Friis gives a slightly different total of 45,613 kerseys in *Cockayne project*, p. 63. In 'Trade of Newcastle', p. 284, Hall gives a very different figure of 42,835 kerseys. Again, our total has been rechecked against the port book. The only other port which exported northern kerseys in fairly large quantities during this period was Newcastle; for example, in 1616, Newcastle exported 13,282½ northern kerseys; Friis, *Cockayne project*, p. 63. Chester's kersey exports, by contrast, were of little significance; see Stephens, 'Overseas trade of Chester', pp. 24–5

[256] Davis, *Trade and shipping of Hull*, p. 7; Hinton, *Eastland trade*, preface p. viii; Fedorowicz, *England's Baltic trade*, pp. 90–1

[257] Davis, *Trade and shipping of Hull*, p. 7

[258] Stephens, 'Cloth exports of the provincial ports', p. 228; see also Stephens, 'Exchequer port books', p. 209

[259] Hinton, *Eastland trade*, pp. 34–5. See also Fedorowicz, *England's Baltic trade*, pp. 93–5. One should note, however, that exports in 1646 were presumably badly affected by the disruption of trade during the English Civil War

[260] Davis, *Trade and shipping of Hull*, p. 22

[261] Exports of northern kerseys from Hull were as follows: 39,470 in 1609; 46,017½ in 1614; 33,268 in 1619; 36,639½ in 1623; 29,609 in 1630; 25,941 in 1631; 28,150 in 1633; 31,804 in 1634; 35,579 in 1637; 32,361 in 1640. These data were obtained from P.R.O. E.190/312/6, E.190/313/8, E.190/314/14, E.190/316/10, E.190/316/12, E.190/317/6, E.190/317/7, E.190/318/1A and B, E.190/318/7. The port book for 1623 is now too damaged for use, but was presumably in reasonable condition when Hall did her Ph.D. thesis in 1933, and so the figure for 1623 is taken from 'Trade of Newcastle', p. 285. For further details of northern kersey exports, see Swain, 'Industry and economy', pp. 233–8

[262] P.R.O. S.P.14/129 fol. 132 (30 April 1622)

[263] See above, p. 117

[264] Mendenhall, *Shrewsbury drapers*, pp. 24, 190

[265] Friis, *Cockayne's project*, p. 414, note 1

[266] P.R.O. D.L.4/94/49. See above, p. 124

[267] See chapter 2, pp. 16–22

[268] Wrigley and Schofield, *Population history of England*, p. 408
[269] Zins, *England and the Baltic*, p. 171
[270] See Chapter 5
[271] For a discussion of the movements of local prices and wages, see Swain, 'Industry and economy', pp. 334–43
[272] See above, p. 129
[273] See Chapter 5, pp. 71–2
[274] See Chapter 3, pp. 36–7, 42–4
[275] P.R.O. D.L.1/156/C2
[276] See Chapter 5, pp. 73–80
[277] For a list of these wills, see Swain, 'Industry and economy', p. 242
[278] See Chapter 2, pp. 25–7
[279] See Chapter 5, pp. 78–9
[280] Bastards can be distinguished by the 'alias x', i.e. the alternative surname given. For a list of these testators, see Swain, 'Industry and economy', p. 243
[281] P.R.O. P.L.6/19/206
[282] See Chapter 2, pp. 25–6
[283] See above, pp. 110, 127–9
[284] See Chapter 2, p. 26
[285] L.R.O. WCW *Supra*, wills and inventories, *passim*
[286] Arable agriculture was far more labour-intensive than pastoral – see Chapter 3, p. 50
[287] See Chapter 5, pp. 71–2
[288] Lawrence Mitton of Great Marsden owned 12 cattle in 1558; L.R.O. WCW *Supra*, will and inventory, 1558. Alexander Parker of Hobstones in Colne possessed 21 cattle in 1574; L.R.O. WCW *Supra*, will and inventory, 1574. Lawrence Blakey of Blacko in Pendle owned 35 cattle in 1574; L.R.O. WCW *Supra*, will and inventory, 1574
[289] James Blakey of Emmott Lane Head owned no cattle in 1604; L.R.O. WCW *Supra*, will and inventory, 1604. John Hargreaves (alias Driver) of Monkroyd in Foulridge possessed 9 cattle in 1604; L.R.O. WCW *Supra*, will and inventory, 1604 (in the will proved at Chester, Hargreaves is described as a yeoman, but a virtually identical will proved at York gives the occupation clothier; B.I., P.C.Y. vol. 29 fol. 407). William Holt of Colne had no cattle in 1610; L.R.O. WCW *Supra*, will and inventory, 1610. John Green of Roughlee had 6 cattle in 1612; L.R.O. WCW *Supra* inventory 1612. James Marsden of Priestfield owned 6 cattle in 1620; L.R.O. WCW *Supra*, will and inventory, 1620. John Hargreaves, a clothier of Whitefield in Little Marsden, owned cattle valued at £19 in 1606, but the numbers are not specified. If we compare other cattle prices in inventories, and assuming for the sake of argument that all of the cattle were cows, then since the mean valuation of cows in inventories of the 1600s was £2 5s 0d (see Swain, 'Industry and economy', p. 337), this represents about 8 cows. L.R.O. WCW *Supra*, will 1606, inventory undated
[290] See above, pp. 136–7
[291] *H. M. C. Sackville MSS*, vol. 2, pp. 30, 31, 54–5, 57, 64–5, 131–2, 195–6 and *passim*; quoted by Endrei, 'English kersey in eastern Europe', pp. 94–6;

Supple, *Commercial crisis and change*, pp. 61, 140; Tawney, *Business and politics*, pp. 58–60

[292] Endrei, 'English kersey in eastern Europe', pp. 96–7; Zins, *England and the Baltic*, p. 184

[293] See above, pp. 136–7

[294] See especially Friis, *Cockayne's project*, *passim*, and Supple, *Commercial crisis and change*, *passim*

[295] For the effects of the Cockayne Project and this prohibition on the export of white cloths, see Heaton, *Yorkshire woollen and worsted industries*, pp. 185–9

[296] Supple, *Commercial crisis and change*, *passim*; Gould, 'Trade depression', *passim*

[297] Supple, *Commercial crisis and change*, pp. 58, 73–98

[298] Hinton, 'Eastland trade', pp. 17–18; Davis, *Trade and shipping of Hull*, p. 20. On foreign competition, see Heaton, *Yorkshire woollen and worsted industries*, pp. 150, 192–3; Fedorowicz, *England's Baltic trade*, pp. 292–4

[299] Zins, *England and the Baltic*, p. 212, note 107

[300] Fedorowicz, *England's Baltic trade*, p. 95

[301] Hinton, *Eastland trade*, p. 36

[302] Davis, *Trade and shipping of Hull*, p. 20

[303] See above, p. 140

[304] See Chapter 5, pp. 93–5

[305] L.R.O. WCW *Supra* inventories, *passim*. However, the size of the sample was only 11 inventories, so we ought not to place too much reliance on these figures. Comparison of Trawden inventories over time is impossible, since we only have 4 inventories for the period from 1601–20 and 9 inventories for the period 1581–1600 (3 of which are damaged). If the pre-1621 Trawden inventories are grouped together, 42% owned cards or combs (5 out of 12), 54% possessed spinning wheels (7 out of 13), and 40% had looms (4 out of 10)

[306] See above, p. 138

[307] See Chapter 2, pp. 22–5

[308] This is a familiar argument; see Kriedte *et al.*, *Industrialisation before industrialisation*, pp. 32, 90, 118–19

[309] See Chapter 4, pp. 61–5

[310] See Chapter 2, pp. 20–22

[311] See above, pp. 132–5

[312] See above, p. 129

[313] L.R.O. QSB 1, *passim*; the size of the sample is 203; for further details, see Swain, 'Industry and economy', Table 6.14, p. 253

[314] See above, pp. 110, 127–9

[315] See above, pp. 127–38, 142–4

[316] See above, pp. 120–1

[317] The size of the sample was 161; see Swain, 'Industry and economy', Table 6.14, p. 253

[318] Of 81 cases in Quarter Sessions, 1626–42, relating to people from the Colne area, 35 concerned bastardy and 10 felony (with 20 unspecified); L.R.O. QSB 1 *passim*. As explained in Chapter 2, p. 26, bastardy cases usually involved the poorer sort

³¹⁹ L.R.O. P.R.3027/1/2. The sample size is 434 for baptisms and 299 for burials. For further details, see Swain, 'Industry and economy', Table 6.15, p. 256

³²⁰ The Padiham register (L.R.O. P.R.2863/1/2) and the transcript of the Newchurch in Pendle register (L.R.O. P.R.2862/2/1) only rarely give occupations; the same is true for the Colne register (transcripts of which were kindly made available to me by Mrs. D. Crowther of Nelson; the original is kept by the rector of Colne)

³²¹ The gentry constitute 8% of the Quarter Sessions sample for Colne chapelry and Pendle forest, and the yeomen 27%; in Burnley and Padiham chapelries (excluding Pendle forest) the proportions were 11% and 19% respectively. The Burnley registers for the period from 1653–60 suggest that the gentry constituted only 4% of the total population, and yeomen 13% to 14%. See Swain, 'Industry and economy', Tables 6.14 and 6.15, pp. 253, 256

³²² Wadsworth and Mann, *Cotton trade and industrial Lancashire*, p. 52. It must be noted that occupations were not stated for 19 of the 80 Radcliffe entries and for 2 of the 246 Rochdale entries, and therefore the actual proportions involved in textile manufacture may have been higher, particularly in Radcliffe

³²³ Drake, 'Elementary exercise', p. 431

³²⁴ See above, pp. 118–21

³²⁵ See above, pp. 113–15

³²⁶ Heaton found that there was a change in the type of kersey produced in the West Riding in the early seventeenth century, from 'broadlist' kerseys of 14 to 17 yards in length and more than 1 yard in width with a very broad list (or waste edge), to kerseys 19 or 20 yards in length (or even longer) and of superior quality. This change occurred during the period 1613–38. Heaton, *Yorkshire woollen and worsted industries*, pp. 197–8

³²⁷ In the Colne area, we have no evidence that this changeover occurred. Indeed, it seems that Colne continued to produce the older type of kersey, for a clothworker, John College of Colne, owned 8 'blue list kerseys' in 1639; L.R.O. WCW *Supra* inventory, 26 July 1639. The only evidence of a change in the type of kerseys produced in Lancashire, is a reference to the export of 30,000 'Lancaster new devised kerseys' in c.1594; P.R.O. S.P.12/250 fol. 147–147v. This predates the change in the West Riding, and may not be related to it; we do not know what was new about the kerseys. The reluctance or inability to diversify may have exacerbated the cloth depression in the Colne area in the 1620s and 1630s

³²⁸ Lowe, *Lancashire textile industry*, chapter 7

³²⁹ Wadsworth and Mann, *Cotton trade and industrial Lancashire*, p. 88, quoting from the inventory of William Roberts of Marsden in 1717 (P.R.O. P.L.7/129)

³³⁰ Heaton, *Yorkshire woollen and worsted industries*, pp. 263–76; Dickinson, 'West Riding woollen and worsted industries', chapter 4; Hudson, 'Proto-industrialisation: the case of the West Riding', especially pp. 38–40

³³¹ Heaton, *Yorkshire woollen and worsted industries*, pp. 296–7

³³² Wadsworth and Mann, *Cotton trade and industrial Lancashire*, p. 88

³³³ Thirsk, 'Industries in the countryside', *passim*. For a discussion of Thirsk's argument, see Chapter 9, pp. 204–5

CHAPTER VII

COAL MINING

It will be demonstrated in this chapter that coal mining in the Colne area during the sixteenth and early seventeenth centuries consisted of a few small-scale and short-lived operations. Whilst coal mining did not constitute an important source of employment for many inhabitants, it nevertheless absorbed large amounts of capital, at least relative to that invested by most households in cloth production.

THE AVAILABILITY OF FUEL

James Roberts, aged 79 of Burnley parish (where he had lived for sixty years) stated in a lawsuit in 1527 that no one had 'any need in time past to get coals for their fuel, by reason they had plenty of wood from the forests and turves at their liberty, which now be decayed and restrained from them'.[1] By 1608, the forest tenants of Rossendale, Pendle, Trawden and Accrington were claiming that there was no building timber in the vicinity.[2] This was probably an exaggeration but suggests that little wood would have been available for use as fuel.

If both wood and turf were becoming in short supply, local inhabitants may have turned increasingly to coal for their fuel requirements. Indeed, inventories provide some evidence of this development. There are 59 inventories of testators from Colne chapelry and Pendle forest which record coal, turf or both, between 1558 and 1640.[3] If we compare the period up to 1600, with that from 1601 to 1640, it is apparent that whilst roughly half of the fuel-owning testators possessed both coal and turf during both periods, just 6% owned only coal in the sixteenth century, compared with 24% in the period from 1601 to 1640. This evidence should be viewed with caution, since the numbers involved are small,[4] but nevertheless it is significant that the proportion of fuel-owning testators with only turf falls over time, and correspondingly that with only coal rises substantially. This suggests that the supply of turf may have become less adequate as the number of copyholders with the right to dig it rose considerably during the sixteenth and early seventeenth centuries.[5]

The tenants' claim to get turf and peat for household use from the wastes and commons without charge was not disputed by the Crown.[6] However, the tenants saw the need to conserve turf resources, as can be seen from the many amercements in the manorial courts for illegal graving of turf, either where the individual had no right, or where excessive quantities had been taken.[7]

Turf was preferred to coal for a number of reasons. In the first place, it was free, whereas the right to get coal as fireboot was disputed.[8] Secondly, it could be obtained more easily than coal, and without such damage to agricultural land. Thirdly, turf was more aromatic and less sulphurous than coal, which was a factor of obvious importance for domestic users. In addition, turf did not require wood to ignite it, and once alight, it had good smouldering qualities and needed less attention than coal.[9]

THE DEMAND FOR FUEL

Fuel was obviously needed for domestic purposes, particularly heating, cooking and lighting. It is likely that coal was increasingly in demand in the home, partly due to population growth, and partly due to the increasing lack of alternative fuels.

Various industrial processes also required fuel. Coal was needed in limeburning, which was an activity of particular importance in this area and one which grew in significance over time.[10] Considerable quantities of coal were needed to produce lime; Nef calculated that half a ton of coal was probably required to make a chaldron of lime.[11] Secondly, smiths needed fuel, preferring coal which was more economical than wood, providing a steady, hot flame suitable for the rougher kinds of iron work.[12] Thirdly, fuel was utilised in the manufacture of woollen cloth, either directly in scouring and dyeing, or indirectly in the production of clothmaking instruments such as wire cards, combs and shears, and also in the making of soap and alum.[13]

RIGHTS TO COAL

The copyholders were particularly concerned to prevent outsiders from obtaining coal in the precincts of the manor and forests. For example, the Colne jury ordered in May 1518 that if any person from

Craven tried to obtain coal within the township of Colne, he was to forfeit 3s 4d.[14] However, far more disputes over rights to coal arose from within the area. This can be seen from an examination of three different categories of land – waste, freehold and copyhold land. The inhabitants of Colne manor do not appear to have disputed the Crown's right to mine coal found on or under the wastes. Thus, whilst they stated in 1618 that 'time out of mind' they had been accustomed to get wallstone, limestone, marl, sods, turf and peat on the commons and wastes for use on their copyhold lands, they made no claim to dig coal there.[15] Indeed, the manorial juries fined those who attempted to obtain coal from the wastes. For example, Henry Emott was fined 4d in 1531 for getting small coals without permission from the King's waste at Cathole Clough in Trawden forest.[16]

The juries were equally anxious to ensure that agriculture was not unnecessarily disrupted by legitimate coal mining. One aspect of this problem was to ensure that old coal pits were filled up so that they did not present a danger either to men or to grazing beasts. Thus the King's farmer of the coal mines, Lawrence Lister Esquire, was fined 5s in 1599 because he had not filled up his old coal pits.[17] A related problem was the need to regulate operational coal mines. For example, the Colne jury fined William Hartley of Stirkhouse in 1608 for polluting Spring Water in Great Marsden with his coal horses.[18]

Freeholders in Colne manor might dig for coal on their lands without seeking permission from the lord or anyone else.[19] Indeed, the Crown lessees of the coal mines, who were later to dispute the copyholders' right to dig coal in their own holdings, did not claim that their lease from the Crown included the right to dig for coal in freehold land without permission. William Lister stated in a lawsuit of 1564–6 that he had obtained permission to dig in Greenfield in order to make a sough, which would enable him to get coal from land outside this freehold area. However, it was proved that Lister had actually obtained a considerable amount of coal (valued at £33 2s 8d) from Greenfield itself without a licence from the owner, Anne Towneley. The Duchy court ordered Lister to pay Anne £15 compensation for the coal obtained, and £6 towards her legal costs.[20]

The situation with regard to copyhold land was less clear-cut. Nef argued that customary tenants, in contrast to freeholders, never appear to have claimed for themselves full ownership of minerals under the ground, but rather two rights; first, the privilege, often based on manorial custom, of allowing them to obtain coal for their own use and to dig surface coal on their own holdings, in return for obligations to the lord; secondly, the right to refuse access to minerals under their holdings because of potential damage to the surface.[21] Both of these rights were claimed by the tenants of Colne manor and the forests of Trawden and Pendle. For example, Henry Barcroft argued in 1599 that the right of copyhold tenure gave the copyholders and their undertenants 'liberty of fireboot of coal mines'.[22] Similarly, Edmund Robinson of Old Laund in Pendle said in 1580 that his ancestors had dug for coal 'time out of mind' for their necessary fireboot for burning on their lands, but denied that either he or his ancestors had sold or given away coal to others.[23]

The danger of damage being done to copyhold land by coal mining was fully realised. Indeed, in some cases copyholders were prepared to offer payment for a lease of a coal mine purely to prevent another damaging their lands. Thus in 1604, John Hartley of Great Marsden offered to take a lease of the coal in his holding for a term of 21 years at 2s 6d annual rent (and another tenant of Little Marsden made a similar offer for his land), 'to stay the spoilage of their lands which would happen if strangers got a lease thereof and make many holes searching for and getting coals, rather than for any benefit which they were likely to get'.[24]

The crucial question, however, which arose at the very end of the sixteenth century was whether a copyholder might legitimately take a lease of the coal in his land and exploit it himself. It was generally agreed among copyholders that the Crown farmers of the coal mines did not have an automatic right of entry into their lands to mine for coal, but might enter only with permission, and even then the copyholder could expect compensation for any damage incurred. On the other hand, they were less clear as to whether they might exploit coal on their own account. John Hartley of Swinden stated in 1600 that he had been advised by his friends against seeking a lease from the Crown of the coal in his copyhold land, because it had been granted already to the Queen's farmer, Lawrence Lister. John Hartley of Waterside thought the same.[25] However, when Henry Barcroft obtained a lease in 1597 of the coal in his copyhold lands in Great Marsden, the attempt by Lister to dispute the validity of the grant clearly failed and other such grants followed.[26] The Crown's need for cash had contributed to a clear redefinition of rights to coal in favour of the copyholders.

(a) *Risk* It should be appreciated that coal mining during this period was, from a financial point of view, 'speculative in the highest degree'.[27] This was partly due to the risk of mining for coal, and either not finding any, or discovering a seam which soon ran out or which proved impractical to exploit. During the first two decades of the seventeenth century, Lawrence Towneley sank seven pits in the copyhold lands of Robert Hartley in Great Marsden and one in the grounds of Robert Walker. Coal was obtained from three of these pits in reasonable quantities, and a few coals were obtained from another; but no coal at all was mined from the other four pits, despite the large sums spent on timbering.[28] Clearly, if this was at all typical, a failure ratio of one pit in two might be expected.

Furthermore, it was possible that a seam which proved productive initially might become extremely difficult or impossible to exploit. For example, Lawrence Towneley was able to mine for six years at Carr Heys in Trawden forest after he had built a sough, but he had to abandon mining in about 1619 because 'the coal-bed at one end of the copyhold land went quite out . . . and at the other end of the copyhold land the current of water could not be drawn off the coal in regard the coal bed dibbed into the hills, notwithstanding all their best endeavours to dry the same'.[29] Some copyholders, coal miners and other persons skilled in coal mining from Great and Little Marsden were called together in 1604 to inquire into the likely profits that would accrue to the King from leasing the coal there, but they refused to make any valuation 'because oftentimes suchlike mines do lie uncertain in the grounds and can very hardly be gotten by reason of great quarrels of stone or abundance of water, which are very chargeable to dig through, and perhaps not possible at all to be gotten through with any reasonable charges'.[30]

The possibility of natural disaster occurring added further to the risks which faced the colliery owner. This most often took the form of flooding. Langton has argued that flooding was responsible for the closure of many pits in south-west Lancashire during this period, and was a reason for the short-lived nature of most of the collieries.[31] The same was certainly true of north-east Lancashire too. For example, it was stated in 1600 that Lawrence Lister had sunk a shaft for coal in the Lee in Great Marsden waste, but had been driven out by 'extremity of water'.[32] In addition, there was the danger that a mine might collapse due to a fall of earth, which would necessitate much costly timbering as a preventative measure.

Coal mining seems to have attracted an inordinate number of disputes, many of which centred around alleged sabotage to the mine or violence perpetrated on the colliers. It was alleged in 1618, for example, that Lawrence Towneley had ordered his workmen John Foster and Lawrence Brigg to sabotage a rival's pit by taking away one pillar, thereby causing a cave-in which hindered his rival's workmen (who were digging for coal on the waste) from digging in Towneley's copyhold land.[33] Sabotage was also alleged in the Greenfield dispute in 1572, in which both sides agreed that the rope of Anne Towneley's mine in Great Marsden had been cut, and the turn, together with an assortment of stone, coal and timber, had been thrown into the pit.[34] Some of these charges may have been invented, but, as Nef argued, the charge of sabotage was made too frequently to be dismissed as mere fabrication.[35] Whatever the nature of the dispute, it could be extremely expensive for both parties if it resulted in litigation before the law courts in London, with the prospect of a protracted suit and the possibility of a counter-suit adding further to the delay and cost.

It is therefore not surprising to find that the life of a typical coal mine in this area could be extremely short. The lease of the Barcrofts' mine in Great Marsden was granted in 1597, but it was apparently in disuse in 1604.[36] Langton found a similar picture in south-west Lancashire where 70% of coal mines during the period from 1590 to 1690 had a working life of less than ten years.[37]

(b) *Initial capital outlay*   The cost of obtaining a lease of a coal mine could be extremely high. For example, Richard Towneley was alleged to have spent about £30 in making a composition with the Duchy court for a lease of a coal mine at Carr Heys in Trawden forest, together with the expense of riding three times to London, according to a deposition of 1627.[38] Expenses could be even higher if a speculator had already obtained the desired lease. Thus it was alleged in 1600 that William Lister had undertaken three journeys to London to obtain coal mine leases; each journey cost about £20, and in addition, Lister agreed to pay £10 to Mr. Ingram Marton, together with a 'hundreth' and an annual rent of £20 to the executors of Mr. Freston. He was also required to pay a small annual rent to the Queen.[39]

Having obtained a lease, further initial expenditure was obviously required for digging pits. This could be extremely high. For example, a witness alleged in 1627 that Lawrence Towneley claimed to have spent at least £100 in digging, sinking, soughing and drying coal in his copyhold lands at Carr Heys, since the beginning of a lease in 1607.[40] The scale of this expenditure depended partly on the type of mine needed. There were three basic types; first, surface diggings, such as those at Castercliff in Great Marsden; secondly, beehive mines made by digging a shaft eight to ten yards deep to reach a suitable seam and then widening the bottom of the shaft by digging outwards and later upwards to form a beehive shape, such as occurred at Swinden and Lee in Great Marsden; thirdly, drift or tunnel pits, made by digging at an incline into the sides of a hill, such as those at Black Hill and Nook.[41] Clearly, the cost of mining increased with depth, mainly due to the need for more timber for support, and the cost of the labour required to install it. Sinking a pit without timbering cost at least 22d a yard, and timbering 10s a yard (including the cost of timber and labour), according to depositions in 1618. Estimates of the depth of pits at Haghead in Great Marsden varied from 16 or 17 yards to 21 or 22 yards; apparently the depth of timbering varied in these mines, but might extend to 18 yards. In the last case, the pit was alleged to be 21 yards deep in all, and therefore the cost of sinking and timbering must have amounted to £10 18s 6d.[42] Timbering was essential, for without it the mine would collapse.

Furthermore, it was often necessary to dig soughs, or trenches to drain off the water, which added still further to initial expenses. A sough was costly to construct; for example, three workmen were employed making a sough at Carr Heys in Trawden which took almost twelve months to construct and which allegedly cost between £18 16s 10d and over £20 in 1612–13, according to different estimates made in 1627.[43] Some soughs were even more expensive, for a deposition of 1600 stated that William Lister's wage bill for building a sough amounted to £50, and in addition he spent more than £50 on timber and stone. The construction of this sough had employed ten carpenters and five miners for about a quarter of a year.[44] Naturally, the cost of such a project would be increased considerably if the raw materials had to be transported from a distance. When making a sough in Great Marsden, Towneley had to bring timber from Carr Heys in Trawden, eight miles away.[45]

(c) *Maintenance costs* Colliery owners also faced considerable expenditure on rent, compensation for damage, and wages. Annual rents to the Duchy were usually low, though, as we have seen, large entry fines might be demanded.[46] This was really a bad bargain for the Crown, for with long leases in operation, usually of 21 years, the opportunity to exploit financially profitable mining enterprises was severely restricted.[47] On the other hand, rents to middlemen or speculators could be extremely high. For example, in 1629 Nicholas Mitchell surrendered two closes containing 12 acres of land in Colne to Richard, Thomas and Anthony Freston, as security for payment of rent for coal mines at Castercliff and Dryhurst in the township of Great Marsden. Mitchell had taken a lease of these mines for seven years, and had agreed to pay a huge annual rent of £46 10s 0d.[48] Clearly, Mitchell must have anticipated substantial profits from these mines to justify this level of rent. The Duchy was benefiting very little from its lease to the Frestons, for they paid just 11s annually for the right to mine for coal in all the wastes of Colne manor and Trawden forest.[49]

Secondly, a colliery owner was required to give compensation if he dug for coal in the copyhold land of another. This was explicitly stated in the ministers' accounts for adjacent Padiham in 1546, where a colliery owner was required to give sufficient coal for fuel to anyone in whose grounds he dug during the period in which he was mining, and was also obliged to give compensation for any damage caused by mining, and after mining was finished, he was required to fill up his pits.[50] Compensation was mentioned in numerous lawsuits. For example, John Hartley, a yeoman of Swinden, alleged in 1600 that he had received eighty horseloads of coal annually from William Lister in return for allowing him to get coal in his copyhold land. Another witness claimed that Lister had lent his workmen and tools to Hartley, to enable him to get the coal.[51]

However, the major component of colliery expenses was the wage bill. It seems that a typical mine in this area employed about six men.[52] James Tattersall had six workmen digging for coal at Limefield in Ightenhill manor in 1598.[53] Similarly, William Lister had seven workmen in his pay in Great Marsden in 1564,[54] and Lawrence Towneley usually kept six men at work at Haghead in Great Marsden, whose wages amounted to £8 each per annum according to a deposition in 1618.[55] Thus annual expenditure on wages in a typical mine at the end of the sixteenth century might amount to about £48 a year. Colliers' wages seem to have been high, relative to other activities. Henry Brigg stated that he had been paid a shilling a day for four years between 1615 and 1619, whilst working at Carr Heys.[56] Presumably there were periods when Brigg was laid off due to bad weather or flooding in the mine, and Stone has shown that colliers took a good deal of time off voluntarily for festivals or holidays.[57] Thus Brigg's wage is not necessarily incompatible with the annual wage for this period of £8 quoted previously. If the two figures are compatible, it would suggest that miners worked on average for 160 days a year. The lack of colliery accounts for this area is a great handicap, since we can only provide a very rough guide to actual working expenses.

There were also what might be described as 'extraordinary' maintenance costs, which were incurred on an irregular basis. For example, Lawrence Towneley was obliged to repair the watergate at Carr Heys several times, according to a deposition in 1618. He apparently spent £3 6s 8d on one occasion, and at other times the cost varied both above and below this figure.[58] Moreover, flooding or a fall of earth not only necessitated expenditure on repair but also represented time (and therefore profit) lost.

(d) *Productivity and profit* The above analysis may have given the erroneous impression that coal mining in the Colne district during this period was a highly unprofitable activity. It is clear, however, that a substantial income might be generated in many cases. Three estimates were given in 1600 of the profits from Lawrence Lister's coal mines on the wastes of Colne manor; these were £40, £20 and £10 per annum, 'over and above all charges'. The last two estimates are probably the more reliable since they were given by witnesses, whereas the first figure was quoted by the defendants in the case, in whose interests it was to show that Lister's profits from his coal mines on the waste were substantial enough already, without having to interfere in other tenants' copyhold lands.[59]

The profits which might be obtained from coal mining were usually greatest during the early stages of mining, whilst the coal was relatively easily accessible. Deeper digging often necessitated additional timbering for support and possibly soughing too, which all added to the expense and therefore reduced the rate of profit.[60] The profits of the Towneley mine at Carr Heys were alleged to have been £28 19s 6¼d between 13 June 1607 and 17 October 1607, but later it seems that profits were less. Towneley apparently received between 10s and 12s a week in clear profit for six months after building a sough (in about 1613), and for six years after the sough's construction, he generally received 10s a week in clear profit.

Another witness estimated that within two years of building the sough, Towneley had recouped his money spent on it, in addition to covering his working expenses for the period; estimates of the cost of the sough varied from £18 16s 10d to over £20, which suggest that annual profits may have been in the region of £10.[61] This also implies that the mine was in operation for perhaps 20 weeks a year.[62]

The Towneley mine at Haghead in Great Marsden appears to have been more profitable. It was alleged in 1617 that Towneley received 20s a week in clear profit and that the annual profit 'above all charges' was £13 6s 8d.[63] This implies that Haghead was operated for a shorter period than Carr Heys, perhaps about 13 weeks a year, but nevertheless yielded greater profits. It seems that coal mining was a highly seasonal activity, and the evidence points to the summer and autumn, when the weather was most favourable, as the usual period of operation. Indeed, explicit reference was made in one case to the 'summer season'.[64] This might continue until early November at least.[65]

An important factor governing profitability of coal mining was the depth of the shaft. It was stated in 1600 that William Lister's pit, which was between 14 and 20 fathoms deep, was suffering greatly from competiton from coal dug in Henry Barcroft's pit, which was only 4 fathoms deep. Thus Barcroft might 'better afford to sell his coals at 12d the score than Mr. Lister for 20d, respecting the charge of the getting of coals'. The situation was so serious that Lister had apparently not even received sufficient income to cover his expenses, and had therefore been compelled to abandon mining before the end of the summer season, and also indulge in the costly business of litigation in an attempt to force Barcroft to close his pit.[66]

Competition, and its effects on the price of coal in the market was therefore another crucial element in determining the level of profit. Before the grant of Barcroft's lease in 1597, Lister had only to worry about competition from the mines in the freehold lands of the Towneleys at Greenfield.[67] Barcroft's lease was to be merely the first of a number of such grants to copyholders.[68] This had a direct effect on prices and hence on profits, for apparently Lister had increased the price of his coal about four or five years previously from 1d to 1½d a horseload, but was forced to reduce his price to 1d again when Barcroft opened his pit.[69] Barcroft's mine was allegedly producing, according to different estimates, 160, 180 or 200 horseloads a day, which converts to a daily income of 13s 4d, 15s or 16s 8d (at 1d a horseload).[70] Naturally, expenses would have to be deducted from this income. Nevertheless, this level of productivity was extremely high and probably exceptional; the mine at Carr Heys produced just 80 loads in a single day in October 1607, only four months after opening.[71]

In 1650, the parliamentary commissioners made estimates of the annual value of the coal mines in this area,[72] which are particularly useful because, in contrast to the statements of litigants or their witnesses, they are relatively impartial. A total of five mines out of eight from Colne manor and Trawden forest were flooded or in disuse.[73] Although this survey was drawn up following a period of Civil Wars, and hence economic dislocation, it might be expected that the valuation of mines which were in operation would bear reasonably close resemblance to normal profitability. The valuations of the three mines which were in working order were put at £60, £30 and £6 13s 4d per annum (over and above the rents paid to the Crown of 11s, 40s and 13s 4d respectively), which were far below some of the pits in the Wigan area, two of which generated £200 each in 1624–5.[74] Moreover, the most profitable mine of the three, that in Trawden, was stated to be in disuse only twelve years later.[75]

THE COLLIERS

A necessary prerequisite for successful coal mining was that there should be a supply of skilled workmen. Indeed, it is evident that there was a tradition of coal mining in certain families, such as the Boothmans of Marsden and the Briggs of Colne. For example, Henry Brigg, a collier of Colne, stated in 1618 that his father had also worked as a collier under Mr William Lister, and he too had worked for Lister and later for his son Lawrence Lister.[76] Similarly, a yeoman of Great Marsden named John Holgate aged 40 in 1618 said that his father had been banksman to both Mr Lawrence Lister and Sir William Lister, and he himself had been banksman to Sir William Lister after his father's death.[77] This tradition was also found by Langton in his work on south-west Lancashire.[78]

It is also likely that just as there was a persistence of coal mining employment in certain families, colliers tended to remain in this activity for the duration of their working lives, changing master when necessary. Lawrence Brigg, a collier of Great Marsden, stated in 1618 that he had been employed in the mine of Lawrence Lister Esquire in Great Marsden wastes, and had also worked for

Lawrence Towneley in copyhold land at Haghead.[79] Some colliers worked for the same master for considerable periods. Henry Brigg of Colne had worked for Lawrence Towneley as a collier for six years, and James Stanfield of Colne had been employed for five years and ten months between 1613 and 1619.[80] Brigg was in his sixties during this period, and thus age was no bar to employment. Colliery owners must have valued the services of skilled older colliers, whose experience would be especially useful in such tasks as the selection of suitable sites for shafts and the training of younger colliers.

The number of colliers employed in the Colne area cannot have been very great. If we assume that there was an average of six colliers per pit,[81] and even if we include the two pits in operation in Little Marsden together with the four in Colne manor and Trawden forest in 1600,[82] the total workforce probably did not exceed forty men. In 1650 there were only three working pits in this district,[83] and therefore the size of the workforce had almost certainly contracted. However, other specialist workmen might also be employed for specific tasks. Carpenters were in particular demand for soughing and general timbering work. Ten carpenters and five miners were employed for about three months constructing a sough for William Lister, according to a deposition in 1600.[84]

It is extremely difficult to draw firm conclusions regarding the standard of living of colliers. Nef calculated that an English collier could expect to receive, by the end of the seventeenth century, between £6 and £8 annually, taking into account unemployed periods and bonuses, and was therefore a little better off than some manual labourers.[85] This estimate is certainly in accord with a collier's annual income of £8 in 1618 previously quoted.[86] Nef also pointed out that few miners could expect to work for more than half the year during the period from 1550 to 1700[87] and this certainly seems to have been the case in the Colne district.[88]

It is therefore unlikely that coal mining can be regarded as a by-employment to be taken up when required, since the skilled nature of the work and the colliery owner's need for a regular workforce would militate against this. Nevertheless, it is probable that many colliers possessed some land and a few animals which would be tended by the rest of the family and which would occupy some of their attention out of the mining season. For example, in 1635, a collier named William Boothman of Marsden mortgaged a messuage, buildings and 11 acres of waste in Marsden to John Hammond for a payment of 50s.[89] Other colliers also occupied cottages on the waste; in 1638, William Watson, a collier of Colne, sold a messuage and garden at Colne Waterside to Edmund Waterhouse for £20.[90]

Some colliers may have been involved in other non-agricultural activities such as clothmaking during the winter and spring. However, the scale of these other pursuits must remain a matter of speculation, since there does not seem to be a single inventory extant of a collier from the Colne area during our period. The only inventory in which coal mining is explicitly referred to is that of the yeoman John Higgen of Little Marsden, who died in 1617. Higgen was a fairly wealthy man whose personal estate including debts amounted to £167 8s 0d; it included two coal picks, but most items were agricultural, with considerable wealth invested in livestock and crops.[91] Higgen was an entrepreneur rather than a collier, for he had taken a lease of the coal in his lands in Little Marsden in the manor of Ightenhill in 1590.[92]

CHANGE OVER TIME

We have noted the important development which occurred at the end of the sixteenth century, when copyholders won the right to take leases of the coal in their lands.[93] The suit *Lister* v *Barcroft et al.* of 1599 was clearly a test case.[94] Henry Barcroft had already been granted a lease of the coal in his copyhold land at Swinden in Great Marsden,[95] and Lister, the Crown farmer of the coal mines in Colne manor, challenged the legality of the grant on the grounds that he had the sole right to exploit coal found both in copyhold as well as waste land. As has been shown, the competition was extremely bad for Lister's business.[96] Apparently Henry Barcroft's father had previously requested Lister's permission to get coal at Swinden and had offered to share half of the cost if he might take half of the coal mined. Lister had refused this offer and also that made five or six years later by Henry himself, who also wished to mine for coal at Swinden.[97] The judgment in this particular case does not appear to have survived, but it must have gone in Barcroft's favour, since he continued to mine, and other grants of coal in copyhold land followed.[98]

This change in policy should be seen as a means by the Crown to obtain additional revenue, rather than as a paternalistic gesture to remove the monopolistic control of Lister. Five grants of the right to mine for coal in copyhold land in Colne manor and Trawden forest were issued by the Duchy in the period from 1605 to 1608.[99] However, we should not assume that all of these mines were necessarily of great importance, for it has already been noted that the offer of John Hartley to take a lease was merely to prevent damage to his holding in Great Marsden by another lessee, rather than for any benefit which he was likely to get.[100] What is important, nevertheless, is that the virtual monopoly of coal mining by Crown lessees (virtual, since they had to face some competition from freeholders, such as the Towneleys at Greenfield) had now been broken. The early seventeenth century was an era of increased competition between collieries which, in at least one case, had the effect of reducing prices.[101] This is likely to have had an important influence on the efficiency of local collieries, and may also have resulted in earlier abandonment of shafts than was usual in the sixteenth century, if deeper and hence more costly mining was required.

An equally important theme was continuity in the types of entrepreneurs involved in coal mining in this area – it was the gentry who predominated as colliery owners. For example, the Listers, who held a lease from the Duchy of the coal mines in Colne from the mid-fifteenth century until the very early seventeenth century,[102] were a West Riding family which also had colliery interests in the Halifax area.[103] Other capital came from gentry resident in the Colne district, for many of the numerous branches of the Towneley family were involved in financing coal mining in the Colne and Burnley areas. Similarly, the Barcrofts of Lodge in Pendle, who mined at Swinden, were a substantial gentry family.

In view of the large capital inputs often required, it is not surprising that it should have been the larger landowners who were most involved in the local coal industry. The cost of reaching the deeper seams was such that few peasants could afford to undertake a colliery enterprise without outside capital. Langton found a similar picture of gentry dominance amongst the coal entrepreneurs of south-west Lancashire during this period.[104] However, he also noted that even the middling gentry did not usually possess sufficient cash resources to run collieries successfully over long periods.[105]

CONCLUSION

It must be remembered that much of this discussion is based on litigation, and that there are a number of reservations about the reliability of this type of evidence. Statements by litigants, or witnesses on their behalf, are not 'objective' in the same way as colliery accounts (which regrettably do not survive for any Colne mine during this period), but are statements by interested parties determined to put forward one point of view. Even where a judicial decision survives, we cannot assume that the claims made by the victorious party were necessarily more accurate than those of their opponents. Furthermore, witnesses' depositions were often recorded after a considerable period of time had elapsed, and since many witnesses were old it may be presumed that memories were failing in some cases. In addition, litigation describes a situation at the time of the 'crisis' which produced the dispute, which may have been untypical of general working conditions. All this may seem somewhat hypercritical. It is certainly true that, without utilising legal sources, information on local coal mining during this period is very sparse. Nevertheless, it is wise to be aware of the deficiencies in the source material, which is a topic on which Nef is notably silent.[106]

Our findings do not suggest that the Colne coal industry experienced a 'revolution' in the levels of production during the period from 1500 to 1650. Nef argued that 'in the hundred and thirty years following the accession of Elizabeth the production of coal, in comparison with previous production, increased scarcely less rapidly than during the hundred and twenty years following 1775, the period commonly thought of as ushering in the Coal Age'.[107] With regard to north-east Lancashire, Nef quoted the example of a colliery at Clayton le Moors, which was said to be worth £200 annually in clear profit in 1672, and claimed that if five or six of the score or more mines in this area operated on this scale, the production of coal in north-east Lancashire must have rivalled even that of south-west Lancashire at the end of the seventeenth century.[108] However, there is no sign, at least by 1650, that Colne mines operated on this scale.

It is quite apparent that the organisation of coal mining contrasts strongly with that of the predominant industry in the Colne area, namely woollen cloth production. Whilst the former was essentially capital-intensive, with a significant cleavage between capital and labour, the latter was far more labour-intensive, with capital playing a relatively small role. In order to participate in coal mining as an entrepreneur, large quantities of capital were needed; conversely, in woollen cloth production, quite modest resources were not a bar to setting up manufacture, since the cost of cloth instruments and raw materials was fairly cheap.[109]

We should not use the example of coal mining to demonstrate the existence of a sharp division between industry and agriculture in this area. It is quite clear that the financing and organisation of coal mining during this period came largely from the gentry, and therefore since most gentry wealth was generated from land, either directly by farming or indirectly from rents, the fortunes of coal mining must have been tied inextricably to the prosperity of agriculture.

NOTES

[1] P.R.O. D.L.3/19/T3, printed in Fishwick, *Pleadings and depositions – Henry VII and VIII*, p. 141

[2] See Chapter 3, p. 38

[3] L.R.O. WCW *Supra* inventories, *passim*. Wood has been excluded from this analysis, since it was used for a variety of purposes, and its exact function (e.g. 'firewood') is seldom stated in the inventories

[4] There are 18 inventories for the period up to 1600 (of which 9 contained both coal and turf, 1 coal only and 8 turf only) and 41 for the period from 1601–40 (of which 21 listed both coal and turf, 10 coal only and 10 turf only)

[5] See Chapter 5, pp. 71–2

[6] P.R.O. D.L.5/27 fols. 1313–14, 1322

[7] Farrer, *Court rolls*, vols. 1 and 2, *passim*; L.R.O. DDHCl3, *passim*

[8] See below, pp. 165–6, 175–6

[9] Crofton, 'Lancashire and Cheshire coalmining records', pp. 26–7

[10] See Chapter 8, pp. 182–3

[11] Nef, *Coal industry*, vol. 1, p. 206

[12] *Ibid.*, vol. 1, pp. 11–12

[13] *Ibid.*, vol. 1, p. 192

[14] Farrer, *Court rolls*, vol. 1, p. 267

[15] P.R.O. D.L.5/27 fol. 1314

[16] Farrer, *Court rolls*, vol. 1, pp. 304–5

[17] L.R.O. DDHCl3/81, Colne manor, 2nd halmote, 12 June 1599

[18] L.R.O. DDHCl3/90, Colne manor, 1st halmote, 27 January 1608

[19] Nef, *Coal industry*, vol. 1, p. 306

[20] P.R.O. D.L.1/131/T4, D.L.4/7/34, D.L.6/14

[21] Nef, *Coal industry*, vol. 1, p. 310

[22] P.R.O. D.L.1/189/L7a

[23] P.R.O. D.L.1/109/A9

[24] P.R.O. D.L.44/648

[25] P.R.O. D.L.4/42/21 m.2

[26] See below, pp. 175–6

[27] Nef, *Coal industry*, vol. 1, p. 377

[28] P.R.O. D.L.4/66/27 m.5
[29] P.R.O. D.L.4/76/19 m.4
[30] *Ibid.*
[31] Langton, *Geographical change and industrial revolution*, p. 67
[32] P.R.O. D.L.4/42/21 m.2d
[33] P.R.O. D.L.4/66/27 m.7
[34] P.R.O. D.L.1/102/T10, D.L.4/15/50
[35] Nef, *Coal industry*, vol. 1, pp. 339–40
[36] P.R.O. IND 17596, p. 344, D.L.1/189/L7a; D.L.44/648
[37] Langton, *Geographical change and industrial revolution*, p. 39. However, Langton admits that it is impossible to tell how far this is due to the patchy nature of the records
[38] P.R.O. D.L.4/76/19 m.2d
[39] *Ibid.*, m.2d
[40] P.R.O. D.L.4/76/19 m.2
[41] Bennett, *History of Marsden*, pp. 104–5
[42] P.R.O. D.L.4/66/27 m.5–5d
[43] P.R.O. D.L.4/76/19 m.2, 4–4d
[44] P.R.O. D.L.4/42/21 m.1d
[45] P.R.O. D.L.4/66/27 m.5
[46] See above, p. 168
[47] See Chapter 4, p. 58
[48] L.R.O. DDHCl3/112, Colne manor, 1st halmote, 20 October 1629. These mines were also known as Height Pits and the Lenches respectively
[49] P.R.O. IND 17596, p. 648
[50] P.R.O. D.L.29/82/1576 (Blackburnshire forest)
[51] P.R.O. D.L.4/42/21 m.2–2d
[52] Thus the mines in the Colne area were probably of a similar scale to that Sheffield mine examined by Stone, where the total workforce was usually five and never more than eight. Stone, 'Elizabethan coalmine', p. 97
[53] P.R.O. D.L.1/185/T12
[54] P.R.O. D.L.4/7/34 m.4
[55] P.R.O. D.L.4/66/27 m.5
[56] P.R.O. D.L.4/76/19 m.4d. Kersey weavers in the 1620s and 1630s were paid at most 9d a day; see Chapter 6, pp. 121–2. Slaters were generally paid 4d a day, and were also given food valued at between 4d and 6d in the 1620s and 1630s. L.R.O. DDPt 1, *passim*
[57] Stone, 'Elizabethan coalmine', pp. 101–2
[58] P.R.O. D.L.4/66/27 m.5
[59] D.L.1/189/L7a, D.L.4/42/21 m.5–5d. Nef quotes only the £40 estimate; Nef, *Coal industry*, vol. 2, p. 70, note 4
[60] Langton, *Geographical change and industrial revolution*, p. 73
[61] P.R.O. D.L.4/76/19
[62] Assuming that weekly profit was 10s
[63] P.R.O. D.L.4/66/27 m.7d
[64] P.R.O. D.L.4/42/21 m.1d
[65] The mining of coal was allegedly taking place on 2nd November 1572 in Greenfield. P.R.O. D.L.1/102/T10
[66] P.R.O. D.L.1/194/L1, D.L.1/189/L7, D.L.4/42/21

[67] See above, p. 165

[68] See below, pp. 175–6

[69] P.R.O. D.L.4/42/21 m.5

[70] P.R.O. D.L.1/194/L1, D.L.4/42/21 m.1d

[71] P.R.O. D.L.4/76/19 m.6

[72] P.R.O. E.317 Lancs.8, m.2–4, 13–16, 43, 78; E.317 Lancs.19; E.320 J/11, ZZ/8, ZZ/22

[73] It should be noted that the mine leased to Jeremy Webster, which was stated to be situated in Great Marsden, was recorded wrongly under Ightenhill manor. P.R.O E.317 Lancs.8, m.2–3

[74] Langton, *Geographical change and industrial revolution*, p. 73

[75] Farrer, *Court rolls*, vol. 2, p. 449

[76] P.R.O. D.L.4/66/27 m.5d

[77] *Ibid.*, m.7d

[78] Langton, *Geographical change and industrial revolution*, p. 72

[79] P.R.O. D.L.4/66/27 m.5d

[80] P.R.O. D.L.4/76/19 m.4–4d

[81] See above, p. 170

[82] These pits are referred to in various depositions in P.R.O. D.L.4/42/21. The pits were at Lee in Great Marsden, Spring in Great Marsden, Trawden, Marsden, together with two pits in Little Marsden

[83] See above, p. 173

[84] See above, p. 169

[85] Nef, *Coal industry*, vol. 2, pp. 195–6

[86] See above, pp. 170–1

[87] Nef, *Coal industry*, vol. 2, p. 183

[88] See above, p. 172

[89] L.R.O. DDHCl3/118, Colne manor, 1st halmote, 20 October 1635

[90] L.R.O. DDHCl3/121, Colne manor, 1st halmote, 25 October 1638

[91] L.R.O. WCW *Supra*, will and inventory, 1617

[92] The lease is recorded in P.R.O. 17596, p. 341 and D.L.29/84/1594 (Ightenhill manor). It was noted in 1604, however, that Higgen had forfeited his lease and refused to pay his rent because he could obtain no more coal due to flooding. P.R.O. D.L.44/648

[93] See above, p. 166

[94] P.R.O. D.L.1/194/L1, D.L.1/189/L7, D.L.4/42/21, D.L.5/22 fols. 516, 526, 573, 762, 804, 883

[95] P.R.O. IND 17596, p. 344

[96] See above, pp. 172–3

[97] P.R.O. D.L.4/42/21 m.2d

[98] That Barcroft continued to mine and was restrained by difficulties of extraction, not by legal means, is implied in P.R.O. D.L.44/648

[99] P.R.O. IND 17596, pp. 637–8; D.L.29/85/1602 (Colne manor and Trawden forest)

[100] See above, p. 166

[101] See above, pp. 172–3

[102] The Listers first appear as lessees of coal mines in 1450–1. P.R.O. D.L.29/77/1509 (Trawden)

[103] Nef, *Coal industry*, vol. 2, p. 9

[104] Langton, *Geographical change and industrial revolution*, p. 74. There were, however, a number of small non-gentry enterprises in the 1620s and 1630s

[105] *Ibid.*, p. 77

[106] Nef consistently fails to note the differing reliability of the various sources which he uses, and in particular, the drawbacks in using litigation. Nef, *Coal industry, passim*

[107] *Ibid.*, vol. 1, p. 20

[108] *Ibid.*, vol. 1, p. 63

[109] See Chapter 6, pp. 115–18

CHAPTER VIII

OTHER INDUSTRIES AND OCCUPATIONS

It would be a mistake to give the impression that industry in the Colne area was limited to participation in cloth production or coal mining, for it will be shown in this chapter that other activities, such as quarrying, building, tanning, the provision of clothing, food, drink and agricultural equipment were of significance.

Many of these activities were intimately linked to agriculture. A number of craftsmen were also farmers, sometimes on a significant scale. Also most trades relied on agriculture to provide them with raw materials; for example with wool for cloth, hides for leather and corn for baking and brewing. In turn, some craftsmen, notably blacksmiths, carpenters, wheelwrights and ploughwrights, supplied farmers with essential tools, whilst building workers constructed not only houses but also barns and stables. Thus we cannot distinguish sharply between an 'industrial' and an 'agricultural' sector.[1]

Limestone was a particularly important natural resource found in many parts of Colne manor and Trawden and Pendle forests, as can be seen from the frequent references to its use in the halmote records.[2] Lime was used both in the making of mortar and also as a fertiliser.[3] Rights to the use of limestone were clearly laid down. The copyholders of Colne manor were permitted to gather limestone on their own holdings, and they were also allowed to obtain some limestone from the wastes, providing such limestone was used only on their own holdings and was not sold.[4] The manorial juries were particularly concerned to ensure that this latter restriction was observed, in order to conserve limestone resources. They decreed that no one was to sell limestones outside the manor of Colne, under a penalty of 2d for each infringement of this custom. This evidently did not deter Edward Mitton, Lawrence Hartley and Geoffrey Hartley who were fined 8d, 6d and 6d respectively in 1575 for selling limestones outside the manor.[5]

The Crown was also concerned in the exploitation of limestone in this area. As part of a general policy to increase revenue, the Duchy leased the right to obtain limestone in the unenclosed portions of the wastes in Burnley and Colne parishes in 1609. The lessee was William Boswell, gentleman, who paid an annual rent of 6s 8d[6] By 1650, the lease, held by Nicholas Towneley Esquire of Royle for the same rent as in 1609, was alleged by the parliamentary commissioners to be worth an additional improved rent of 33s 4d.[7] However, we have no further information on the scale of operations of these Crown lessees during our period.

An index of the increasing importance of limestone is provided by an examination of probate inventories. In the period from 1558 to 1600, only 8% of inventories from Colne chapelry and Pendle forest record limestone or lime amongst the goods listed; this compares with 22% between 1601 and 1640.[8] The greater use of limestone in the early seventeenth century can be attributed largely to the rise in population, which must have increased the demand for buildings, and hence mortar. In addition, the period from 1570 to 1640 is known to have been one of rebuilding, both nationally and in north-east Lancashire.[9] Secondly, and more speculatively, it is possible that lime was increasingly in use as a fertiliser as tenants attempted to increase productivity per acre to offset losses in income due to fragmentation of holdings.[10]

Other natural resources available in this area included slate, which was used especially for roofs and walls. Rights to its use were defined in exactly the same way as for limestone.[11] However, in contrast to limestone, the Duchy had granted the right to mine slate in the wastes of Marsden in the later Middle Ages,[12] and this continued throughout our period.[13] Nevertheless, not all resources exploited in the Middle Ages were also utilised in the early modern period, for there are references to the mining of iron in the forests of Trawden and Pendle in the early fourteenth century,[14] but no record of such mining during the period from 1500 to 1640,[15] possibly due to exhaustion of the ore or difficulties of extraction. The copyholders were entitled to use or sell timber if it grew on their own holdings, but it was apparently in very short supply.[16]

The availability of lime and slate greatly assisted the development of the building industry. A number of inventories of building workers from the Colne area have survived which cast interesting light on their economic activities. It is clear from all of these inventories that building workers had relatively little personal estate tied up in the tools of their trade. For example, the necessary tools of a waller named James Whittaker of Fence in Pendle were valued at just 7*s* in 1601, whilst John Nutter, a carpenter of Trawden, owned tools worth 30*s* in 1636. By comparison, their personal estates, excluding debts, were valued at about £72 and £55 respectively.[17]

We should not infer, however, that the low cost of building workers' tools ensured easy entry into the trade, for obviously a considerable degree of skill and training was required. A usual way of obtaining such training was by undergoing a period of apprenticeship or service. For example, James Leigh, a mason of Catlow in Great Marsden, recorded in his will in 1617 that he had hired an apprentice named Lucas for a year for a wage of £3 6*s* 8*d*. It is interesting to note that half of this wage had been paid in advance, and though the reason for this arrangement is not stated, it is possible that it was designed to help Lucas buy necessary tools.[18] Servants were also employed in the building trades. James Parker, a carpenter of Edge in Colne, employed a servant named John Bancroft, to whom he owed a quarter's wages of 15*s* 10*d* in 1619.[19] Parker also provided Bancroft with food, drink and lodging.

Building workers often earned part of their income from other activities, especially from agriculture. The waller James Whittaker owned 9 cattle, 2 horses, 2 swine, and poultry at his death in 1601. He also possessed corn and hay valued at £16, and ploughs, harrows, oxen gear and work tools for husbandry. In addition, his household was involved in at least two other activities, tanning and cloth production, for Whittaker owned tanned leather at the Barkpit, and also cards, combs and spinning wheels. Whittaker was a reasonably prosperous man whose inventory was valued at about £72.[20] Some masons, however, were relatively poor; a mason named Richard Tootall of Winewall in Trawden died in 1595 leaving possessions worth just over £13, including a solitary cow, though he was also owed debts of over £34.[21] Indeed, not all masons were also involved in agriculture. Anthony Whitehead alias Hanson of Emmott owned neither cattle nor crops nor husbandry equipment at his death in 1608. His goods amounted to just £35 12*s* 8*d*, yet Whitehead was also owed debts worth £185 9*s* 0*d*.[22]

Inventories of carpenters confirm the generally close ties between industry and agriculture. For example, in 1576 John Craven of Alkincoats in Colne kept 2 cattle, a swine and hens. Most of his personal estate lay in debts owed to him (which amounted to over £77, compared with goods worth nearly £15).[23] John Nutter of Trawden kept 3 cattle and a mare in 1636. He also owned cards, spinning wheels and a pair of looms. However, mere ownership of instruments of textile production by a carpenter does not prove that they were being used for cloth manufacture, for they may have been made for sale. In this case, Nutter was obviously making cloth, for his inventory included wool, yarn and raw cloth valued at £19. Nutter's personal estate (excluding debts) was valued at about £55, but he owed debts of nearly £38.[24]

It is difficult to draw firm conclusions on the wealth of construction workers from inventories, for we have shown that inventories are typical largely of the 'middling sort'.[25] Furthermore, the levels of personal estate displayed in inventories would vary with the life cycle; thus the low level of wealth of Richard Tootall referred to above may have been due to the fact that he had retired; this is suggested by the absence of masonry tools amongst his goods.[26] Whilst it is true that most building workers were also involved in farming (if only in some cases to a limited extent), they were more usually subtenants rather than copyholders. Ten wills of building workers have survived for our period, and only one refers to real estate. On the other hand, at least four of the eleven testators for whom we possess wills or inventories were leaseholders.[27] Thus it is possible that a considerable number of building workers were recruited from the ranks of those men who could expect no inheritance of land.

Another activity pursued in this area was tanning. Of 215 *supra* inventories, 53 (25%) record possession of leather; of these 53 references, 12 (6%) list leather 'at tanning' or 'hides in the Barkpit', 20 (9%) record 'tanned leather' and 21 (10%) note just 'leather'.[28] Clearly, some of those testators who possessed 'leather' or even 'tanned leather' may have purchased the leather and not tanned it themselves. Conversely, some testators may have been involved in tanning at some stage, but may have owned no leather at the time that the inventory was drawn up. This latter possibility is especially likely, since the number of hides 'at tanning' was usually small, often only one; those involved in tanning on a bigger scale would have been more likely to have left some record of it in their inventory.

It seems that tanning was largely an incidental activity, and was combined with other occupations, particularly farming. For example, John Mangnolls of Great Marsden died in 1624 with leather 'at tanning and ready tanned' worth 14s. Mangnolls was a prosperous yeoman whose inventory was worth over £241, including debts owing to him.[29] Furthermore, as we have shown, some craftsmen also tanned leather.[30] However, tanning does not seem to have been a very prominent industry in this area. The absence of large-scale tanning activities can be attributed largely to the nature of pastoral agriculture practised, which tended to concentrate not on cattle fattening, but rather on stock raising for sale elsewhere.[31]

Naturally, leather was used to a considerable extent in the clothing trades, particularly in the making of gloves and shoes. Shoemakers' wealth varied considerably. At one end of the scale, Robert Taylor of Great Marsden possessed a single cow, hay, tools, leather and other household equipment valued at £6 7s 6d in 1616.[32] At the other extreme, the total value of the personal estate of John Clayton of Colne was just over £140 in 1605 (this includes the debts owing to him). Clayton's prosperity seems not have been derived from agriculture, for he owned just one cow. Nevertheless, he had accumulated money and gold worth £113 7s 0d.[33] Significantly, no shoemaker referred either to real estate or to leases taken of land in their wills, and no shoemaker's inventory listed a lease of land.[34]

Other occupations relating to the provision of clothing for which we possess wills or inventories include tailors, linen drapers and hat-makers. Here too, there was not a clear-cut division between agriculture and industry, as the following examples show. A tailor named John Habergham of Colne referred to a cottage, outhouse and garden in his will in 1631.[35] John Mitchell, a linen draper of Colne, was involved in farming in a small way; he owned a cow and a mare, as well as a swine and a goose. Mitchell's inventory, including debts owing to him, was valued at over £72 in 1611.[36] Henry Boothman, a hat-maker of the Hill, stated in his will in 1618 that the profits from his lands were to be used to pay the debts which his goods would not cover.[37]

A number of the more expensive or exotic items of merchandise, including cloth, were sold by mercers.[38] We are fortunate that an extremely detailed mercer's inventory has survived; it belongs to Lawrence Parker of Colne, who died in 1597. Parker sold many types of cloth, including taffeta, silk and lace, as well as the more mundane white kerseys. He also marketed finished clothware such as gloves, girdles and worsted stockings, and items for clothmaking such as cards, combs, buttons, thimbles, pins and thread. In addition, Parker sold many other types of merchandise, including candlesticks, purses, pepper, nutmeg, ginger, sugar, brimstone, quicksilver, soap, wax, parchment, a Bible, psalm books, primers, grammars and 'Catoes'. He does not appear to have been involved in agriculture, for he owned neither crops nor husbandry equipment, and the only animal which he possessed was a mare. In all, Parker's goods were valued at about £121, but he was also owed over £135 by 126 individuals.[39] This again illustrates the importance of credit in the local economy. Parker's inventory was drawn up in July; presumably many of his debtors would have paid up after the harvest, when cash would have been more readily available.

Obviously, another important activity was the provision of food and drink. A number of individuals from the Colne district were licensed at Quarter Sessions to act as 'badgers' to deal in corn. Between 1627 and 1639, 51 licences to trade in corn were granted to 33 men from Colne chapelry and Pendle forest.[40] In addition, a further three individuals were refused licences in 1638.[41] Corn dealers were of particular importance in an area such as Colne where crop cultivation was precarious and where, judging by the data on the distribution of land and wealth, many must have been forced to buy a large proportion of their food requirements.[42] It is regrettable that we do not have further information concerning the activities of local 'badgers'.

Turning to those who dealt with the actual processing of food (as opposed to its supply), one key specialist occupation was that of miller, who was responsible for shelling and grinding corn. As a consequence of population expansion, at least nine corn mills had been built in Colne chapelry and Pendle forest by 1640; by contrast there were one or possibly two mills in Colne in 1500.[43] Clearly the number of millers and their assistants must therefore have risen over time. Whilst some millers were paid servants of the local gentry who owned the mills or leased them from the Duchy, others purchased the right to operate on their own account. As an example of this latter practice, Henry Baldwin, a clothier of Great Marsden, alleged in 1617 that he had previously been the miller at Bradley mill, for which privilege he had paid as much as £7 per annum to Thomas Towneley.[44] Nevertheless, not all millers were such wealthy men. For example, the personal estate of a miller named Bernard Wood of Wheatley Lane in Pendle, who died in 1617, was valued at about £31, including net debts. Wood was also involved in agriculture in a small way, for he possessed kine and heifers valued at £14 and also some hens. In addition, he owned cards and a spinning wheel.[45]

No Colne or Pendle butchers' inventories appear to have survived, but occupational data derived from Quarter Sessions recognisance rolls indicate that this was a specialist employment too.[46] This is not at all surprising, for agriculture in this area was primarily pastoral and concentrated on stock-raising.[47] No reference at all to bakers has been discovered, and the ubiquitous presence of such items as bakestones and sieves in probate inventories suggests that baking was not a professional activity.[48]

Licences were issued at Quarter Sessions not only for badgers but also for alehouse-keepers. The earliest surviving example of this appears to be that of Henry Mitton of Colne, who was licensed in 1601.[49] The Justices were also concerned to regulate the activities of alehouse-keepers, and were prepared to remove the licences of those who misbehaved. Thus the alehouse of a yeoman named William Rumthwaite of Colne was suppressed in 1632 because he had permitted 'evil order' to prevail on his premises.[50] However, lack of a licence did not deter some, for 16 individuals from Colne, Marsden and Pendle were found to be keeping unlicensed alehouses at Quarter Sessions in 1601. Three years later, 17 Colne alehouse-keepers (including some of those named in 1601) were charged with this offence.[51] It is significant that four of the offenders were women. It seems that keeping an alehouse was one way for women, particularly widows, to make a living.[52] For example, Janet Radcliffe was a fairly prosperous widow of Heyhouses in Pendle whose personal estate including debts was valued at about £120; her goods included meal and malt in a brew-house.[53] Brewing was also an activity pursued by the very rich, for Richard Towneley Esquire of Carr Hall owned a brew-house in 1630, which presumably produced ale for the use of his household and servants.[54]

Another important group was that of craftsmen who made and serviced agricultural and domestic equipment, notably blacksmiths, coopers and wheelwrights. John Sharp of Wheatley Lane in Pendle was a reasonably prosperous blacksmith whose goods amounted to just over £104 in 1639. However, work as a blacksmith was not the sole source of Sharp's income, for his household was also involved both in agriculture and in textile production, as is shown by his possession of kine and calves valued at £22, 4 horses, a swine, hens, geese, a spinning wheel and a pair of looms.[55] As Brigg noted, not all who followed a blacksmith's trade were actually described as blacksmiths, for Anthony Wilson of Barrowford in Pendle owned a smithy in 1641 and yet was designated a yeoman.[56]

The dangers of relying too readily on occupational descriptions as the sole guide to economic activity, have already been outlined. Such an analysis conceals the fact that many households followed two or more activities.[57] However, occupational data are useful in two ways. First, an occupation structure illustrates the range of activities practised. Secondly, if we assume that, although many pursued more than one occupation, most men described themselves or were described by others in accordance with their main occupation, then occupational information does give us a very rough idea of the relative importance of one sector compared with another.

An examination of the occupations recorded in the Quarter Sessions recognisance rolls underlines the importance of craftsmen in the local economy. Non-agrarian occupations (excluding gentry, cloth producers and colliers) in Colne chapelry and Pendle forest between 1626 and 1642 accounted for 13% of the sample.[58] Similarly, occupational data derived from wills and inventories show that non-agrarian occupations (excluding gentry, clergy, cloth producers and colliers) comprised 9% of the sample.[59] As we have explained, both of these sources are socially selective,[60] but must be utilised in the absence of occupational information obtainable from parish registers, such as that available for Burnley between 1653 and 1660. In Burnley, the proportion of these non-agrarian occupations was much higher, for the parish register data suggest that between 24% and 28% of the male working population pursued these activities.[61]

One important activity, money-lending, is certainly not revealed by occupational analysis. Yet an examination of *supra* wills and inventories emphasises the crucial role which credit played in the local economy; 48% of *supra* wills recorded credits owed to the testator, and 31% listed debts which he owed.[62] Furthermore, it would be incorrect to conclude that the remaining testators had little involvement in credit and debt transactions, for analysis of those testators who recorded no credits in their wills and for whom we possess inventories has shown that 52% were owed money.[63] The equivalent figure for those will-makers who owed debts in their inventories but not in their wills was only 17%[64] (but it should be noted that appraisers were not obliged to put into the inventory the debts which the deceased owed).[65] In addition, we have 34 inventories for which wills do not appear to have survived; 28 (82%) of these contained credits and 16 (47%) debts. Altogether, 73% of *supra* testators possessed credits in their wills or inventories, and 42% had recorded debts.[66]

Furthermore, not only were the vast majority of testators participating in credit and debt relationships, but also many held a considerable proportion of their assets as credits. The total valuation of 220 *supra* testators' credits amounted to 25% of their assets (excluding debts).[67] This average conceals the extent of the range involved; 22 testators (10%) had more than two-thirds of their assets in the form of credits, 41 (19%) possessed credits worth between one-third and two-thirds of the valuation of their assets, 105 (48%) were owed credits worth up to a third of their assets, and there is no reference made to credits in the wills or inventories of the remaining 52 testators (24% of the sample).[68]

The picture drawn from *infra* inventories illustrates that many of the poor were also involved in credit and debt transactions, though our conclusions are at best tentative due to the small size of the sample. Credits were listed by 8 out of 18 will-makers (44%), and one (6%) referred to debts which he owed. In total, 14 out of 26 *infra* testators (54%) recorded credits in their wills or inventories, and 3 (12%) owed debts.[69]

These figures are not as informative as they at first appear, since the actual purpose or method of credit and debt transactions in wills and inventories are rarely stated. There were basically two different categories of money-lending; first, delayed payment for a commodity purchased, service provided or rent owed (and where interest was not often charged), and secondly loans of money (usually at interest).[70] The former type of loan was particularly important to pre-industrial communities where specie was in relatively short supply[71] and where a large proportion of the income of many families was generated only at certain times of the year, particularly after the harvesting and sales of cattle.[72] The latter type of loan might arise where a large payment of money was required; for example, for the purchase of land or the provision of dowries and children's portions.[73]

It is regrettable that we cannot determine the relative significance of these two types of loan,[74] though some light is cast on this problem by analysis of the importance of credits to different occupational groups. Credits expressed as a proportion of assets were of particular importance to those described as clothmakers and tradesmen; clothmakers held 41% and tradesmen 37% of their assets as credits. Women (predominantly widows) and husbandmen also had a relatively large amount of their assets as credits – in both cases 30% – whilst yeomen and gentry had just 19% and 10% respectively of their assets as credits.[75]

Tradesmen were found to be especially likely to have many credits, which though often relatively insubstantial sums individually, amounted to a considerable total of credits, as can be seen from Table 8.1.

Table 8.1   Mean number and valuation of credits, by occupational group, in supra wills and inventories from Colne chapelry and Pendle forest, 1558–1640[76]

Occupational group	No. usable	No. with credits	Mean no. of credits per testator with credits	Mean value of each credit (£)	Mean total value of credits per testator with credits (£)
Gentry	5	4	12·3	2·6	31·5
Yeomen	99	67	8·6	4·3	36·5
Husbandmen	34	25	6·1	4·7	28·7
Clothmakers	10	10	10·6	4·1	42·9
Tradesmen	16	14	19·6	2·1	40·4
Women	26	21	5·1	6·9	35·1

At one extreme, the small number and high mean valuation of women's credits suggests that they were more concerned with lending larger sums of money, and hence probably at interest. This confirms other studies which have emphasised the importance of women, especially widows, as money lenders.[77] Conversely, judging by the sheer number of credits and their relative and absolute valuation, it seems likely that most tradesmen and probably many clothmakers must have sold a substantial proportion of their wares and services on credit. The most extreme example of this is that of the mercer Lawrence Parker, who was owed sums by 126 individuals.[78] The fact that tradesmen seem to have been forced to wait for payment from their customers implies that when they first embarked on their working career, either they must have possessed a reasonable amount of working capital or that others were prepared to grant them credit to defray their expenses. Thus the availability of sufficiently large children's portions is likely to have been crucial in encouraging and facilitating sons to turn to trades and crafts.

Although no example has been found where the rate of interest is specified in an inventory, we know from other sources that some individuals were making a living, in part at least, by the financing of substantial loans at interest. For example, it was alleged in a Star Chamber lawsuit of 1621 that a husbandman named Roger Folds of Wycoller in Trawden had lent £20 four years previously to Edward

Marsden and Nicholas Mitchell, both yeomen of Colne. Folds seems to have been a professional money-lender, for it was claimed that he 'had a stock of money which he did and for a long time before had usually lent upon interest after the rate of ten pounds per centum'. In this case, the loan was to last for a year at a rate of interest of 10%; it was secured by a bond for the payment of £40, if £22 was not repaid at the end of the year. Marsden and Mitchell were granted an extension of the loan for a longer period, but subsequently litigation resulted from a dispute over repayment and the arrest of Marsden.[79]

As an alternative to a bond, a mortgage of land might be used as collateral.[80] Mortgages were naturally preferred for large loans, since they provided additional security for the money-lender. For example, in 1638 a yeoman named Richard Wilson of Lee in Great Marsden surrendered a holding of 10 acres and an acre of waste in Great Marsden to Anthony Wilson of Barrowford for a payment of £40. The terms of the mortgage stipulated that Richard was to continue to occupy the premises so long as he paid £3 4s 0d annually for the next seven years (which is 8% interest) and then repay the £40 in 1645. The surrender was then to be void, but if Richard defaulted in payment at any stage, Anthony was to be permitted to occupy the land for the next twelve years. Clearly Anthony Wilson was well protected by this arrangement.[81]

The examples found of local interest rates suggest that the statutory maximum rate of interest was adhered to. Interest was permitted in 1571 up to a limit of 10% (previously it was illegal to charge interest, apart from the period from 1545 to 1552, when interest up to 10% was allowed); in 1625, the maximum rate of interest was reduced to 8%.[82] Whilst such rates of interest might seem attractive as a means of generating wealth, money-lending was certainly not without its risks, particularly if expensive litigation was necessary to recover the loan or interest. Nevertheless, on balance, many must have felt that the benefits of lending money at interest greatly outweighed the possible risks.

In conclusion, it appears that the households of most tradesmen and craftsmen pursued two or more activities to make a living. They were particularly likely to be involved in agriculture to some extent; for example, all but two of the 19 inventories of tradesmen and craftsmen from this area listed some cattle.[83] In turn, households of yeomen and husbandmen also participated in a range of other activities, including not only clothmaking, but also quarrying, tanning, brewing and money-lending.

NOTES

¹ See Coleman, *Economy of England*, p. 71
² Farrer, *Court rolls*, vols. 1 and 2, *passim*; L.R.O. DDHCl3, *passim*
³ For the use of lime as a fertiliser, see Chapter 3, p. 39
⁴ P.R.O. D.L.5/27 fols. 1314, 1322
⁵ L.R.O. DDHCl3/58, Colne manor, 1st halmote, 13 December 1575
⁶ See Chapter 4, p. 58
⁷ P.R.O. E.317 Lancs.8, m.15; E.320 J5
⁸ L.R.O. WCW *Supra, passim*. The samples were 59 and 158 inventories respectively
⁹ Hoskins, 'Rebuilding of rural England', pp. 47–50. For a detailed analysis of house building in this area, see Sarah Pearson, *Rural houses of the Lancashire Pennines*, to whom I am extremely grateful for the opportunity to read a draft version of her text. She argues that a considerable amount of rebuilding by the gentry and yeomen occurred in this area, especially from the early seventeenth century
¹⁰ See Chapter 3, pp. 38–9 and Chapter 5, pp. 71–2
¹¹ P.R.O. D.L.5/27 fol. 1322
¹² See Chapter 1, p. 7
¹³ P.R.O. D.L.29/81/1562 – D.L.29/88/1629 (Blackburnshire Foresters' Accounts)
¹⁴ See Chapter 1, p. 7
¹⁵ P.R.O. D.L.29/81/1562 – D.L.29/88/1629, *passim*
¹⁶ In 1591, it was alleged that the copyholders and customary tenants of the manors might lawfully cut down and sell timber growing upon their copyhold land. P.R.O. D.L.1/154/H2a. However, timber was in short supply; see Chapter 3, p. 38 and Chapter 7, p. 163
¹⁷ L.R.O. WCW *Supra*, wills and inventories, 1601 and 1636
¹⁸ B.I. P.C.Y. vol. 34, fol. 668
¹⁹ L.R.O. WCW *Supra*, will 1618, inventory 1619
²⁰ L.R.O. WCW *Supra*, will and inventory, 1601
²¹ L.R.O. WCW *Supra*, will 1594, inventory 1595
²² L.R.O. WCW *Supra*, will 1607, inventory 1608
²³ L.R.O. WCW *Supra*, will and inventory, 1576
²⁴ L.R.O. WCW *Supra*, will and inventory, 1636
²⁵ See Chapter 6, pp. 132–5
²⁶ L.R.O. WCW *Supra*, will 1594, inventory 1595
²⁷ For a list of these wills and inventories, see Swain, 'Industry and economy', p. 296. It should be noted that the absence of references to real estate in a will does not prove that a testator did not have real estate
²⁸ L.R.O. WCW *Supra*, testators from Colne chapelry and Pendle forest, *passim*
²⁹ L.R.O. WCW *Supra*, will 1612, inventory 1624
³⁰ See above, p. 184
³¹ For a discussion of pastoral farming, see Chapter 3, pp. 41–51
³² L.R.O. WCW *Infra*, inventory 1616
³³ L.R.O. WCW *Supra*, will 1603, inventory 1605
³⁴ L.R.O. WCW wills and inventories, *passim*

[35] L.R.O. DDHCl3/114, Colne manor, 2nd halmote, 7 May 1632 (will dated 25 June 1631)

[36] L.R.O. WCW *Supra*, will and inventory, 1611

[37] B.I. P.C.Y. vol. 35 fol. 234

[38] For a transcription of the inventory of another Lancashire mercer and a discussion of its significance, see Bagley, 'Matthew Markland', *passim*

[39] L.R.O. WCW *Supra*, inventory 1597

[40] L.R.O. QSB 1, *passim*

[41] L.R.O. QSB 1/193/33

[42] See Chapters 3 and 5, *passim*

[43] For further details of the exact location of these mills and the sources for their existence, see Swain, 'Industry and economy', p. 301

[44] P.R.O. D.L.4/65/25 m.9–9d

[45] L.R.O. WCW *Infra*, will 1613, inventory 1617

[46] L.R.O. QSB 1, *passim*. See Swain, 'Industry and economy', Table 6.14, p. 253

[47] See Chapter 3, *passim*

[48] L.R.O. WCW probate inventories, *passim*

[49] Tait, *Lancashire Quarter Sessions records*, p. 104

[50] L.R.O. QSB 1/109/33

[51] Tait, *Lancashire Quarter Sessions records*, pp. 117, 213

[52] Brigg has also noted the role of women as alehousekeepers in seventeenth century Pendle. Brigg, 'Forest of Pendle', Part 1, p. 77; Part 2, p. 80

[53] L.R.O. WCW *Supra*, will and inventory, 1636

[54] L.R.O. WCW *Supra*, will and inventory, 1630. Towneley's personal estate was valued at over £603

[55] L.R.O. WCW *Supra*, will 1638, inventory 1639

[56] Brigg, 'Forest of Pendle', Part 1, p. 89

[57] This is particularly true for clothmaking. See Chapter 6, pp. 118–21

[58] L.R.O. QSB 1, *passim*. The sample size is 203. For further details, see Swain, 'Industry and economy', Table 6.14, p. 253

[59] L.R.O. WCW; DRCh; DDX/19/19; DDBd/60/1, 60/2, 60/6; DDWh/3/5, 3/14; DDHCl3, *passim*. B.I. P.C.Y. *passim*. The sample size is 279

[60] See Chapter 6, pp. 132–5, 145–6

[61] L.R.O. P.R.3027/1/2. The baptism register gives a total of 24% of occupations in these categories, and the burial register 28%. See Swain, 'Industry and economy', Table 6.15, p. 256

[62] L.R.O. WCW *Supra* wills, *passim*. Of 213 usable wills of testators from Colne chapelry and Pendle forest, 102 recorded credits owed to the testator, and 65 noted debts owed by the testator

[63] *Ibid.* Of the 111 testators who did not have credits mentioned in the will, 98 had usable inventories and 51 of these had credits recorded in the inventory

[64] *Ibid.* Of the 148 testators who did not have debts mentioned in the will, 130 had usable inventories and 22 of these had debts recorded in the inventory

[65] Camp, *Wills and their whereabouts*, xviii

[66] L.R.O. WCW *Supra*, wills and inventories, *passim*. A total of 181 testators out of 247 possessed credits, and 103 out of 247 had debts

[67] 'Assets' are defined as the total valuation of the testator's goods plus the credits owed to him and recorded in the inventory (or if no credits are recorded in the inventory, those in the will, if any, have been included, since some appraisers clearly did not bother to record credits in the inventory if they were already listed in the will)

[68] L.R.O. WCW *Supra*, wills and inventories, *passim*

[69] L.R.O. WCW *Infra*, wills and inventories, *passim*

[70] Holderness, 'Credit in English rural society', p. 99

[71] Clarkson, *Pre-industrial economy in England*, p. 148

[72] Holderness, 'Credit in a rural community', p. 94 and Holderness, 'Credit in English rural society', pp. 97–8, in both cases quoting from Tawney's introduction to Wilson's *Discourse upon usury*, pp. 19–25, and Tawney, *Religion and the rise of capitalism*, pp. 43–4. However, Holderness does claim, but without stating any evidence, that English data do not necessarily suggest that village borrowing increased significantly in the period before the harvest; Holderness, 'Credit in English rural society', p. 98. We cannot use credits and debts in wills and inventories to analyse the question of seasonality in these transactions, since we do not know when they were first contracted

[73] Marshall, 'Domestic economy of the Lakeland yeoman', pp. 212–15, discusses the reasons why mortgages of land might occur

[74] Holderness, 'Credit in English rural society', p. 99

[75] L.R.O. WCW *Supra*, wills and inventories, *passim*. The size of each sample was as follows; clothmakers 10, tradesmen 16, women 27, husbandmen 34, yeomen 101, gentry 5. For further details, see Swain, 'Industry and economy', table 8.2, p. 307

[76] *Ibid.* No attempt has been made to correct for inflation in estimating the value of credits, since data on inflation are too imprecise. The gentry sample is much too small for analysis and is probably distorted by inflation (in that two of the four testators with credits died in 1569 and 1575; the average valuation of credits of the other two testators, who died in 1588 and 1607, was 6.41)

[77] On the role of widows as money lenders, see Holderness, 'Credit in English rural society', p. 105; Holderness, 'Credit in a rural community', pp. 100–2; Clarkson, *Pre-industrial economy in England*, p. 148

[78] See above, p. 187

[79] P.R.O. STAC 8/213/17. Marsden was also described as a gentleman

[80] For a discussion of the numbers of sales and mortgages recorded in the court rolls, see Chapter 5, pp. 80–4

[81] L.R.O. DDHCl3/121, Colne manor, 1st halmote, 25 October 1638. It is unclear whether the two men were related

[82] Clarkson, *Pre-industrial economy in England*, p. 167

[83] L.R.O. WCW *Supra* and *Infra* inventories of blacksmiths, carpenters, glovers, linen drapers, masons, millers, shoe-makers and wallers from Colne chapelry and Pendle forest, 1576–1639, *passim*

CHAPTER IX

CONCLUSION

For purposes of analysis, it has proved convenient to organise our discussion thematically by chapter, but the effect of this may have been to blur or hide some of the connections between the various branches of the local economy. We now attempt to highlight the most important of these interrelationships.

The underlying structure of industry in the Colne area during the period from 1500 to 1640 remained essentially the same. The most prominent industry, in terms of numbers employed, was cloth manufacture, which consisted chiefly in the making of kerseys.[1]. No less than 70% of *supra* testators owned cards, combs, spinning wheels or looms. Weaving was especially concentrated in Colne chapelry and Roughlee, where approximately half of such testators were found to possess looms, compared with only a fifth of *supra* will-makers in the rest of Pendle forest.[2]

The basic unit of kersey production was the household. Proto-factory conditions were nowhere evident, for the maximum number of looms found in any household was four, and the overwhelming majority kept just one or two. Female and child labour was of fundamental importance in this structure, since women and children seem to have performed the bulk of carding and spinning (where workers outnumbered weavers by five to one).[3] Each household was independent in the sense that it owned and was responsible for the disposal of the cloth which it made; no evidence whatsoever has been discovered that an extensive putting-out system operated.[4]

Though cloth was made in very many households, it rarely constituted the sole or main source of income for households of middling wealth levels. Some practised a craft in combination with cloth manufacture,[5] but it was agriculture which occupied the attention and much of the capital of most *supra* testators.[6] Nevertheless, many testators whose main occupation was agricultural were also involved in cloth production; for example, approximately half of those yeomen and husbandmen from Colne chapelry and Roughlee who left a *supra* inventory owned looms.[7] Hence it is not surprising to find that the extent of cloth production seems to have varied with the season, for output appears to have increased during the less labour-intensive periods of the agricultural year, and contracted during the haymaking and harvesting seasons.[8]

Lack of capital does not appear to have been a major deterrent to involvement in cloth manufacture, for the instruments of production, especially cards, combs and spinning wheels, were relatively inexpensive.[9] Ultimately, however, the amount of capital which might be generated in a household economy based entirely or predominantly on cloth manufacture was limited; for example, those *infra* weavers who had minimal agricultural assets remained very poor.[10]

By contrast, coal mining was an activity which required large amounts of initial capital.[11] Thus we find that the gentry predominated amongst colliery entrepreneurs.[12] Coal mining was only one of a range of possible options for the investment of surplus gentry capital; in turn, the amount of such capital available depended in part on the level of agricultural and seigneurial income which the gentry derived from their lands. An important factor influencing any decision to invest in coal mining was the high degree of risk involved. It was not easy to find a seam which would prove productive in the long term, and the measures necessary to prevent flooding and subsidence or to repair any damage caused added greatly to colliery expenses and could not be anticipated well in advance.[13] Nevertheless, a few local coal mines were reasonably profitable, though they did not operate on the scale of some of those mines in the Wigan area, still less those on Tyneside.[14]

Colliers did not constitute a sizeable proportion of the adult male population, and probably numbered just a few dozen men (though other workmen, notably carpenters, might be employed on specific tasks such as soughing).[15] Coal miners were highly skilled workmen, and, doubtless as a consequence of this and the dangers involved, received relatively high daily wages compared with those in other industries and crafts.[16] Colliers might expect to work for perhaps a maximum of six months in a year, and therefore may have worked in other capacities during the winter.[17] Local colliers cannot have been too dissatisfied with their lot, for a number remained as coal miners for long periods, and in some cases their sons followed them into the craft.[18]

Other industries and activities present during our period included the quarrying of limestone and slate, building and tanning, in addition to the usual occupations relating to the provision of clothing, food and drink, and agricultural equipment. Many of these activities were practised as by-employments, and therefore occupational data minimise the extent of such involvement. Furthermore, occupational data conceal the existence of a substantial amount of money lending, both with and without interest, particularly amongst those described as clothmakers, tradesmen and craftsmen.[19]

Thus far, we have concentrated on an examination of the enduring structures in industry, but there were also clearly defined patterns of change over time. These were especially apparent in the textile industry, but notable changes occurred in other industries too. As the local population grew throughout the sixteenth and early seventeenth centuries,[20] the demand for fuel must have risen, and it seems that coal was used increasingly as the supply of turf and timber became short.[21] The number of coal mining ventures rose particularly in the years around 1600, in response to this growing demand for coal. This increase in the number of local collieries was facilitated and promoted by the Crown's grants of the right to mine for coal in copyhold land.[22] Nevertheless, colliery ventures remained small, largely due to shortage of capital and difficulties of extraction; there were no really large collieries in the Colne area by the middle of the seventeenth century.[23] Thus we have found little support in our area for Nef's 'revolution' thesis.[24] Population growth seems to have given a similar stimulus to other industries; for example, the construction industry must have benefited from the growing need for dwellings, as well as from the rebuilding of the homes of the gentry and richer yeomen.[25]

It is in the field of textiles, however, that change over time can best be measured. There was a very significant increase in the 1600s and 1610s in the number of *supra* testators from Colne chapelry and Pendle forest who owned cards, combs and spinning wheels. However, possession of these instruments in the 1620s and 1630s fell to a similar level to that found during the later sixteenth century. The proportion of testators from Colne chapelry and Roughlee who owned looms followed the same pattern, though to a very restrained extent. These fluctuations in the ownership of instruments of textile production strongly suggest that aggregate output of local cloth had risen substantially by the 1600s and 1610s, but contracted during the 1620s and 1630s.[26] These same developments are also found in export data for northern kerseys, which were shipped overseas in increasingly large numbers until the mid-1610s, but were subsequently exported in significantly smaller quantities.[27]

The reasons for the expansion in kersey production in the Colne area, which was clearly evident by the 1600s and 1610s, are far more complex than those for the textile depression of the 1620s and 1630s. The demand for cheaper cloths such as kerseys must have risen locally, and indeed throughout the country, as population grew and the standard of living fell for very many households.[28] But given a demand for inexpensive cloths, why should an area not naturally endowed with plentiful wool supplies[29] and situated a considerable distance from the large concentrations of population and important ports be so heavily involved in textile production, and actually increase that degree of involvement?

The explanation must surely lie in the fact that a large and growing proportion of the inhabitants of the Colne area looked to textiles as a means of making a livelihood or as a source of supplementary income. This was certainly true of many who held copyhold land, which was the predominant form of land tenure in this area.[30] It was not, however, high levels of entry fines and annual rents which compelled many copyholders to seek additional income. On the contrary, rents and entry fines were fixed and became increasingly nominal in real terms as prices rose.[31] Nevertheless, copyholders faced two crucial difficulties.

First, many copyholds in Colne manor and north-east Pendle forest became subdivided during the sixteenth and very early seventeenth centuries. In Colne manor, the number of copyholds doubled between 1527 and 1617, and this resulted in a disproportionate increase in the number of very small copyholds; by 1617, nearly half of the copyholds in Colne manor were five Lancashire acres or less in size, upon which subsistence would have been practically impossible without recourse to additional income.[32] Fragmentation of holdings was the product of a number of factors, notably sales and mortgages, and the demographic consequences of primogeniture. A few examples of partible inheritance have been found, particularly in the forests following the disafforestation of 1507, but, apart from north-east Pendle, these were not areas where holdings fragmented significantly in the sixteenth century, and, increasingly, many in the forests turned away from partible inheritance strategies in the direction of primogeniture.[33]

The significance of a severe reduction in the size of many copyholds was that such holdings could support a smaller area of arable cultivation, which was especially serious with extra mouths to feed and with the price of food escalating rapidly. Furthermore, a smaller holding meant that fewer livestock might be supported on it over the winter, and, in addition, a smaller herd might be pastured on the commons and wastes over the summer (since pasture rights in these areas were stinted according to the size of copyholds). As a consequence, median herd sizes fell in Colne manor and north-east Pendle by the 1600s and 1610s.[34]

Secondly, many copyholders faced severe financial difficulties on inheriting their holdings. If they had younger brothers and sisters, in many cases they found themselves responsible for providing them with substantial cash portions, as a condition of the father's will. This was a time of rapidly rising population, and the number of families with large numbers of children increased so many heirs had to raise a good number of portions. Indeed, not all heirs received a share in their fathers' personal estate to help them defray these financial commitments. Furthermore, an heir with a widowed mother was obliged to provide her with at least a quarter of the holding and a third of her husband's personal estate as dower. Thus the years immediately following inheritance could be extremely difficult ones for an heir (particularly if there were serious economic problems to face, such as harvest failure), and could necessitate sale or mortgage of part of the holding, which might stave off immediate disaster but only at the cost of greater problems in the long term.[35] Hence many copyholders must have welcomed the opportunity in the late sixteenth and very early seventeenth centuries to obtain supplementary income from kersey manufacture.

Involvement in textile manufacture was not limited to those who inherited copyhold land but was found amongst all levels of society, including subtenants. We have found that an increasing number of households leased plots of copyhold land, often on long leases. Many of these plots of land were extremely small; this was especially true in Colne manor and north-east Pendle forest. Moreover, those who held land as subtenants not only found that their holdings were insufficient in size to provide adequate support for their families, but also faced considerable expenditure on rent payments. Indeed, those who took on new leases of copyhold land in the later sixteenth and early seventeenth centuries did so on increasingly disadvantageous financial terms. As population rose and land became relatively scarce, copyholders, who benefited from fixed rents and entry fines, found it increasingly lucrative to sublet part of their lands.[36] Thus many lessees might look to industry to provide an essential source of supplementary income.

There were also two distinct groups who could not normally expect to inherit either copyhold or leasehold land and who might therefore turn to industry. First, the most usual type of inheritance strategy practised, certainly by those who left wills in the later sixteenth and early seventeenth centuries, was primogeniture. By definition, therefore, many younger sons could not expect to inherit land. Furthermore, the number of younger sons increased as population grew. The prospects of younger sons, particularly those of copyholders, were not entirely bleak, for they might expect a cash portion which could be used to finance a textile or craft workshop and which might extend to a lease or even the purchase of a small amount of land.[37]

Secondly, it has been shown that illegitimacy was extremely high in this area, particularly in Colne chapelry and Roughlee in the early seventeenth century. For example, nearly one in eight baptisms in Colne chapelry between 1600 and 1639 were of bastards. Whilst some men readily accepted financial responsibility for the welfare of their illegitimate offspring and also left reasonable legacies to them, others were not or could not be so generous, and many fathers had to be compelled by the J.P.s to give financial support for the upbringing of their bastards. Furthermore, those bastards born to copyholders were not normally eligible to inherit land, unless special provision had been made for this by a will or deed. Thus many bastards turned to industry as a means of making a living; it is notable that the areas in which bastardy was most prominent (Colne chapelry and Roughlee) were also those most involved in weaving.[38]

One possibility for those without land, who could not afford to buy or lease it, was to squat on a portion of common. The attractions of this were obvious – the commons were plentiful and no entry fines or rents were levied. Moreover, the Duchy was extremely slack in detecting squatters and even more inefficient in obtaining rent from encroachments when they had been discovered. Even when the commons of Colne manor were granted by copyhold tenure in 1618, the cottagers on the waste were not evicted, but, on the contrary, it was agreed in 1621 that they should remain in their cottages with security of tenure and pay only nominal rents. The manorial juries increasingly seem to have turned a blind eye to encroachments, presumably because most consisted of tiny plots of land, which did not constitute a great threat to communal interests.[39] Yet the fact that these encroachments were so small and also that they were situated on very marginal land compelled their occupants to seek other sources of income.

However, the opportunities for earning a living from agricultural wage labour were more restricted in pastoral than arable areas; this was certainly true of the predominantly pastoral Colne district, where it was unusual to find a man described as a labourer. Furthermore, pastoral farmers and their families had relatively more time on their hands than those in specialist corn-growing districts, and might usefully occupy their spare time in industrial by-employments, if the opportunities arose.[40]

Thus all levels of society, rich and poor, male and female, young and old, participated in cloth production in the Colne area to an increasing extent. This became manifest by the 1600s and 1610s in the greater incidence of ownership of instruments of cloth production amongst all levels of *supra* testators, and in the frequent recording of such instruments amongst the goods of *infra* testators in these decades.[41] However, whilst *infra* weavers and spinsters made cloth out of sheer necessity, kersey manufacture was no more than useful additional income for the more prosperous yeomen.

The reasons for the depression in the kersey trade in the 1620s and 1630s seem to be entirely exogeneous, namely a collapse in the export trade in kerseys.[42] It is impossible to estimate what proportion of kerseys produced in the Colne area were destined for overseas markets, but it is likely to have been high; for example, we know that 30,000 Lancashire kerseys were exported in 1594[43] and yet kerseys were made only in the north-east of the county.[44] Furthermore, it was stated in 1638 that three-quarters of Yorkshire kerseys were exported[45] and since many kerseys made in the Colne area were finished and sold in the Heptonstall and Halifax district of the West Riding,[46] it would be surprising if a considerable proportion of Colne kerseys did not also reach the Continent via West Riding merchants. Indeed, the bulk of kerseys shipped overseas were exported from Hull,[47] and therefore the reasons for the close ties between Colne and the West Riding become even clearer.

The export trade in kerseys was hit by two severe blows. First, the Cockayne Project of 1614–17 had disastrous consequences, for many kerseys were exported undyed, and hence kersey manufacturers suffered from the ban on the export of white cloth. Secondly, a long term depression in kersey exports set in after 1620 due in part to monetary manipulation on the Continent (following the outbreak of the Thirty Years' War), which priced English goods out of the market. In addition, rival production of cheaper kerseys developed apace in Prussia and Silesia. Hence the demand for English kerseys fell considerably in the Baltic in the 1620s and 1630s, and the attempt by English merchants to find alternative markets, such as the United Provinces, did not compensate for this.[48]

The effects of a depression in the kersey export trade were clearly disastrous for areas such as Colne, where many households depended on cloth manufacture as a principal or supplementary source of income. Indeed, it is probable that the increased opportunities for textile manufacture until the mid-1610s had persuaded many to remain in the Colne district, when otherwise they might have seriously considered moving elsewhere in search of a living. Now they found themselves in dire economic straits.

The consequences of the textile depression were even more serious when combined with other unfavourable elements, such as large composition payments to the Crown and severe harvest failures. The forest tenants had been obliged to pay twelve years' rent in 1609 for confirmation of the security of their copyholds, but those in the manors were required to pay twenty years' rent in 1618 for confirmation of the certainty of their entry fines and copyhold estates, and additional new rent for the commons. A good proportion of these burdens fell on subtenants, who could least afford to pay them.[49] However, it was the effects of the harvest failures of 1621 and 1622 which proved to be far more catastrophic. Many subtenants were unable to meet the cost of escalating food prices and still pay their rents, and in consequence a large number of lessees defaulted on their rent payments in 1622–4.[50] Furthermore, some copyholders tried to stave off a calamity by mortgaging or selling land in 1622–3.[51] Nevertheless, disaster was not averted, for we have strong evidence that the crisis mortality of 1623–4 was the product largely of famine.[52]

The difficulties of the period 1621–40 seem to have been responsible for the large increase in the number of sales and mortgages recorded in the court rolls, and it was particularly in the areas hit hardest by the textile depression (Colne manor and north east Pendle) that this increase was most apparent. By contrast, the richer inhabitants of Trawden forest, for whom cloth production was no more than useful supplementary income, were hardly affected at all by this development.[53] It is therefore not surprising to find that many inhabitants of Colne chapelry decided to leave the area, particularly in the 1620s, as is indicated by the sharp decline in the number of marriages celebrated.[54]

These conclusions cast interesting light on a number of hypotheses which have been advanced to explain the reasons for the location and development of industry in the countryside in the pre-industrial period. Undoubtedly, the most significant and influential hypothesis put forward on this subject is that of Joan Thirsk. Thirsk has argued that, with the exception of the extractive industries (which by definition were located in areas endowed with mineral deposits), many industries tended to be situated in areas where labour was in abundance, rather than where the raw materials were produced. The reasoning behind this hypothesis is that raw materials, such as wool, could be transported easily to an area where labour was plentiful. The inhabitants of such areas might be especially likely to turn to industry, or to attract entrepreneurs wishing to employ them in industrial activities, if there was much unemployment and underemployment, and hence cheap labour.[55]

These circumstances, Thirsk argues, were most likely to occur in pastoral areas, which were less labour-intensive than arable regions, and which therefore offered fewer opportunities for regular employment. Such pastoral districts often had abundant and open commons and wastes which attracted immigrants, and hence encouraged population growth. Settlement on the wastes was especially likely to occur if manorial control was weak and if little attempt was made to control squatting. Apart from squatters, others who might also be particularly able and willing to turn to industry included those tenants who had only smallholdings. The small size of these farms may have been the product of partible inheritance, which led to fragmentation of holdings. In turn, partible inheritance might be a further spur to population growth, since the expectation of a future inheritance might discourage many from leaving the area. Partible inheritance was particularly likely to be practised in communities where many held land either on freehold terms, or on a type of tenure almost as good as freehold, where there was little seigneurial pressure on families to adopt unigeniture inheritance strategies.[56]

Several aspects of Thirsk's model have received considerable support within these pages. We have shown the intimate connection between the pastoral economy and the development of industry.

Moreover, it was especially in areas where fragmentation of holdings occurred most noticeably, and where many farms were as a consequence extremely small, that clothmaking was particularly prominent. Our area exhibits many of Thirsk's preconditions for the rise of industry – a pastoral economy, abundant and open commons (until 1618 in Colne manor), small farms, fragmentation of holdings, weak lordship and secure copyhold tenure (apart from the copyhold disputes). There is one notable exception, however, namely the relative absence of partible inheritance. Though partible inheritance was practised to a certain extent in the forests following the disafforestation in 1507, it became increasingly rare, and most inheritance strategies observed during the later sixteenth and early seventeenth centuries were based on the principle of primogeniture.

It appears that tenants in the Colne area actually chose to practise primogeniture, though they ensured that generous cash portions were available to their daughters and younger sons as compensation. Given the choice, it does not seem that households would necessarily choose partible inheritance strategies (as Thirsk argues),[57] particularly if they felt that this might produce excessive fragmentation of their holdings to the point where none of their sons might expect to make a successful livelihood. This in no way undermines Thirsk's hypothesis that areas where partible inheritance and the other preconditions of her model were present were likely to be particularly receptive to the growth of rural industry. However, perhaps we might replace partible inheritance by fragmentation of holdings as one element likely to promote rural industry, since this would obviously occur where partible inheritance was practised, but might also develop in districts of unigeniture, for reasons already discussed.

In the final analysis, however, the long term depression in the kersey trade evident in the 1620s and 1630s demonstrates that the rise of industry was not primarily dependent on the supply of labour but rather on the existence of a demand for particular industrial goods, the awareness of that demand by those who needed additional income, and the ability to satisfy that demand at a profit. If the demand for a product declined substantially, then the number of people who had time on their hands or who needed supplementary income was ultimately irrelevant.

Some have attempted to revise Joan Thirsk's hypothesis, or to place a different emphasis on the various elements in her model. For example. R. B. Smith has stressed the importance of the availability of capital rather than labour as a precondition for the rise of industry. Thus with reference to the West Riding, he argues that additional capital was available for the establishment of industry especially in areas of weak lordship, where tenants had to pay relatively light dues to the lord. Favourable tenurial conditions might also attract settlers to the area and hence increase the supply of labour available for industry.[58]

Pat Hudson also lays great emphasis on the importance of weak lordship in helping to explain the development of industry, but argues that weak or strong lordship helped to determine not the existence but rather the type of industry which was practised. On the one hand, she argues that weak lordship and its eventual collapse in the West Riding encouraged the enclosure of the wastes (which fell largely into the hands of a small number of substantial tenants), permitted the enfranchisement of many copyholds and the practice of partible inheritance. All contributed to a greater degree of polarisation between rich and poor peasants. This facilitated the growth of the worsted industry organised on a putting-out basis, since the richer peasants had accumulated enough capital to finance putting-out, whilst the poor had insufficient resources to set up production on their own account. Conversely, she argues that polarisation between rich and poor was retarded in areas where manorialisation was stronger, which were normally districts of more fertile land. In such areas, cloth manufacture was generally undertaken by independent artisans who combined agriculture with woollen cloth production.[59]

Both Smith's and Hudson's arguments are to some extent in sympathy with a Marxist approach which notes that industry, or the more economically advanced types of industrial organisation, were most likely to be stimulated in areas where feudalism disintegrated most rapidly. However, we have discovered little evidence to support either Smith or Hudson in our examination of industry in north east Lancashire between 1500 and 1640. It has been shown that small capital resources do not appear to have been a deterrent to involvement in the textile industry, whilst low rents did not permit many yeomen to accumulate capital sufficient to engage in substantial colliery enterprises. Secondly, we have found that weak lordship did not inevitably lead to partible inheritance, but, on the contrary, the tenants might choose primogeniture inheritance strategies even when under little seigneurial pressure to do so. Indeed, the division between lord and tenant so prevalent in much

Marxist writing is totally inadequate, for even stronger divisions were often present between tenants on the one hand, and subtenants and the landless on the other. Whilst tenants in the Colne area benefited from weak lordship, their subtenants and the landless were increasingly at the mercy of unfavourable market forces as population rose and land become more scarce in the sixteenth and early seventeenth centuries.

There are a number of important findings which emerge from this study of industry in north east Lancashire in the Tudor and early Stuart period. The most fundamental conclusion to be drawn is the overwhelming importance of industry, particularly cloth manufacture, in the local economy. It is clear that those not involved in some type of industrial or craft activity were in a minority. Thus we cannot make a clear-cut distinction between early modern and industrial Lancashire in terms of the proportion of people involved in industry.

The chief difference, however, between sixteenth and nineteenth century Lancashire is that very many inhabitants of Tudor Lancashire pursued an agricultural livelihood in conjunction with industry, whereas the industrial revolution largely destroyed this combination. Braudel has argued that the survival of the peasant in pre-industrial society was usually due to taking on by-employments,[60] whilst Thirsk has suggested that about half of the pastoral farmers in seventeenth century England were also involved in industry.[61] This study has confirmed the crucial interrelationship between agriculture and industry in the pre-industrial economy.

The exceptionally high degree of participation in industry is largely hidden if undue reliance is placed on occupational data to provide a guide to the importance of industry.[62] For example, probate inventories demonstrate that very many of those who were described as farmers rather than cloth manufacturers nevertheless owned not only cards, combs and spinning wheels, but also looms. If we were to rely on occupational data alone, we should greatly underestimate the extent of textile production, for in only 6% of *supra* inventories were male testators described as cloth manufacturers.[63] Thus, the importance of industry in the sixteenth and seventeenth centuries, particularly as a by-employment, is underlined.

The level of industrial participation was far from static, for notable changes over time have been observed, particularly in the extent of cloth production. This is in accord with the findings of

Braudel, who has noted extensive fluctuations in the proportion of the population involved in industry in the pre-industrial period.[64] Thus considerable expansion in breadth was possible by multiplying the units of production (usually the workforce). This might be achieved either by keeping a fixed proportion of the population employed in industrial activities during a period of population growth, or by increasing the proportion involved in industry, or both, as in the case of the expansion in textile production in the Colne area, evident by the 1600s and 1610s. However, industrial activity in the early modern period cannot be seen as an uninterrupted or inevitable march from feudalism to capitalism, as the depression in the kersey trade in the 1620s and 1630s shows. In the final analysis, therefore, it appears that the ability to derive an income, in part at least, from industry, was of crucial importance for the well-being of the household economy, well before the Industrial Revolution.

NOTES

[1] See Chapter 6, pp. 108–9
[2] *Ibid.*, pp. 127–8
[3] *Ibid.*, pp. 110–12
[4] *Ibid.*, pp. 113–15
[5] *Ibid.*, p. 120
[6] See Chapter 3
[7] See Chapter 6, p. 120
[8] *Ibid.*, pp. 120–1
[9] *Ibid.*, pp. 115–18
[10] *Ibid.*, pp. 119–22
[11] See Chapter 7, pp. 168–9
[12] *Ibid.*, p. 176
[13] *Ibid.*, pp. 167–8
[14] *Ibid.*, pp. 173, 177
[15] *Ibid.*, p. 169
[16] *Ibid.*, pp. 170–1, 174
[17] *Ibid.*, pp. 171–2, 174–5
[18] *Ibid.*, pp. 173–4
[19] See Chapter 8
[20] See Chapter 2
[21] See Chapter 7, pp. 163–4
[22] *Ibid.*, pp. 166, 175–6
[23] *Ibid.*, pp. 173, 177
[24] *Ibid.*, p. 177
[25] See Chapter 8, p. 183
[26] See Chapter 6, pp. 127–36

[27] *Ibid.*, pp. 136–8
[28] *Ibid.*, pp. 138–9
[29] *Ibid.*, pp. 115–17
[30] See Chapter 5, p. 70
[31] See Chapter 4, pp. 56–7
[32] See Chapter 5, pp. 71–2
[33] *Ibid.*, pp. 72–84
[34] See Chapter 3, pp. 36–7, 41–7
[35] See Chapter 5, pp. 73–84
[36] *Ibid.*, pp. 84–91
[37] *Ibid.*, pp. 73–80, 97–8 and Chapter 6, pp. 138–9, 147–8
[38] See Chapter 2, pp. 25–7; Chapter 5, pp. 78–9; Chapter 6, pp. 140–1
[39] See Chapter 5, pp. 91–3
[40] See Chapter 3, p. 50
[41] See Chapter 6, pp. 127–9
[42] *Ibid.*, pp. 137, 142–3
[43] *Ibid.*, pp. 125–6, 159n
[44] *Ibid.*, p. 108
[45] *Ibid.*, p. 136
[46] *Ibid.*, pp. 122–5
[47] *Ibid.*, pp. 136, 159n
[48] *Ibid.*, pp. 142–3
[49] See Chapter 4, pp. 60–5 and Chapter 5, pp. 80–2
[50] See Chapter 5, p. 90
[51] *Ibid.*, pp. 80–1
[52] See Chapter 2, pp. 22–5
[53] See Chapter 5, pp. 81–3
[54] See Chapter 2, pp. 20–2
[55] Thirsk, 'Industries in the countryside', pp. 71–3, and *passim*
[56] *Ibid.*, pp. 70, 76–8, 83–4, 86–7
[57] Thirsk, 'Industries in the countryside', p. 78; 'Younger sons in the seventeenth century', p. 361
[58] Smith, *Land and politics*, pp. 119–22
[59] Hudson, 'Proto-industrialisation: the case of the West Riding', pp. 40–4
[60] Braudel, *Wheels of commerce*, p. 255
[61] Thirsk, 'Seventeenth century agriculture and social change', p. 172
[62] Mendels, 'Proto-industrialisation; theory and reality', pp. 73–4
[63] See Chapter 6, p. 120
[64] Braudel, *Wheels of commerce*, p. 308

BIBLIOGRAPHY

MANUSCRIPT SOURCES

Public Record Office, Chancery Lane, London

(a) *Duchy of Lancaster*

	D.L.1	Pleadings
	D.L.3 & 4	Depositions
	D.L.5	Decrees and orders
	D.L.6	Draft decrees and orders
	D.L.7	Inquisitions post mortem
	D.L.29	Ministers' and Receivers' Accounts
	D.L.30	Court rolls
	D.L.41	Miscellanea
	D.L.42	Miscellaneous books
	D.L.43	Rentals and surveys
	D.L.44	Special commissions
(b) *State Papers Domestic*	S.P.12	Elizabeth I
	S.P.14	James I
	S.P.16	Charles I
(c) *Other legal and financial records*		
(i) *Chancery*	C.1	Early Chancery proceedings
	C.3	Chancery proceedings
(ii) *Exchequer*	E.101	Accounts
	E.134	Depositions
	E.159	King's Remembrancer memoranda rolls
	E.179	Lay subsidies
	E.190	Port books
	E.317	Parliamentary surveys
	E.320	Augmentation office
(iii) *Palatinate of Lancaster*	P.L.6	Bills

(iv) *Requests* Req.2 Proceedings, Henry VII–James I

(v) *Ministers' accounts* S.C.6

(vi) *Star chamber* STAC 8 Proceedings, James I

(d) *Maps and plans* M.P.C.

British Library, London
(a) *Additional manuscripts*
(b) *Harleian*
(c) *Lansdowne*
(d) *Stowe*

Lancashire Record Office, Preston

(a) *Wills and inventories* DRCh
  WCW
  Infra
  WCW
  Supra

(b) *Honor of Clitheroe* DDHCl3 Court rolls
  DDHCl3 Thomas Barclay's map of
  Map 5 Clitheroe Honor

(c) *Quarter Sessions* QSB Recognisance rolls
  QSP Petitions

(d) *Bishops' transcripts* DRB Chapelry register transcripts

(e) *Parochial records* P.R.

(f) *Deposited documents* DDB Parker of Browsholme
  DDBd Badgery of Colne
  DDF Farington of Worden
  DDFr Francis and Co., Cambridge
  DDIn Blundell of Ince Blundell
  DDK Derby
  DDKe Kenyon of Peel
  DDPt Petre
  DDTa Tatton of Cuerdon
  DDTo Towneley
  DDWh Whittaker of Simonstone
  DDX Miscellaneous
  DX Miscellaneous

(g) *Microfilms* MF

Borthwick Institute of Historical Research, York
   Prerogative Court of York Act Books (wills)
Cheshire Record Office, Chester
   Ecclesiastical Courts, E.D.V. 1, Correction books
Manchester Central Library
   The William Farrer collection
Wigan Record Office, Leigh
   Towneley manuscripts, D/DZ A.4, Honor of Clitheroe

PRINTED SOURCES

Acts of the Privy Council of England, 1542–1631, ed. J. R. Dasent and
   others. 46 vols. (London, 1890–1964)
Bestall, J. M. and Fowkes, D. V. ed., *Chesterfield wills and inventories,
   1521–1603*, Derbyshire Record Society 1 (1977)
Brears, P. C. D. ed., *Yorkshire probate inventories, 1542–1689*. Y.A.S.R.S.
   134 (1972)
Calendar of state papers domestic, Edward VI–Charles I, 1547–1640, ed.
   R. Lemon and others. 30 vols. (London, 1856–97)
Cash, M. ed., *Devon inventories of the sixteenth and seventeenth centuries*
   Devon and Cornwall Record Society, New Series 11 (1966)
Crossley, J. ed., *Potts' discovery of witches in the county of Lancaster*
   Chetham Society, Old Series 6 (1845)
Ecroyd, T. B. ed., *The registers of the parish church of Colne in the county of
   Lancaster. Christenings, weddings and burials, 1599–1653* L.P.R.S.
   (Rochdale, 1904)
Ecroyd, T. B. ed., *The registers of the parish church of Whalley in the county
   of Lancaster. Christenings, weddings and burials, 1538–1601* L.P.R.S.
   (Rochdale, 1900)
Emmison, F. G. ed., *Jacobean household inventories* Publications of the
   Bedfordshire Historical Record Society 20 (1938)
Farrer, W. ed., *Lancashire inquests, extents and feudal aids Part 1. A.D.
   1205–A.D. 1307* R.S.L.C. 48 (1903); *Part 2. A.D. 1310–A.D. 1333*
   R.S.L.C. 54 (1907)
Farrer, W. ed., *Some court rolls of the lordships, wapentakes and demesne
   manors of Thomas, Earl of Lancaster in the county of Lancaster. A.D.
   1323–4* R.S.L.C. 41 (1901)
Farrer, W. ed., *The court rolls of the Honor of Clitheroe in the county of
   Lancaster* 3 vols. (Manchester, 1897; Edinburgh, 1912, 1913)
Farrer, W. ed., *The registers of the parish church of Burnley in the county of*

Lancaster. *Christenings, weddings and burials, 1562–1653* L.P.R.S. (Rochdale, 1899)

Fishwick, H. ed., *Lancashire and Cheshire church surveys, 1649–1655* R.S.L.C. 1 (1878)

Fishwick, H. ed., *Pleadings and depositions in the Duchy Court of Lancaster. Time of Henry VII and Henry VIII*, R.S.L.C. 32 (1896); *Time of Henry VIII*, R.S.L.C. 35 (1897)) *Time of Edward VI*, R.S.L.C. 40 (1899)

Fishwick, H. ed., *The survey of the manor of Rochdale* Chetham Society, New Series 71 (1913)

Grosart, A. B. ed., *The Towneley Hall MSS: the spending of the money of Robert Nowell of Reade Hall, Lancashire, brother of Dean Alexander Nowell, 1568–1580* (Manchester, 1877)

Harland, J. ed., *The house and farm accounts of the Shuttleworths of Gawthorpe Hall in the county of Lancaster at Smithils and Gawthorpe, from September 1582 to October 1621* 4 vols. Chetham Society, Old Series 35 (1856), 41 (1856), 43 (1857), 46 (1858)

Harland, J. and Wilkinson, T. ed., *Lancashire legends, traditions, pageants, sports etc. with an appendix containing a rare tract on the Lancashire witches* (London, 1873, reprinted Wakefield, 1973)

Havinden, M. A. ed., *Household and farm inventories in Oxfordshire, 1550–1590* Oxfordshire Record Society 44 (1965)

Historical Manuscripts Commission, fourteenth report, appendix part IV. The manuscripts of Lord Kenyon ed., W. J. Hardy (London, 1894)

Historical Manuscripts Commission. Volume 80. Calendar of the manuscripts of the Honourable Lord Sackville of Knole, Sevenoaks, Kent. Volume 2. Letters relating to Lionel Cranfield's business overseas, 1597–1612 ed., F. J. Fisher (London, 1966)

Holt, J., *General view of the agriculture of the county of Lancaster* (London, 1795, reprinted Newton Abbot, 1969)

Laycock, J. A. ed., *The registers of the parish church of Padiham in the county of Lancaster. Christenings, burials and weddings, 1573–1653* L.P.R.S. (Wigan, 1903)

Letters and papers foreign and domestic, Henry VIII, ed., J. S. Brewer and others 37 vols. (London, 1920–32)

Lyons, P. A. ed., *Two 'compoti' of the Lancashire and Cheshire manors of Henry de Lacy, Earl of Lincoln, XXIV and XXXIII Edward I* Chetham Society, Old Series 112 (1884)

Norcliffe, C. B. ed., 'Inventory of the goods of John Pawson', *Publications of the Thoresby Society* 4 Miscellanea (1895), 163–6

Preston, W. E. ed., *Wills proved in the court of the manor of Crosley, Bingley, Cottingley and Pudsey in co. York, with inventories and abstracts of bonds* Bradford Historical and Antiquarian Society Local Record Series 1 (1929)

Raines, F. R. ed., 'The state, civil and ecclesiastical, of the county of Lancaster, about the year 1590, by some of the clergy of the diocese of Chester' in Raines, F. R. ed., *Chetham miscellanies. Volume 5* Chetham Society, Old Series 96 (1875)

Raines, F. R. ed., 'The rent roll of Sir John Towneley of Towneley, Knight for Burnley, Ightenhill, etc., in the County Palatine of Lancaster, A.D. 1535–6', in Raines, F. R. ed., *Chetham miscellanies. Volume 6* Chetham society, Old Series 103 (1878)

Ramsay, G. D. ed., 'The distribution of the cloth industry in 1561– 2', *Eng.H.R.* 57 (1942), 361–9

Rylands, J. P. ed., *Lancashire inquisitions returned into the Chancery of the Duchy of Lancaster and now existing in the Public Record Office*, London 3 vols. R.S.L.C. 3 (1879), 16 (1887), 17 (1888)

Tait, J. ed., *Lancashire Quarter Sessions records. 1. 1590–1606* Chetham Society, New Series 77 (1917)

Tawney, R. H. ed., *A discourse upon usury* by Thomas Wilson (London, 1925)

Vaisey, D. G. ed., *Probate inventories of Lichfield and district, 1568–1680* Staffordshire Record Society, 4th Series 5 (1969)

Maps

Clitheroe, sheet 68, drift edition 1:50,000, geological survey of Great Britain (England and Wales). Ordnance Survey, 1975.

Clitheroe, sheet 68, solid edition, 1:63,360, geological survey of Great Britain (England and Wales). Ordnance Survey, 1960.

Soil association map of the county of Lancashire, 1:250,000, Soil survey of England and Wales. Ordnance Survey, 1970.

PRINTED SECONDARY WORKS

Ainsworth, H., *The Lancashire witches* (London, 1849, reprinted London, 1980)

Alexander, G. G., 'The custom of the Province of York', *Publications of the Thoresby Society* 28 (1928), 417–30

Appleby, A. B., 'Disease or famine? Mortality in Cumberland and Westmorland, 1580–1640', *Ec.H.R.* 2nd Series 26 (1973), 403–31

Appleby, A. B., *Famine in Tudor and Stuart England* (Liverpool, 1978)

Arkell, V. T. J., 'An enquiry into the frequency of the parochial registration of Catholics in a 17th Century Warwickshire parish', *L.P.S.* 9 (1972), 23–32

Bagley, J. J., 'Matthew Markland, a Wigan mercer: the manufacture and sale of Lancashire textiles in the reigns of Elizabeth I and James I', *T.L.C.A.S.* 68 (1958, printed 1959), 45–68

Baines, P., *Spinning wheels, spinners and spinning* (New York, 1979)

Baker, A. R. H. and Butlin, R. A. ed., *Studies of field systems in the British Isles* (Cambridge, 1973)

Barley, M. W., *The English farmhouse and cottage* (London, 1961)

Batho, G., 'Landlords in England. A. The Crown', in Thirsk, J. ed., *The agrarian history of England and Wales. Volume IV, 1500–1640* (Cambridge, 1967), 256–76

Batho, G., 'Landlords in England. B. Noblemen, gentlemen and yeomen', in Thirsk, J. ed., *The agrarian history of England and Wales. Volume IV, 1500–1640* (Cambridge, 1967), 276–306

Bennett, W., *The history of Marsden and Nelson* (Nelson, 1957)

Berry, B. M. and Schofield, R. S., 'Age at baptism in pre-industrial England', *Population Studies* 25 (1971), 453–63

Blackwood, B. G., *The Lancashire gentry and the Great Rebellion* Chetham Society, 3rd Series 25 (1978)

Bowden, P. J., 'Agricultural prices, farm profits and rents', in Thirsk, J. ed., *The agrarian history of England and Wales. Volume IV, 1500–1640* (Cambridge, 1967), 593–695

Bowden, P. J., 'Statistical appendix', in Thirsk, J. ed., *The agrarian history of England and Wales. Volume IV, 1500–1640* (Cambridge, 1967), 814–70

Bowden, P. J., *The wool trade in Tudor and Stuart England* (London, 1971)

Braudel, F., *Civilisation and capitalism, 15th–18th century. Volume II. The wheels of commerce* (London, 1982)

Brigg, M., 'The forest of Pendle in the seventeenth century', Part 1, *T.H.S.L.C.* 113 (1961, printed 1962), 65–96; Part 2, *T.H.S.L.C.* 115 (1963, printed 1964), 65–90

Camp, A. J., *Wills and their whereabouts* 4th edn (London, 1974)

Carus-Wilson, E. M., 'An industrial revolution of the thirteenth century', *Ec.H.R.* 11 (1941), 39–60

Clarkson, L. A., 'The organisation of the English leather industry in the late sixteenth and seventeenth centuries', *Ec.H.R.* 2nd Series, 13 (1960), 245–56

Clarkson, L. A., *The pre-industrial economy in England, 1500–1750* (London, 1971)

Coleman, D. C., *Industry in Tudor and Stuart England* (London, 1975)

Coleman, D. C., 'Textile growth', in Harte, N. B. and Ponting, K. G.

ed., *Textile history and economic history. Essays in honour of Miss Julia de Lacy Mann* (Manchester, 1973), 1–21

Coleman, D. C., *The domestic system in industry* Historical Association aids for teachers series, No. 6 (1960 reprinted 1963)

Coleman, D. C., *The economy of England, 1450–1750* (Oxford, 1977)

Coleman, D. C., 'Proto-industrialization: a concept too many', *Ec.H.R.* 2nd Series 36 (1983), 435–48

Cornwall, J., 'English country towns in the 1520s', *Ec.H.R.* 2nd Series 15 (1962), 54–69

Cornwall, J., 'English population in the early sixteenth century', *Ec.H.R.* 2nd Series 23 (1970), 32–44

Crofton, H. T., 'Lancashire and Cheshire coalmining records', *T.L.C.A.S.* 7, (1889, printed 1890), 26–73

Crump, W. B., 'The wool-textile industry of the Pennines in its physical setting', Parts 1 and 2, *Journal of the Textiles Institute* 26 (1935), 367–74, 383–94

Crump, W. B., 'The yeoman-clothier of the seventeenth century: his home and his loom shop', *The Bradford Antiquary* New Series 5 (1933), 217–39

Davis, R., *The trade and shipping of Hull, 1500–1700* East Yorkshire Local History Society 17 (1964)

Dietz, F. C., *English government finance, 1485–1558* 2nd edn. (London, 1964)

Dietz, F. C., *English public finance, 1558–1641* 2nd edn (London, 1964)

Drake, M., 'An elementary exercise in parish register demography', *Ec.H.R.* 2nd Series 14 (1962), 427–45

Drake, M., *Historical demography: problems and projects* (Milton Keynes, 1978)

Earwaker, J. P. ed., *An index to the wills and inventories now preserved in the Court of Probate at Chester from A.D. 1545 to 1620* R.S.L.C. 2 (1879)

Earwaker, J. P. ed., *An index to the wills and inventories now preserved in the Court of Probate at Chester from A.D. 1621 to 1650* R.S.L.C. 4 (1881)

Endrei, W. G., 'English kersey in eastern Europe with special reference to Hungary', *Textile History* 5 (1974), 90–9

Everitt, A., 'Farm labourers', in Thirsk, J. ed., *The agrarian history of England and Wales. Volume IV, 1500–1640* (Cambridge, 1967), 396–465

Eversley, D. E. C., 'Exploitation of Anglican parish registers by aggregative analysis', in Wrigley, E. A. ed., *An introduction to English historical demography* (London, 1966), 44–95

Farrer, W. and Brownbill, J. ed., *Victoria county history of Lancashire* 8 vols. (1906–14, reprinted London, 1966)

Fedorowicz, J. K., *England's Baltic trade in the early seventeenth century* (Cambridge, 1980)

France, R. S., 'A history of plague in Lancashire', *T.H.S.L.C.* 90 (1938, printed 1939), 1–175

Freeman, T. W., Rodgers, H. B. and Kinvig, R. H., *Lancashire, Cheshire and the Isle of Man* (London, 1966)

Friis, A., *Alderman Cockayne's project and the cloth trade. The commercial policy of England in its main aspects, 1603–1625* (London, 1927)

Frost, P., 'Yeomen and metalsmiths: livestock in the dual economy in South Staffordshire 1560–1720', *Ag.H.R.* 29 (1981), 29–41

Fussell, G. E., *The English dairy farmer 1500–1900* (London, 1966)

Gould, J. D., 'The trade depression of the early 1620s', *Ec.H.R.* 2nd Series 7 (1954), 81–90

Haigh, C., *Reformation and resistance in Tudor Lancashire* (Cambridge, 1975)

Haigh, C., 'The continuity of Catholicism in the English Reformation', *P.&P.* 93 (1981), 37–69

Halliwell, J. O., *A dictionary of archaic and provincial words* 7th edn (London, 1924)

Harrison, C. J. 'Elizabethan village surveys: a comment', *Ag.H.R.* 27 (1979), 82–9

Heaton, H., *The Yorkshire woollen and worsted industries from the earliest times up to the industrial revolution.* 2nd edn (Oxford, 1965)

Hewart, B., 'The cloth trade in the north of England in the sixteenth and seventeenth centuries', *Economic Journal* 10 (1900), 20–31

Hinton, R. W. K., *The Eastland trade and the common weal in the seventeenth century* (Cambridge, 1959)

Holderness, B. A., 'Credit in a rural community, 1660–1800. Some neglected aspects of probate inventories', *Midland History* 3 (1975), 94–115

Holderness, B. A., 'Credit in English rural society before the nineteenth century, with special reference to the period 1650–1720', *Ag.H.R.* 24 (1976) 97–109

Hollingsworth, T. H., *Historical demography* (New York, 1969)

Hoskins, W. G., 'The rebuilding of rural England 1570–1640', *P.&P.* 4 (1953), 44–59

Howell, C., 'Peasant inheritance customs in the Midlands, 1280–1700', in Goody, J., Thirsk, J. and Thompson, E. P. ed.,

Family and inheritance. Rural society in western Europe, 1200–1800
(Cambridge, 1976), 112–55

Howson, W. G., 'Plague, poverty and population in parts of
north-west England, 1580–1720', *T.H.S.L.C.* 112 (1960; printed
1961), 29–55

Hudson, P., 'Proto-industrialisation: the case of the West Riding
wool textile industry in the 18th and eary 19th centuries', *History
Workshop Journal* 12 (1981), 34–61

Irvine, W. F. ed., 'An index of 'infra' wills now preserved in the
probate registry, Chester, 1590–1665', in Irvine, W. F. Price,
W. H. and Beazley, F. C. ed., *Miscellanies relating to Lancashire and
Cheshire. Volume the fifth* R.S.L.C. 52 (1906)

Irvine, W. F. ed., 'List of the wills, inventories, administration
bonds and testamentary depositions now preserved at the
Diocesan Registry, Chester, from the year 1487 to 1620
inclusive', in Irvine, W. F., and Radcliffe, R. D. ed., *Miscellanies
relating to Lancashire and Cheshire. Volume the third* R.S.L.C. 33
(1896)

Jones, B. C., 'The Lancashire probate records', *T.H.S.L.C.* 104
(1952; printed 1953), 61–73

Jones, E. L., 'The agricultural origins of industry', *P.&P.* 40
(1968), 58–71

Kenyon, J. P., *The Stuart constitution, 1603–1688, documents and
commentary* (Cambridge, 1976)

Kerridge, E., *Agrarian problems in the sixteenth century and after*
(Birkenhead, 1969)

Kerridge, E., *The agricultural revolution* (London, 1967)

Kerridge, E., 'The movement of rent, 1540–1640', *Ec.H.R.* 2nd
Series 6 (1953), 16–34

Kriedte, P., Medick, H. and Schlumbohm, J. ed., *Industrialisation
before industrialisation. Rural industry in the genesis of capitalism*
(Cambridge, 1981)

Kussmaul, A., *Servants in husbandry in early modern England*
(Cambridge, 1981)

Langton, J., *Geographical change and industrial revolution. Coalmining in
south west Lancashire 1590–1799* (Cambridge, 1979)

Laslett, P., *Family life and illicit love in earlier generations* (Cambridge,
1977)

Laslett, P., 'Introduction: comparing illegitimacy over time and
between cultures', in Laslett, P., Oosterveen, K. and Smith,
R. M. ed., *Bastardy and its comparative history* (London, 1980), 1–65

Laslett, P., *The world we have lost* 2nd edn (London, 1971, reprinted, 1979)

Laslett, P. and Oosterveen, K., 'Long-term trends in bastardy in England', *Population Studies* 27 (1973), 255–86

Laslett, P., Oosterveen, K. and Smith, R. M. ed., *Bastardy and its comparative history* (London, 1980)

Latham, R. E., 'Hints on interpreting the public records. III. Inquisitions post mortem', *Amateur Historian* 1 (1953), 77–81

Levine, D., *Family formation in an age of nascent capitalism* (New York, 1977)

Levine, D. and Wrightson, K., 'The social context of illegitimacy in early modern England', in Laslett, P., Oosterveen, K. and Smith, R. M. ed., *Bastardy and its comparative history* (London, 1980), 158–75

Lipson, E., *The history of the woollen and worsted industries* (London, 1921)

Lowe, N., *The Lancashire textile industry in the sixteenth century* Chetham Society, 3rd Series 20 (1972)

Macfarlane, A. D. J., 'Illegitimacy and illegitimates in English history', in Laslett, P., Oosterveen, K. and Smith, R. M. ed., *Bastardy and its comparative history* (London, 1980), 71–85

Macfarlane, A. D. J., *Reconstructing historical communities* (Cambridge, 1977)

Macfarlane, A. D. J., *Witchcraft in Tudor and Stuart England. A regional and comparative study* (London, 1970)

Mann, J. de L., Review of Lowe, N., *The Lancashire textile industry in the sixteenth century*, in *Textile History* 4 (1973), 146–7

Manning, B., *The English people and the English revolution* (Harmondsworth, 1978)

Marshall, J. D., 'Agrarian wealth and social structure in pre-industrial Cumbria', *Ec.H.R.* 2nd Series 33 (1980), 503–21

Marshall, J. D., *Lancashire* (London, 1974)

Marshall, J. D., 'The domestic economy of the Lakeland yeoman 1660–1749', *Transactions of the Cumberland and Westmorland Antiquarian and Archaeological Society* New Series 73 (1973), 190–219

Marshall, J. D., 'The study of local and regional "communities". Some problems and possibilities', *Northern History* 17 (1981), 203–30

Mendels, F. F., 'Agriculture and peasant industry in Flanders' in Kriedte, P., Medick, H. and Schlumbohm, J. ed., *Industrialisation before industrialisation. Rural industry in the genesis of capitalism* (Cambridge, 1981), 161–77

Mendels, F. F., 'Proto-industrialisation: the first phase' of the industrialisation process', *Journal of Economic History* 32 (1972), 241–61

Mendels, F. F., 'Proto-industrialisation: theory and reality', in *A themes. Eighth international economic history congress* (Budapest, 1982), 69–105

Mendenhall, T. C., *The Shrewsbury drapers and the Welsh wool trade in the XVI and XVII centuries* (Oxford, 1953)

Nef, J. U., *The rise of the British coal industry* 2 vols. (London, 1932)

Neill, R., *Mist over Pendle* (London, 1951, reprinted London, 1977)

Palliser, D. M., 'Tawney's century: Brave New World or Malthusian trap?' *Ec.H.R.* 2nd Series 35 (1982), 339–53

Pearson, S., *Rural houses of the Lancashire Pennines, 1560–1760* H.M.S.O. (1985)

Porter, J., 'A forest in transition: Bowland, 1500–1650', *T.H.S.L.C.* 125 (1974, printed 1975), 40–60

Porter, J., *The making of the central Pennines* (Ashbourne, 1980)

Price, W. H. ed., 'List of wills, inventories, etc., now preserved at the Diocesan Registry, Chester, from the year 1621 to the year 1700 inclusive', in Irvine, W. F. and Price, W. H. ed., *Miscellanies relating to Lancashire and Cheshire. Volume the fourth.* R.S.L.C. 43 (1902)

Ramsay, G. D., *The Wiltshire woollen industry in the sixteenth and seventeenth centuries.* 2nd edn. (London, 1965)

Ramsay, G. D., *The English woollen industry, 1500–1750* (London, 1982)

Ramsey, P., *Tudor economic problems* (London, 1972)

Richardson, R. C., *Puritanism in north-west England. A regional study of the diocese of Chester to 1642* (Manchester, 1972)

Rodgers, H. B., 'Land use in Tudor Lancashire: the evidence of the final concords, 1450–1558', *The Institute of British Geographers' Transactions and Papers* 21 (1955), 79–97

Rogers, C. D., *The Lancashire population crisis of 1623* (Manchester, 1975)

Rogers, J. E. T., *A history of agriculture and prices in England.* Volumes 3–6 (Oxford, 1882–7)

Rowlands, M. B., *Masters and men in the West Midland metalware trades before the Industrial Revolution* (Manchester, 1975)

Russell, J. C., *British medieval population* (Albuquerque, 1948)

Schofield, R. S., 'The geographical distribution of wealth in England, 1334–1649', *Ec.H.R.* 2nd Series 18 (1965), 483–510

Shaw, R. C., *The royal forest of Lancaster* (Preston, 1956)

Shrewsbury, J. F. D., *A history of bubonic plague in the British Isles* (Cambridge, 1971)

Skipp, V., *Crisis and development. An ecological case study of the forest of Arden, 1570–1674* (Cambridge, 1978)

Slicher van Bath, B. H., *The agrarian history of Western Europe, 500–1850* (London, 1963)

Smith, E. H., 'Lancashire long measure', *T.H.S.L.C.* 110 (1958, printed 1959), 1–14

Smith, R. B., *Blackburnshire. A study in early Lancashire history* Department of English Local History Occasional Papers, Leicester University, 15 (1961)

Smith, R. B., *Land and politics in the England of Henry VIII. The West Riding of Yorkshire: 1530–46* (Oxford, 1970)

Smith, R. M., 'Population and its geography in England, 1500–1730', in Dodgshon, R. A. and Butlin, R. A. ed., *An historical geography of England and Wales* (London, 1978), 199–237

Somerville, R., *History of the Duchy of Lancaster. Volume 1, 1265–1603* (London, 1953)

Spufford, M., *Contrasting communities. English villagers in the sixteenth and seventeenth centuries* (Cambridge, 1974)

Spufford, M., 'Peasant inheritance customs and land distribution in Cambridgeshire from the sixteenth to the eighteenth centuries', in Goody, J., Thirsk, J. and Thompson, E. P. ed., *Family and inheritance. Rural society in Western Europe, 1200–1800* (Cambridge, 1976)

Stephens, W. B., *Sources for English local history* (Manchester, 1973)

Stephens, W. B., 'The cloth exports of the provincial ports, 1600–1640', *Ec.H.R.* 2nd Series 22 (1969), 228–48

Stephens, W. B., 'The Exchequer port books as a source for the history of the English cloth trade', *Textile History* 1 (1969), 206–13

Stephens, W. B., 'The overseas trade of Chester in the early seventeenth century', *T.H.S.L.C.* 120 (1968, printed 1969), 23–34

Stone, L., 'An Elizabethan coalmine', *Ec.H.R.* 2nd Series 3 (1950) 97–106

Supple, B. E., *Commercial crisis and change in England, 1600–1642. A study in the instability of a mercantile economy* (Cambridge, 1959)

Tawney, R. H., *Business and politics under James I. Lionel Cranfield as merchant and minister* (Cambridge, 1958)

Tawney, R. H., *Religion and the rise of capitalism* (London, 1926)

Tawney, R. H., *The agrarian problem in the sixteenth century* (London, 1912)

Tawney, R. H. and Power, E. ed., *Tudor economic documents* 3 vols. (London, 1924)

Thirsk, J., 'Sources of information on population, 1500–1760',
Amateur Historian 4 (1959), 129–33, 182–4
Thirsk, J., 'Industries in the countryside', in Fisher, F. J. ed., *Essays
in the economic and social history of Tudor and Stuart England in honour of
R. H. Tawney* (Cambridge, 1961), 70–88
Thirsk, J., 'Farming techniques', in Thirsk, J. ed., *The agrarian history
of England and Wales. Volume IV, 1500–1640* (Cambridge, 1967), 161–
99
Thirsk, J., 'The farming regions of England', in Thirsk, J. ed., *The
agrarian history of England and Wales. Volume IV, 1500–1640*
(Cambridge, 1967), 1–112
Thirsk, J. ed., *The agrarian history of England and Wales. Volume IV,
1500–1640* (Cambridge, 1967)
Thirsk, J., 'Younger sons in the seventeenth century', *History* 54
(1969), 358–77
Thirsk, J., 'Seventeenth-century agriculture and social change', in
Thirsk, J. ed., *Land, church and people. Essays presented to Professor
H. P. R. Finberg. Ag.H.R.* 18 (1970) Supplement, 148–77
Thirsk, J. and Cooper, J. P. ed., *Seventeenth century economic documents*
(Oxford, 1972)
Thirsk, J., *Economic policy and projects. The development of a consumer
society in early modern England* (Oxford, 1978)
Thomas, K., *Religion and the decline of magic* (London, 1971)
Tupling, G. H., *The economic history of Rossendale*. Chetham Society,
New Series 86 (1927)
Tupling, G. H., 'The origin of markets and fairs in medieval
Lancashire', *T.L.C.A.S.* 49 (1933, printed 1935), 75–94
Tupling, G. H., 'An alphabetical list of the markets and fairs of
Lancashire recorded before the year 1701', *T.L.C.A.S.* 51 (1936,
printed 1937), 86–110
Tupling, G. H., 'Lancashire markets in the sixteenth and
seventeenth centuries', Part 1, *T.L.C.A.S.* 58 (1945–6, printed
1947), 1–34; Part 2, *T.L.C.A.S.* 59 (1947, printed 1948), 1–34
Tupling, G. H., 'The early metal trades and the beginnings of
engineering in Lancashire', *T.L.C.A.S.* 61 (1949, printed 1951), 1–
34
Tupling, G. H., 'The causes of the Civil War in Lancashire',
T.L.C.A.S. 65 (1955, printed 1956), 1–32
Wadsworth, A. P. and Mann, J. de L., *The cotton trade and industrial
Lancashire, 1600–1780* (Manchester, 1931, reprinted Manchester,
1965)

Whitaker, T. D., *An history of the original parish of Whalley and Honor of Clitheroe in the counties of Lancaster and York to which is subjoined an account of the parish of Cartmell. 3rd edn.* (London, 1818)

Wightman, P., *Bonnie Colne* (Nelson, n.d., between 1975 and 1981)

Wild, M. T., 'The Yorkshire wool textile industry', in Jenkins, J. G. ed., *The wool textile industry in Great Britain* (London, 1972), 185–234

Willan, T. S., *Elizabethan Manchester.* Chetham Society, 3rd Series 27 (1980)

Willan, T. S., 'Manchester clothiers in the early seventeenth century', *Textile History* 10 (1979), 175–83

Willan, T. S., *The inland trade. Studies in English internal trade in the sixteenth and seventeenth centuries* (Manchester, 1976)

Woodward, D., 'Wage rates and living standards in pre-industrial England', *P.&P.* 91 (1981), 28–46

Wright, J., *The English dialect dictionary* 6 vols (London, 1898)

Wrightson, K. E., 'The nadir of English illegitimacy in the seventeenth century', in Laslett, P., Oosterveen, K. and Smith, R. M. ed., *Bastardy and its comparative history* (London, 1980), 176–91

Wrightson, K. E., *English society 1580–1680* (London, 1982)

Wrigley, E. A., 'Fertility strategy for the individual and the group', in Tilly, C. ed., *Historical studies of changing fertility* (Princeton, 1978), 135–54

Wrigley, E. A. and Schofield, R. S., *The population history of England, 1541–1871. A reconstruction* (London, 1981)

Yelling, J. A., 'Probate inventories and the geography of livestock farming: a study of East Worcestershire, 1540–1750', *The Institute of British Geographers' Transactions and Papers* 51 (1970), 111–26

Youd, G., 'The common fields of Lancashire', *T.H.S.L.C.* 113 (1961, printed 1962), 1–41

Youings, J., *Sixteenth-century England* (Harmondsworth, 1984)

Zell, M. L., 'The Exchequer lists of provincial clothmakers fined in London during the sixteenth century', *Bulletin of the Institute of Historical Research*, 54 (1981), 129–30

Zins, H., *England and the Baltic in the Elizabethan era.* (Manchester, 1972)

UNPUBLISHED DISSERTATIONS, ETC

Dickinson, M., 'The West Riding woollen and worsted industries, 1689–1770. An analysis of probate inventories and insurance policies'. Ph.D. thesis, Nottingham University (1974)

Fedorowicz, J. K., 'Anglo-Polish relations in the first half of the seventeenth century: a study in commercial diplomacy'. Ph.D. thesis, Cambridge University (1976)

Frost, P. M., 'The growth and localisation of rural industry in south Staffordshire, 1560–1720'. Ph.D. thesis, Birmingham University (1973)

Hall, B., 'The trade of Newcastle upon Tyne and the north-east coast, 1600–1640'. Ph.D. thesis, London University (1933)

Harrison, C. J., 'The social and economic history of Cannock and Rugeley, 1546–1597'. Ph.D. thesis, Keele University (1974)

King, W., 'The economic and demographic development of Rossendale, c.1650–c.1795'. Ph.D. thesis, Leicester University (1979)

Long, P. R., 'The wealth of the magisterial class in Lancashire, c.1590–1640', M.A. thesis, Manchester University (1968)

Lowe, N., 'The Lancashire textile industry in the sixteenth century'. M.A. thesis, Manchester University (1966)

Overton, M., 'Agricultural change in Norfolk and Suffolk, 1580–1740'. Ph.D. thesis, Cambridge University (1981)

Porter, J., 'The reclamation and settlement of Bowland, with special reference to the period A.D. 1500–1650'. Ph.D. thesis, London University (1973)

Swain, J. T., 'Industry and economy in north east Lancasire, *circa* 1500–1640'. Ph.D. thesis, Cambridge University (1983)

Wrightson, K. E., 'The Puritan reformation of manners, with special reference to the counties of Lancashire and Essex, 1640–1660'. Ph.D. thesis, Cambridge University (1974)

INDEX